THE STORY OF

CHICAGO MAY

THE STORY OF

CHICAGO MAY

Nuala O'Faolain

MICHAEL JOSEPH
an imprint of
PENGUIN BOOKS

MICHAEL JOSEPH

Published by the Penguin Group

Penguin Books Ltd, 80 Strand, London WC2R 0RL, England

Penguin Group (USA) Inc., 375 Hudson Street, New York, New York 10014, USA

Penguin Group (Canada), 90 Eglinton Avenue East, Suite 700, Toronto, Ontario, Canada M4P 2Y3
(a division of Pearson Penguin Canada Inc.)

Penguin Ireland, 25 St Stephen's Green, Dublin 2, Ireland (a division of Penguin Books Ltd)

Penguin Group (Australia), 250 Camberwell Road,

Camberwell, Victoria 3124, Australia (a division of Pearson Australia Group Pty Ltd)

Penguin Books India Pvt Ltd, 11 Community Centre,

Panchsheel Park, New Delhi – 110 017, India

Penguin Group (NZ), cnr Airborne and Rosedale Roads, Albany,

Auckland 1310, New Zealand (a division of Pearson New Zealand Ltd)

Penguin Books (South Africa) (Pty) Ltd, 24 Sturdee Avenue,

Rosebank, Johannesburg 2196, South Africa

Penguin Books Ltd, Registered Offices: 80 Strand, London WC2R 0RL, England

www.penguin.com

First published in the United States of America by Riverhead Books
(a division of the Penguin Group (USA)) 2005
Published in Great Britain by Michael Joseph 2005

1

Copyright © Nuala O'Faolain, 2005

The moral right of the author has been asserted

Printed in Great Britain by Clays Ltd, St Ives plc

A CIP catalogue record for this book is available from the British Library

ISBN: 0-718-14524-0

FOR JOHN

Contents

Prologue

I was in the west of Ireland when I heard about the Irishwoman who ran away from home toward the end of the nineteenth century and became famous in America as a crook known as "Chicago May." I was told that a book about May, written by a local historian from her part of the country, was based on the life story May published in the 1920s. I knew that, before my own time, there was very little autobiography by Irish women, and almost none by women who were neither saintly nor patriotic nor literary, so I had only to hear about May's book to want to read it. But it seemed that no library in her native land had ever heard of her, much less had a copy of her book. I went online and found it in the New York Public Library on Fifth Avenue, the words thrilling me as they came up: *Chicago May, Her Story: A Human Document by "The Queen of Crooks,"* May Churchill Sharpe, 1928.

Manhattan, however, was three thousand miles away.

But the book about May by the local historian was in the main library of the county she came from, County Longford. So early one morning in late summer, soon after I first heard her name, I got ready, to a profusion of aerial whistles and squelchy, companionable squawks from the crows on the electricity line above my cottage, to drive halfway up Ireland to read it. A blackbird pecked around in grass that had been mowed the night before and lay like hair-partings, slicked down by the heavy dew. The poet Keats, who watched a sparrow pecking, said that a person should be capable of being in uncertainty "without any irritable reaching after fact and reason"—that you can wait, in other words, to find out what your purpose is. But I didn't even feel the need of a purpose. It was second nature to me to go after May.

When I was a producer with Irish television, I made a series called *Plain Tales,* in which older women looked into the camera and told their life stories uninterrupted, the editing cuts covered by their own innocent snapshots, little pictures faded to sepia of fat babies and girls in old-fashioned coats swinging arm in arm along out-of-focus streets. I found those women and coaxed them into talking—partly for myself, who had never felt myself enrolled into the company of women by my solitary mother, and partly as an act of redress on behalf of the millions and millions of women stuffed and crammed into graveyards who might as well never have been born for all anyone knows about them. Millions of men die unknown, too, but at least they once had an audience in a tavern or a marketplace. What they were like was of some consequence in the world.

I might not have gone after May if she'd written her life story when she was still young. Now that I'm not young myself, I see retrospection as the one source of insight available to everyone. Or I might not have gone if May had lived in one of the eras I have to struggle to imagine—among the dogs and sheepskins of a medieval towerhouse, or wearing beauty spots on her powdered face in the eighteenth century. But she ran away into her adult life just as the past turned into our present. In Proust, the richest of consequences unfold at the beginning of the last movement, when the narrator returns to Paris after the First World War and stands here in our time, where there are telephones and taxis and airplanes, and opens a perspective back onto the world which, up to this, he and the readers have been within. May would have as wide a span. She could look back on an antique, agricultural society from the vital chaos of the new cities of America.

She died in 1929, the year of the stock market crash. So—she was a famous criminal in the era of long skirts and big hats, but she was also a contemporary of my mother's.

THE LINEAMENTS of the town that would have dazzled the eyes of little May Duignan when she was a country child—gray roofs rising from marshy fields, old storefronts along the main street—can still be made out in Longford. But sun bounced off the glass and steel of the shopping center where I ran up the stairs to the Local Studies library, eager to start reading. Below in the car-park, women marshaled their broods—slender daughters in full makeup, little boys in soccer shorts, calm, round-eyed infants. A mother bowled a buggy along, issuing instructions over her shoulder with such confidence that she never even looked around. What skills did May command, I wondered as I opened the book, that could compare to the way these women organized children and shopping and households? What was she good at?

Then—I hardly noticed half a day pass.

I hadn't been prepared for the sheer amount of story, the number of places May had been, the number of things she'd done, the coincidences that had happened, the wonderful highs and terrible lows— the sheer speed of her tumultuous life. I hadn't realized that her world was much wider than Ireland and America—that it was in Paris, for example, with the most dangerous of her lovers, that she first came to real grief. But there was frontier America, too, Egypt, England, South America. There were marriages and murders, diamonds and absolute poverty, exotic places and here—home. I lifted my head and reminded myself where I was. Longford. Just under a hundred years earlier, then, the May of this book had come through this very town, a tall, straight-backed woman, fabulously dressed, and with a purse bursting with money for all to see.

But pallid, with a jail pallor.

And that was when she was only in her early thirties. There were extremes of experience still to come. I raced through the pages, shaking my head as I read the way people do when they can hardly believe what they're being told. Imprisonment. An oblique encounter with the Easter Rising. A lethal, obsessive jealousy. Collapse on the icy streets of Prohibition Detroit. And then—a miracle. May had lived down at grassroots level, looking up at important events and people; now, the eye of a great person fell on her—a caring eye—and against all the odds, she had it in her to respond. But even that was not the end. There was a last act still to come, and even, at the very last minute, another development.

How like her, I thought, when death was staring her in the face, to be starting off in a new direction.

But as I closed the book, I was already asking myself what I meant by that.

What did I mean by "like her"?

I HAD NO real sense of May. She was indomitable, certainly; simply to have survived the twists and turns of her life proved that. But I had no real grasp of the self that was the only thing to connect so many people and events. It was as if May—the flavor of her, her appeal for other people, her interests, her characteristic ways of thinking and feeling, her beliefs, her tastes—was obscured by the drama of her life. And by the author's indifference. The local historian who wrote the book in front of me had not been interested in the mystery of personality. "She was a truly evil person" were his first words about May, and his analysis never got much further than that. His account of her life was a remarkable achievement in fact-finding by a gifted researcher, but it was the chase, not the quarry, that had interested him. It was as if this woman had been called forward out of the ranks of the forgotten, had opened her mouth to speak, and had then been told to be silent.

It was beyond me to leave it at that.

I looked around for some other avenue of approach. It turned out there was a history of May's home parish, written by a retired schoolmaster named James MacNerney, and I sat on in the library and read that. The book is a labor of love full of the most minute details of schools built, matches won, ambushes set, dances held, churches dedicated, and of poignant snapshots of haymaking and visiting relatives laughing in print frocks, and windblown children with flower faces outside one-room schools, and barns once used for dancing, and stern football teams in baggy white shorts. It is a book to restore the reader's faith in the beauty and strength of community; and the community of the townland of Edenmore, stretching from Saint Patrick to the present day, included even May. Though May was approached somewhat gingerly. What exactly she did was left vague, other than that she emigrated and "lived a flamboyant lifestyle. She was an attractive young woman ill-prepared for the lures and pitfalls of life and of money." A remote and largely unchanging community survives by not saying things rather than by saying them, and readers would understand, of course, that what was not being said was that May turned to crime and that the crime, since it involved money and attractiveness, had something to do with sex.

The few lines conclude: "Perhaps the most charitable approach to the subject is to breathe a prayer for her and not to judge her."

The kindly evasion almost laid a duty on me to enter another protest.

Why was she assumed to be a victim? Might it not be the case that her life was chosen by her, insofar as she was free to choose?

THERE WAS NOTHING more to read. If I wanted to go further with May, I'd have to visit where she came from. So I contacted James MacNerney, and a few days later I drove north again, this time to be shown around Edenmore by himself and his friend, another retired gentleman, who also expresses his affection for his native place by writing about it, though what he writes are humorous, nostalgic ballads. The two of them climbed banks and jumped over stiles and reversed the car up lanes at speed and stood on the tops of breezy hills as if they were in their first youth, tripping over themselves with pride. Here was the schoolhouse—thatched then—that May attended, there a holy well Saint Patrick himself blessed beside a thornbush covered in the rags and socks and dishcloths of petitioners. There a mill, here a view of five counties, there the church where the Duignan family went to Mass, here an ancient wattle path across marsh ground.

They even saw to it that I was welcomed into the very house—blackish-green trees around, the stone of the original four rooms as thick as a fortress—where May was born and grew up. It was the most isolated dwelling in a lonely place, facing a hill, behind it a wilderness of purple bog.

We were received with the courtesy and hospitality of an Ireland of long ago and sat in "the room"—the room off the kitchen—drinking tea out of china cups and eating sandwiches and cake that the lady of the house and her daughter had prepared for us. They said nothing except to press their visitors to more. No doubt they're full of opinions in private—the young woman was a college student—but on this semipublic occasion, only the men were making statements.

When they arrived at May in their unhurried talk, their tone became tentative.

"She was a fine person," James said, but he looked around a little helplessly, because there was no getting away from the fact that the fine person did become a notorious criminal.

Our host, the man of the house, said gravely, "They were very decent people, the Duignans. Tremendous decent people."

"She was a fine person, but she fell into bad company," the balladeer added helpfully.

The three men nodded. They had found a formula that preserved her for the community even if it took away her free will.

I LEFT EDENMORE and took the road through the water meadows of the basin of the River Shannon—evening mist coiling slowly across them—heading for home.

It made me uneasy that I was sliding toward involvement with May before I knew anything about her at first hand, since I hadn't yet read her own book. Already, something within was trying to enlist me. Something that was more impulse than reason was telling me to stand beside her, to re-open the file on her, to call people back to look at her again. It was true of nearly everyone who ever lived that a careful estimate of what they had been had never been made. But though there was nothing to be done about their silence, May happened to live when there was a mass literate audience—an audience who wanted a vicarious thrill from crime the way audiences have always done, but who had to get it from books. There wasn't much radio or many films in that brief period, and there was no television—so she got her autobiography published. That made her different from all the billions of people, including every one of my forebears, who left absolutely nothing behind.

If I were to retell her life, I would have several natural advantages. I was Irish like her. I was a woman, and a woman who, like her, had never been a mother. That we'd both written life stories was no doubt due to that—that we hadn't done the work of mothers, or in any

7

other way applied ourselves to what was called, by the Catholic Church of her childhood and mine, "the duties of our station in life."

And we had both looked to America as a place of transformation. She got there when she was young; I'd made visits there from time to time in the hope of changing myself, and now, as it happened, I was seriously engaged with the place. Orthodox biographers never talk about their personal reasons for embarking on such-and-such a piece of work. They present themselves as pure mind. But I was very conscious that May had spent a great part of her life in the States and that her book was in a library in New York and that I had been going to Brooklyn on and off for the last few years to stay with a friend and his young daughter. Time and again I almost became committed to them, but then I'd back off, and come back to Ireland. If I followed May, I'd be where I should be—where the unanswered question in my own life was.

I TURNED OFF west toward home, and drove along a straight stretch of road between somber trees. Suddenly, flash upon flash, the lights of the car were caught by streaks of vermilion and gold. Posters! The posters for a circus. For a mile or so there was a poster every few yards, bright as parakeets lined up in greeting. The smell of warm canvas and crushed grass came back from when, when I was a child among dull green fields, the circus arrived from another world. The astonishing elephant. The acrobats like seals flipping and diving in the shadows under the Big Top. The circus people themselves, with their lurid makeup and their caravans that spilled tin basins and puppies and exotic pieces of cloth onto the rough ground.

May had no information, I thought. How could she have—a barefoot child out on the edge of the bog in a forgotten corner of a forgotten country? But if she somehow knew, if she sensed that there was a world out there that had color and oompah music and glittering women who balanced perfectly on the backs of plumed ponies, what would stop her from taking off?

Couldn't I take a risk? I never meant to write about a crook—I don't even read about crooks, insofar as there are celebrity crooks nowadays. I'm a bookish person; I'm not attracted to the street. But wouldn't there be something exciting about throwing away my old supports—as she would have done—and starting off in a new direction? Especially as I wouldn't be alone—I'd have her company, after I read her book.

After all, I want the circus in my life, too.

People run away, I thought; that's how it's always described. But there's also running toward.

The posters disappeared. I drove on through the soft night.

PART ONE

1890 to 1893

One

From Edenmore
to the New World

Millions of presumptuous girls, intelligent or not intelligent, daily affront their destiny, and what is it open to their destiny to be, at the most, that we should make an ado about it?

HENRY JAMES, Preface to *The Portrait of a Lady*

Imagine a young woman running. There, where the little hills of Edenmore are patchworked on their flanks by silky fields no bigger than gardens, and where on the lakes hidden between them, in the evening—and she wouldn't have begun her run till it began to get dark—moorhens glide silently across the pale water to their homes in the reeds. The house where May was born wasn't on any road. But once she got safely away, she could take a path lined with hedges so plump with moisture that even in spring their branches block out the light. No one on the path, unless they stood in front of her to force her to stop, would have seen more than the paleness of a face and a gleam of auburn hair when her shawl slipped back. And the last of the light catching the white fingers—the nails, of course, dirty—that clutched the shawl under her chin. But they'd have heard the steady thump of her boots as she ran toward them and then her panting—

Irish women of May's time

part of it fear, part of it elation—and the slap of the heavy cloth bag against her skirt.

May was strong. She was used to making long, barefoot journeys to fairs and to the town. The miles to the railway halt where her father wouldn't think of looking for her were no trouble to her. Yet she wouldn't have been a light runner. The preferred looks of that time— the year was 1890—were womanly, and she said herself that she was buxom. She was tall for those times, and a man who had no reason to praise her said that she was perfectly proportioned, which meant that her hips were as rounded as her breasts. But her face contradicted her body. The taste then was for women with baby faces, and May fulfilled the ideal—the same man described her "complexion of delicate pink and cream, large blue eyes shaded with long lashes and a mouth the upper lip of which formed a perfect Cupid's bow." We don't respond today to that sweet kind of look, though the appearance of innocence still has a powerful effect. But the shapely curve of a mouth or the spring of a hairline from a forehead or the set of a white throat can be almost painfully pleasing, though they are not classically beautiful. It must have been that May had the vivid well-being of a country girl—that she possessed great physical charm.

What she looked like matters to her story. They say in Edenmore that she was a bright child, very good at school. But she was a girl, and on what else but looks could a girl, who owned nothing, base the belief that she was exceptional? And would she have run if she hadn't believed she was exceptional?

THE MOON comes up. Her shadow is black on a bleached causeway raised above flooded meadows, but there is no one to see her. There is no sound except the poignant call of a curlew disturbed by something out in the dark marsh. She grew up among cabins collapsed on themselves, their thatch rotted to lumps of weed, saplings growing through their dirt floors. In the townland of Edenmore, before the potato famine known as the Great Hunger, there were 259 houses tucked away among the little hills and lakes. But in one decade the country lost half its population to death from hunger and fever, or to emigration promoted by the landlords who represented England's interests in Ireland. And the decline continued. By the time May was born, only 49 of the 259 houses were inhabited.

She must have pushed open frail doors into empty rooms where cobwebs made the light opaque and the ashes of last fires were caught at the back of decayed stoves and the enamel of basins lacy with rust gleamed through nettles. She must have learned very early to be furtive but unafraid—to mix play with transgression. She saw the domestic scene in ruin. And when she was seven years old, there was a miracle in a village fifty miles to the west—a place just as remote and humble as Edenmore—when the Mother of God and her spouse, Saint Joseph, manifested themselves on the gable end of the local church. Though it was raining all around, the rain did not fall on them. People understood the wordless tableau to be proclaiming through the Holy Family the holiness of family—and the reinforcement was needed, because families were being torn apart. One in every two children born in Ireland at that time was destined for emigration. May grew up where not just the houses of families but the family itself was in ruin. And health recoils from ruin.

ON THE DAY she ran away, her mother was splayed on her bed, in childbirth. May was a big nineteen-year-old, almost a woman herself. She was needed to look after her three young brothers and dress them and feed them and get them out to school, and to boil water, find cloth rags, hoist potatoes over the fire, prepare tea and bread and bacon for the father and the neighbor midwife woman, clean the lamp and fill it with oil, feed the calves and pigs and hens, wash clothes and spread them to dry on the bushes around the yard and pluck them in from showers like the one I imagine spinning in across the hills from the Atlantic Ocean and lightly bathing the running girl's lifted face. We don't know whether the baby who was born that day arrived before or after May slipped away, but May didn't have to hold a baby in her arms to see the future. She knew that if she didn't marry, she faced a life as a celibate dependent of her father. Letters from America spoke of jobs in abundance for cash wages, but in Edenmore—in all Ireland— there was no money to be made on the smallholdings, there were no factories, there were too many females offering themselves for domestic service.

And yet—a marriage was not so easily arranged. Before the Famine three-quarters of the Irish married, but by May Duignan's time, two-thirds of the marriageable population either could not or would not marry. And though May's father would offer her to the man of his choice, the looks that made her exceptional might prevent a trade being made. "Fine looks never boiled a pot" is one of the many contemptuous sayings of hardscrabble places. A subsistence farmer wants a partner in toil, not a lover. What's more, the other men will jeer at him if he picks a woman for qualities as immaterial as charm or prettiness. Only an old man might face the others down and marry May so as to own her youth.

She knew that, of course. She had seen the effect of her looks in the eyes of men, but she also knew that her looks wouldn't translate into power. Maybe, when she heard the first muffled groan of her mother's labor, she felt her fate approach, massive as a bog slide when rain undermines the slope of a hill and a front of peat bog begins to move, impervious, downward. They say in Edenmore—there are people alive who knew people who knew her—that she ran away because she didn't want to mind another of her mother's babies. This would have been the fourth one given over to her care when the mother resumed the heavy work of the place. Many daughters of poor families will re-member having to walk up and down, soothing an infant almost too heavy to carry, and how the big safety pin for the nappy is always lost and the hole in the teat of the bottle is too small and then too big, and how hot milk squirts into the baby's face, and under the panel of the false floor of the pram a detritus of wet crusts collects. But May was used to work. Extra work wasn't the reason she ran. What might have mattered is resentment. The rest of the work is just work, but the mother and father's babies are an imposition.

She didn't even need to know why she was getting out. The run-ning itself was her consciousness.

BY THE END of the nineteenth century, when half of all the people born in Ireland emigrated, a majority of those emigrants were women, and 90 percent of the women were single. It was England's fault that they were forced to leave—so it was deeply believed. England had controlled Ireland for centuries, but it had never been accepted as other than an occupying power. When you leave your occupied country you are betraying it, so it is incumbent on you to swear that you hate having to go and that someday you will return. So if May sprang into the guard's van with a smile, she was out of the ordinary. Usually, the boys and girls who went to America were escorted to the local train by a crowd stinking of sweat from the dancing and drinking of a night of wild farewells. But no grief-stricken parents, wailing and groaning, ran along beside the track to see the last of this daughter, and she would not have paused to breathe in a final draft of her native air. It has been said that family and community laid on the Irish emigrant a burden of heartbreak that only a lifetime of loyal regret and nostalgia could repay.

Not on May.

She wasn't planning to come home.

The fact is that when May Duignan ran away from Edenmore on the night her mother gave birth to her sister, she took with her the sixty sovereigns—the equivalent of more than five thousand dollars in today's money—that were the entire savings of her father and mother, put together over decades of backbreaking work, and the family's only security. In *Her Story,* she admits that she stole the money: *My father ought to have agreed with me when I hinted about emigrating, and handed me the money with his blessing,* she wrote, like any sulky teenager. *It wasn't my fault I was born.*

She must know that she can no more go home again after stealing that money than the baby born that night can go back into the womb. She is not only an emigrant, but a fugitive. She belongs to nowhere and to nobody now. To her, of course—and perhaps her mouth curves in contentment even as she sleeps, the cloth bag held to her chest—such losses would seem like gains. She's on her way. She's young, healthy, and good-looking, she has no ties and she has money.

To her, what she has must feel like freedom.

I THINK she probably left from Liverpool. Years later, her mother gave an interview—the only one any of the Duignan family ever gave—to a local newspaper, and she said in it that May ran away the night her sister was born and that she took the family money and that the next thing was a postcard from London. But anyone can get a postcard mailed, and Liverpool was the port with constant ships for New York.

THERE WAS BOUND to be a man when May set out on her travels—a gorgeous, disheveled girl on her own would have been scented by a man.

Say she took the train from Holyhead to Liverpool.

"Are we nearly there, sir?" she says.

He hears it as "sorr." Another Paddy.

The timepiece is fished out of his waistcoat.

"Another half-hour," he says. If she hadn't been a Paddy with dried mud all along the hem of her skirt he'd have added "Miss."

She begins to slump back into sleep. He notes, fascinated, that in the evening glow her eyelashes cast their exact shadow on the near-transparent skin under her eyes. The hat slides back off her red-gold hair and releases—he watches it happen—small tendrils along the oval of her hairline. She comes awake again as easily as a baby.

"I'm going to buy another hat," she says, as if they had been talking all along. "I done a swap with a girl on the boat for this one because I had only the shawl, but the crown of it's miles too small."

In the echoing station hall he stands still and allows her to move through the evening crowd, only his rapacious gaze following her. May hurries along a street lined with stores. What was usually done at home was that the girls and boys bought clothes and shoes for America in the same place that sold tickets for the passage, and their people guaranteed the debt until the new emigrant could send money back. But May had cash, and behind the curtains at the back of a Fashion Emporium some shopgirls must have witnessed, by the golden glow of lamplight, a transfiguration. The rough underwear of a subsistence farmer's daughter exchanged for batiste and lawn, May's waist pulled in for the first time by embroidered stays, her bosom made newly assertive in a gauzy blouse with leg-o'-mutton sleeves, the curve of her buttocks smoothed into a long skirt that is tight over the hips but flares neatly just above the boots. The boots! May insists on a pair of cream-colored cloth boots, though the shop assistant says that they will never do, that there isn't a week's wear in them. So I imagine. I see her wearing the cloth boots already as she makes her way, naphtha lamps hissing white in the dark night, to the steamship offices on the quay.

AND THERE she did the thing that sets her apart. The expressive thing.

We have only her word for it, of course, but it fits everything we come to know about her. It was also what she needed to do to hide. What she says herself is that it was because of *not wanting to mix with common steerage emigrants* that she bought herself a cabin-class ticket. This was something that only about two percent of all the people who sailed from Europe to America in the nineteenth century did, and nothing could better show that May had a big idea of herself. It makes her more American than Irish even before she steps aboard—that belief in abundance, that confidence that, when this money is spent, there'll be more money.

A comedy of manners must have ensued. Picture May in her cabin—a jewel box lined in precious woods, brochures of the time say—of bird's-eye maple, perhaps, banded with satinwood. Through a doorway there'd have been a deep bath in a mahogany surround;

beside it on a delicate chair, a pile of folded damask towels. What did she make of these things? What did she make of the silence when she was left standing in the cabin by an impassive porter? I imagine her peering up and down the corridor, and I imagine a little bellboy passing, and May asking him where would she get a drop of tea and what time did he get off work? She had never, after all, been more than a few feet away from someone she knew.

Then a maid might have knocked to see whether the lady needed help with her gown—while three decks below, May's emigrating Irish sisters dreamed of being lucky enough to get jobs as maids. And then there was dinner in the first-class dining room, for a girl who'd barely seen a knife and fork in her life, much less a dinner service. Her gait would already have changed as she walked across the Palm Court, she who'd gone barefoot in summer and worn hobnailed boots in winter. This would be her first time to walk on carpet, since she would never have been in the homes of any of the men and women of the middle class for whom she stepped off the pavement in Longford as they passed in their hats and muffs, shopboys following with their purchases. All May knew about etiquette was whatever she'd observed as one of the little crowd of onlookers kept back by officious shouts when white-gloved servants held open the doors of the Granard Arms Hotel for the gentry descending from their carriages.

She doesn't understand, when she enters the dining room, that the reason everyone is looking at her so intently is because they can't believe their eyes.

She returns a beaming smile. So I confidently imagine.

The orchestra strikes up a selection from *The Gondoliers* and the waiters silently jostle to be the one who will roll the hors d'oeuvres trolley to where she sits. "Look at those beads!" the ladies whisper. "And chiffon! At this hour!" They cannot bring themselves, when May is shown to her table, to return her hearty greeting with even a nod. But the men jump up for her. They find amusing the very things that make the women grow more pinched throughout the meal. That she did not know why the waiter was holding her chair and took it roughly away from him. That she ate her meal with much help from a soup spoon she would not give up. That she gulped the wine as if it were water and held out her glass for more. That she was finished ahead of everyone else and was in no way embarrassed.

"Isn't this a grand place?" she might have said, delighted, looking around the brilliant room. Or, "What's this when it's at home?" poking at her plate.

"You never saw a lobster before, miss?" an elderly man inquires.

"I never saw seawater before today!" May says, and throws her head back and laughs. Her eyes gleam through the silky wisps of hair coming down over her flushed face. But when the passengers move out to the salon for liqueurs and hothouse fruits, the women insistently claim their husbands' arms. She has to walk by herself. No one holds the door for her.

Something very like this must have happened. But in her book *the steamer took ten days to cross the pond,* she blandly writes, *and I thoroughly enjoyed every moment of the trip. I laid myself out to be agreeable and succeeded fairly well.*

ANYONE WHO HAS KNOWN an emigrant journey will remember that the space between countries is full of emotion. The overnight boats to Liverpool and Holyhead that I once knew were full of men drinking and weary women dabbing on a bit of cheap perfume in the toilets that smelled of vomit and combing their hair and going back to sit beside their cardboard suitcases in the bar. Sorrow made them lax. There were also young people, shocked at being out of home but free for the first time ever in their lives from watchful elders. Late at night when the air was thick with smells of engine oil and spilled Guinness, a person desperate for kindness or physical relief might meet a stranger just as needy and the pair of them would go up on deck past the bodies asleep or drunk and push open the iron door against spray flying in from the black night, and give and take some kind of consolation, standing there against a funnel dimpled with years of paint, the man's big coat pulled around both bodies.

Where would these people, after all, have learned the skill of managing liberty?

Runaway May was made vulnerable by her body, and there was nothing for her to protect herself with, in those days, except knowledge. She says in her book, *I was dreadfully afraid of having a baby. I hadn't been on a stock-farm for nothing. I didn't think a stork brought babies unexpectedly. This made me very careful in my dealings with boys.* She may also have known about prostitution—Longford had an army barracks, and therefore it had its women who lived by servicing soldiers. The camp followers who lived near army headquarters, sixty miles away, are documented; they were called "wrens" because their existence was as pitiably exposed to the elements as if they had been birds—they and their children living in holes half scooped out of the earth under gorse bushes and trying to keep warm by sitting on pots of water they heated over fires of sticks, their skirts around the pots. And the Longford ones, too, would have been visible even if they were kept in old cottages down some back lane, because their defense against their terrible lives was drunkenness. Maybe May caught glimpses of them and knew that women sold their bodies to stay alive before she knew much else about men and women.

She was living in luxury, on the voyage to America. She had rich food pressed on her from morning to night. Wine. She was idle for the first time in her life. It is hard to believe that if in that half-fantastical world a gentleman wanted to caress her or have her caress him, May pushed him away. The men would certainly have offered her money, because they wouldn't have known how else to deal with a girl of her class. And she might well have thought that a present in exchange for allowing herself to be caressed was something for nothing. And also—flirting would have passed the time. No lady would have spoken to her. Her presence was an absolute affront to the ladies.

Then one bright morning there must have been a shout—"There! There!"—and a last flamboyant *whoosh* down the scales from the accordionist on the lower deck and a cheer from the dancing crowd. "Look! There now!"

On her island, straight ahead.

Liberty.

THE SHIP TIES UP at Castle Garden. The little bellboy peers from behind a potted palm at the table in the ship's salon where an immigration officer is interviewing May—that's where cabin-class passengers entering America at that time were questioned. She says in her book that she showed the officer some of her cash and gave him the name and address of the uncle she was going to in Nebraska. Edenmore people would have been familiar from their emigrants with the great crossroads that Nebraska was, but none of the 15,963 people of Irish origin in the state census for 1890 have any of May's family names. That doesn't mean that there wasn't an uncle—May herself, after all, is using whatever name she gave in Liverpool when she bought her ticket, and we don't know what that was.

It's not important. The essence of the new world that hustled and shouted and pulsed with energy on the quayside below was self-invention. It was in process of formation—like May. She would never have seen black people before, heard peddlers cry their wares in Yiddish, seen diamonds in the cravats of men like these ones lounging where they could look over the people from steerage as they took their first hesitant steps between the ship and the immigration office. This was no city for girls; the age of consent, until the year before, had been ten; now, it is sixteen.

But May sashays down the gangplank.

She sets a foot—its cream-colored boot distinctly dirty by now—on the soil of the United States.

A study done for a Catholic charity around that time found that of three thousand arrivals of single Irish females, only seventy-six were not met by friends. But May is one of that minority. She is absolutely on her own.

I WENT to America myself, not long after I first heard about her. I crossed a cityscape not wholly different from the one she encountered back then the day I set off from Brooklyn to read her book in the library in Manhattan, taking note again of what surprised me when I first arrived, that must have surprised her, too—houses that are liver-colored, not gray, ceilings made of patterned tin, etched-glass doors, pavements made of blue stone. The F train came out of a tunnel high above warehouses and weedy vacant lots and clanked on stilts around a curve above a canal, the clutter of the New York waterfront off to the left, the Statue of Liberty a somber idol far away across shimmering water. We tipped forward into the dark underwater, and ran across the bed of the East River in a pipe that I imagined swathed in languorous weeds, and stopped and started our way to 42nd Street. I climbed into the golden haze of an autumn morning and strode out to the library. I was very happy to have a destination, and not be a tourist, condemned to wander all day from one weightless experience to another. I had never been in the great Reading Room before, but now, with the satisfaction of an insider, I thought about where I'd sit so that the sun when it moved would not flood my laptop screen with brilliance.

I collected the book and opened it with a silent flourish. Old-fashioned type on cheap, mealy paper. *Chicago May, Her Story.*

At last.

IT'S TRUE that I didn't stop reading for hours. But I traveled home to my friend's house that evening—for the first time in New York a commuter—full of confusion. The train tunneled beneath the sneaker stores and takeout joints of downtown Brooklyn and sloped up into the sunset on a viaduct where cellphone after cellphone woke into tinny melody. I had nothing to celebrate. In Edenmore, May had taken on life in my imagination as a vibrant, impatient, auburn-haired girl whose mixture of arrogance and ignorance I understood very well and was touched by. But that girl hadn't written this book. What I'd believed—that I'd have a warm, easy identification with May—had been foolish.

I had forgotten that the autobiographies of crooks are all plot and no theme. Her book existed because May was a crook, and crooks do things; they don't reflect on them. It brought me face to face with the tedium of the picaresque and reminded me how unsatisfying it is, nowadays, to read an account of experience that is propelled by event, not character. What I wanted to know was what May was like. But she wasn't interested in that question. I myself, and almost all modern memoirists, wrote to discover myself and to reveal myself to the complicit reader, but May hardly mentioned her thoughts or feelings. She presented herself—though her own material sometimes defeated her—as a bluff, practical person with as little inner life as possible. And this no more fits contemporary taste than round faces and Cupid's-bow lips.

What was more, parts of *Her Story* had been overwritten by some editor in an all-purpose, gangster vocabulary, a kind of *Guys and Dolls* language. The men who pick up women are "johns" and "suckers" and "skunks," and the aim in robbing them is to get the "berries" so as to dress in "sparks." It was so hard to read that every few minutes I'd have to take a break and look around at giggling teenagers pitting themselves against the decorum of the library, or at tourists craning up at the painted ceiling, or at job hunters interrogating the screens of computers while they chewed cookies they took from rustling paper bags. It wasn't until I registered how many different kinds of faces I was looking at and how many languages were being whispered around me that it occurred to me that early American crooks were first- or second-generation immigrants and that what I was struggling with was a slang they had invented in order to communicate. Thinking of it as part of the heroic immigrant effort reconciled me to it.

The book was more thrown together than written. After the first chapter, it was full of irrelevancies, repetitions, inconsequential remarks, sudden blunt statements. Paragraphs began, "I forgot to say." Characters arrived and disappeared and arrived again. Admittedly, the artlessness of the narrative had the virtue of winning my trust: May wasn't seriously in the business of persuading the reader of anything, true or false. She was just pouring out, with slapdash vigor, as much about the events of her life as she could get down. When she did, sometimes, try to mislead, you could see her going about it. It was obvious.

But the first chapter was different from the rest. There, the account of her childhood was such a flowery fake that I started to laugh. May gives herself an imaginary birthplace and a pretty English name instead of her workaday Irish one, and promotes herself a few social classes—she says she grew up in *a large, well-kept house* and attended a convent boarding school, which only the daughters of the bourgeoisie did in Ireland in the nineteenth century. She is also, here, the adored and adoring daughter of parents who were as happy as they were good. *Mother was a handsome, buxom young woman as I remember her,* she wrote. *She was singing all the time, attending to her household duties, and making life happy for all around her.* Her father, according to May, was even better; he was *sociable, kindly and agreeable. He loved his neighbors and was a good neighbor to all in the vicinity, were they Catholics or Protestants.* Even today, loving your neighbor is not so easy if he's a Protestant with good, drained land on the hillside and you're a Catholic farming the waterlogged valley or the marginal land out on the edge of the bog. But presumably May thought she might as well make everyone in her ideal childhood happy.

I was the pet of the family, she wrote.

Which means, of course, that her actions when she stole the money and ran away were perfectly inexplicable.

BUT THAT EVENING I started thinking. What if she was protecting her real family? Wouldn't that be a reason for all those lies?

And later it occurred to me that what she'd done in that first chapter was sad. It was sad to see a solitary, middle-aged woman—which is what May was when she was writing—sketch so detailed a fantasy of a loved and loving childhood.

THERE'D BE MORE of that if I went ahead with her, I realized—of interpreting her without ever being sure I was right. I'd be trying to make her express herself as she had not done—I'd be like the talkative one of a pair of twins, who answers for both. I'd have to take her book and fillet it and stick parts of it together and sort it into sequences and abbreviate its anecdotes—assault it, put my ear close to it, coax its meanings out of it. I wasn't worried about being unfair to her writing; this wasn't some rare text, this was a workaday piece of writing that would be nothing but improved by editing. But would my readers be able to trust a biography that proceeded this way? Would I myself be able to stay true to her?

And for what—for what reason, for what reward—would I make the effort? None of us make that kind of effort, except for love. Or, of course, because there's something important about the person under scrutiny. May was important because she lived; but she didn't have a spectacular career—not at all. She wasn't, on the other hand, representative; you'd never call her Everywoman. And she wasn't exceptionally bad or good or clever or stupid—her life was exceptional in the places she knew and the people who came her way and the things she did, but she didn't seem to me to be exceptional the way geniuses are. Then again—that was reassuring. I felt she was not beyond my comprehension.

THE DAYS went by—warm, fall days when I used to come out of the library and sit in Bryant Park and watch the squirrels intent on their squirrel lives—and I read *Her Story* again, this time slowly, and with growing shame at what I had once expected of it. How could I, whose life had never known the perilous edges and black depths and mayhem that May knew, have been so thoughtless as to expect from her the kind of shapely, insightful autobiography that educated women can write today?

A flicker of excitement began within me.

I'd accept the terms that had presented themselves. Of course I would.

There was more here than I'd realized, only it was more deeply hidden.

I would write about her, and I would stay close to her book. To keep myself straight I'd observe my own rules. I'd pick bits and pieces out—I'd have to—but I wouldn't edit within each bit. I'd make things up—her words already prompted all kinds of scenes in my head—but when I did, I'd signal it. I wouldn't use her story as the basis for some kind of semifiction of my own—that would be as bad as if a woman climbed out of a grave and brushed the clay from her mouth and spoke, and I substituted words of my own for hers. I would respect the fact—which, after all, was astonishing—that a book about herself existed, by May Duignan of Edenmore. It had waited more than seventy-five years for a reader as willing to be sympathetic as I was. If sympathy has a meaning—if it is not a fickle emotion but has the heft of the political idea of inclusion, of according careful attention to every human being and enrolling every one of them in the human community—then wanting to reach her would help me reach her, even though she was hidden behind the passage of time, and behind the conventions of the crook's memoir genre, and behind her own chosen image.

Maybe a biography worthy of the name couldn't be constructed across the many voids between us; I had nothing to go on, after all, but her book. But wouldn't it be worth trying to find out how much you have to know about and feel for another person to move toward that person? There was an emotional challenge here that began to seem almost indistinguishable from a moral one.

THERE WAS no question, once I saw the project of writing about May like that, of turning it down. So I set about following her. I was in a library, but I had such a sense of forward movement that I might have been on that quayside near Castle Garden and falling into line behind the boy who's carrying her bag. I follow the glint of sun on the coil of red-gold hair under the splendid tulle hat. She makes her way, straight-backed and tall, through the bustle of the quayside, and I am the only one who knows that her money—her freedom—is hidden between her chemise and her bodice. She's moving fast because she's elated, but I almost see her turn, without breaking her stride, and beckon me on. That was how it often was in real life, in the days of emigration. One woman went ahead and learned the ropes and, as soon as she could, helped another woman make the journey.

It wouldn't have taken May three minutes to get to the line of horse-drawn cabs outside the Custom House. Let's suppose that she paused there to pat a horse's melancholy nose while the driver leaned down for her bag.

She pays the boy with an unfamiliar dollar.

She steps up into the first cab of her life.

The boy slams the door, there's a whipcrack, and the horse wheels around and begins to clip-clop up Broadway.

She's on her way.

Two

Nebraska to Chicago

How does a young person put together an idea of what love is, in a culture where feelings are rarely expressed and where there are no books or films? *Animal spirits,* May wrote, *and romantic, chivalrous love, carried me through the entry-way into crime.* But what did she mean by love when she was nineteen? What love had she seen in Edenmore? Had she listened to what she was told about Christ's all-encompassing love? Or had she noticed the wordless love that shows itself in the way a mother's untiring hand presses a baby into the fold between shoulder and throat? Or was sentimental love what had impressed her in the songs sung, perhaps, by the wife of one of Longford's professional men—the doctor's wife, or the accountant's—to her husband's piano accompaniment late on a summer evening, "I Dreamt That I Dwelt in Marble Halls" or "M'Apparì" drifting from the open windows of the villa to the country people waiting on the roadway for the cart to home?

In a House of Correction in New York at the end of the nineteenth century, 279 prostitutes were interviewed as to how they began in their profession. Some said they were forced, some said it was for pay, some "yielded where there was no love and where neither money nor force was used, but succumbed through weakness of will," and twenty-seven of them, who must have had terrible lives, "could not remember why" they had become prostitutes.

Of the 279 prostitutes, 108 "claimed that their first wrongdoing was because they yielded to a man whom they loved."

No doubt. But no doubt, too, they had no money. Love always has a context.

May's story is that after a while in a hotel in Manhattan her money ran low, so she got the train to Nebraska, to her uncle's house, but she didn't like it there. It was in those circumstances, penniless and dissatisfied, that she fell in love. The boy was called Dal Churchill. She chose him, she wrote, *against the field*; but a partner is a necessity rather than a choice for a young woman adrift in a man's world.

The Nebraska of the 1890s that Willa Cather writes about is a house-making and farm-making place where the energy and personal preferences of the people are fiercely bent toward putting down roots. But settler America was also restless with people in movement—claims lawyers, homesteaders who'd sold or been pushed out, entertainers, enforcers, government agents, horse traders, peddlers, land-grabbers, dentists. And outlaws, men for hire. Dal Churchill, May says, was one of these. She chose him, she said, *knowing him to be a robber, highwayman, safe cracker, cattle rustler and general all-round crook*. She says that he rode with the Dalton Brothers, which was one of the gangs that roamed the lands west of the Mississippi, moving around to attack the early cash-moving system based on railroads and banks. The records that survive from those permeable and shifting territories have no mention of a Dal Churchill. The one organization of that time where the names of men like Dal were recorded was the Pinkerton Detective Agency, a forerunner of the FBI. It was in the

The City Hotel, Sargent, Nebraska

business of guarding banks and tracking bank robbers, but it has no record of him or of any of the actions May mentions.

She says she ran away with him, and I'm sure that there was a lawless young man and that May and he journeyed as a couple along the spreading railroads and lay together in wooden rooms in hotels at the edges of clearings where tracks crossed or diverged—places that you see in old photos mottled by time.

When he was away with the gang, she would have had nothing to do but play cards for cents and eat fatty sausage and boiled potatoes in some settlement where thirsty dogs howled and howled because they were kept from the well by a board fence and where men building houses struggled with sheets of tin in the hot wind. Newly settled America must have been full of people waiting. For tools and livestock to come from the East. For wives and children who would climb down onto the platform, wraithlike in the smoke from the engine, and shy. Sometimes, she says, when the boys went off, they'd send her to a village they knew in the Badlands, or they'd send her back to Chicago where one of them had a sister. So when Dal wanted her to work with him, just the two of them together, *I was for the plan, full of enthusiasm and anxious to prove myself.* It was as his comrade that she learned how to rob men and banks, out there in pioneer America.

They married, though according to May she stipulated that they had to pull off a big job together before she'd do it. I believe all this, partly because many years later, when she was recalling her life so as to write her book, she remarked to someone she never lied to that she had been married, once, in Salt Lake City. But also because she drops a rare remark that shows her analyzing personality. *Dal laughed his hearty, boyish laugh and agreed. It tickled him for me to assume the big-woman attitude and "mother" him.* What exactly was she doing with her proviso? Was she saying that she was his equal, not his dependent?

We're hearing her voice in her book now, but when she describes Dal she might as well be every girl who ever fell for a boy. *He fearlessly rode the countryside,* she wrote, *and forded the rivers where fords there were none, dealing out rough justice to oppressors of the common people. He was strong, muscular and quick as a panther. Children and women were safe in his hands. His friends could count on him to the death and so could his enemies. An inveterate gambler, he rarely touched liquor and never indulged in dope of any sort. He was quick on the trigger and a good pistol shot. Add to all this that he had black eyes that fairly bored through you and wavy chestnut hair, with a complexion that was bronzed with exposure, and there is little wonder that I fell desperately in love with him.*

He sounds like the fantasy hero of a tomboy heroine—Calamity Jane, for instance, who'd been making appearances in dime novels since as far back as 1880. But when it comes to heroes, words need do no more than prompt. At the time that May was writing—toward the end of the 1920s—the frontier world that she had known with Dal was on its way into myth. Its real wildness had been tamed, and its career in vaudeville and cinema had begun—one of the Dalton brothers, even, was employed in Hollywood as an advisor to movies that sanitized the hard life he once actually knew. Silent cowboy movies were all the rage; May wrote part of her book when she was living beside a cinema, and the movies she would have seen were the same then as now—exemplary tales replete with noble, handsome heroes, stern sheriffs, unshaven bandits, and swarthy natives who watch the unsuspecting good men approach the canyon below, then topple backward off their horses in a hail of arrows. Trains are held up by wild young men like Dal, wheeling in on their horses in clouds of dust. In the dark of the cinema she could be both the bad girl who kicks up gartered legs in the saloon and the freckled miss in a gingham frock at the door of the cabin to whom the handsome horseman turns to wave one last time.

But in reality there was little that was heroic about the bandits of the time. Butch Cassidy had no teeth left at the age of thirty-two. And "it was hell proper," one of the Wild Bunch wrote about his life.

In the daytime we would sweat, fry or sizzle under the hot desert sun, or ride for whole days with our clothes soaking wet in rainy weather, or sleep in wet clothes on cold nights under one saddle blanket. The sweat would roll down our bellies and backs, and the hard, heavy money belts would gall a raw ring clear around our bodies. And while we was frying, freezing, starving and depriving ourselves of every comfort and pleasure of existence, here was all that stolen money in our belts while we was nearly perishing for the things it could buy for us.

Gangs like the Daltons were often quite popular, because the settlers didn't much care if banks, which they resented, were robbed, and they appreciated the gestures bandits made, such as—I once read— contributing barrels of oysters to a community's harvest celebration dances. But they endured the roughest of lives for desperately small pickings. There's a photograph of the bodies of four members of the

The bodies of two Dalton brothers and two associates, Coffeyville, Kansas, 1892

Dalton gang propped against a board fence, after the debacle of their final robbery attempt. Four thin men with unruly hair in crumpled dark suits—poor, unbeautiful men. They were shot by the neighbors when they tried to rob the banks in their hometown.

Being a whore isn't glamorous either, though it is constantly glamorized. And a whore and a thief is what May became. That was when she became a young widow, after she heard, when she was waiting for Dal in Chicago, that he was dead.

Dal Churchill was lynched by the locals, she says she was told, when they caught him robbing a train near Phoenix. There's no record of such an event.

That's all.

He leaves her story.

IT IS A FALLACY of biography to make it seem that decisions succeed each other along a chosen path, when from within a life a decision may simply have been whatever it took to survive this situation or that. May was alone in the city of Chicago, an immigrant now, and face to face with harsh circumstance. For generations, Irish people

have emigrated—all my mother's siblings and most of mine, for example, did—yet the collective experience cannot protect the individual migrant from loneliness and fear. My young brother Dermot, the
eighth of the nine of us children, was put on the night boat from Ireland to get himself to London, though he was barely fifteen and did
not know how to make the journey. In the middle of the night, the
train from the Irish ferry stopped for a few minutes at a junction
somewhere in England and he thought he'd arrived in London and got
out; and when day came, a railwayman found him on the deserted
platform, weeping and hungry. May may never have wept; but as a
young woman of twenty-one or twenty-two, alone in her first city,
with no money, her situation was not very different from Dermot's.

It never occurred to me to look for honest employment, she wrote.
*Did I not know that the rewards of steady industry were pitiful com-
pared with the easy, if uncertain, windfalls of crime? I had become a
spendthrift, and the element of luck appealed to me.* But she's talking
as if she were a man. She was a woman. She was not going to use guns
and fast horses in pursuit of the "windfalls of crime"; she was going
to use her person. She was going to make a crude instrument out of
the tender flesh that connected her sexual self, through a tracery of
subtle nerves, to her whole sensibility. Opening a woman's body to a
stranger is as grossly physical an event as being shot to death. May's
bladder and bowels, her heartburn, her period cramps, her runny
nose, her aching ankles were as much part of her as her pink flesh and
red-gold hair, as she began her independent life in Chicago, perhaps
in a lodging house with stained lace curtains where a train juddered
down the center of a dirt street in a cloud of choking smoke, and
trousers stiff with dirt were pulled on in unheated rooms where the
cold water in tin basins had sewage in it.

There are downward passages that seem to happen by themselves.
A person who has lived under the restraints of custom can discover
that sluttish behavior feels perfectly familiar. Maybe May never noticed the line she was crossing—maybe she was tired and half drunk

and she'd been moving from place to place ahead of the landlords and her hair needed a wash and she hadn't a dollar and the man who wanted her held a roll of notes right under her nose and flicked it with his fingernail. Maybe she was with a man she looked on as a protector, and he instructed her to go to the back of the saloon with the man with the roll of notes. She doesn't tell us anything about the crucial moment in her life, the moment of fall, the moment of disjunction from an ordinary fate. The moment when she first agreed to sell her body.

She owned nothing else she could sell, except a different kind of labor, for which she would be paid one-tenth the wage. And life with Dal must have confirmed her self-image as being a reckless girl. And maybe she did it, too, because it was something she could decide to do or not to do, by herself. All her life she'd seen men preach, in-struct, police, judge, travel, get drunk, buy animals, choose occupa-tions, choose wives, and she'd seen women move around the narrow enclave of the home, the only place in which they were allowed agency. Selling herself kept at least some agency in her own hands.

And maybe—this of all things we can never know—she was bet-ter able to do it because something had already happened to her, at home or somewhere else around Edenmore, that had made her will-ing to use her body as a thing. After all, millions of other young women who came to America also found themselves penniless and fearful in big cities. But they washed dishes, swept floors, minded children, begged, sold individual paper flowers by day and slept in doorways by night, or did anything else that would protect their bod-ily integrity and preserve the hope of a better future. Why was May the one who went into the sex trade?

Mustn't her past have had something to do with the choices she made? The aggression—or at least the alienation—behind stealing the family money always stood out for me in May's story. And also, the improbable ease of the theft. Would her father's life savings have been so easy to steal? What if she didn't steal them but was in a posi-tion to demand them? Or what if they were paid to her so she would go away? Wouldn't some kind of family ugliness explain better than anything else the fantasy of the blissful childhood with wonderful parents with which she began *Her Story*? There was never any local gossip about May's home. But the very intimacy of rural Ireland made its people expert in concealment.

Most of my speculations about May are based on fragments of evidence, but for this there's no evidence, so I won't return to it. But the veil has been drawn back too often from seemingly impeccable families not to prompt at least a question when the daughter of a respectable, devout family grows up to laugh in false enjoyment on a bed in a hotel room while a stranger tears at her clothes. That's what May came to, when she graduated to using a whore's skills to rob men.

THE FIRST *big crooked job I did in Chi,* she wrote, *was with Dora Donegan. It turned out to be a big one for me. I pulled a john into the Sherman House. After I got him there I did not know how to land him. Dora came to the rescue. She saw that I was too modest in handling the prey. I lacked brass. She bawled me out for "not playing square by the gentleman." She said it was not decent to not go ahead with the job and suggested that we have a drink all round. Incidentally, she winked at me, so I would not have my spirit broken, the way puppies get if their first rat is too much for them.*

I went through with the job, and Dora lifted nearly a thousand dollars out of the gent's clothes, while I was putting up a barrage of laughs, shrieks and expostulations. Dora also helped me in this enterprise by steering the gink away from the place and allowing me to escape. I got my split and felt quite big. It was comparatively easy after it was done.

I imagine May and Dora fleeing in a flurry of skirts down Wabash or State to one of the lounges where unaccompanied women were allowed to drink. Maybe they called for champagne—with what else would you celebrate a thousand dollars for an hour's work? Anyway, all the girls drank champagne—it was the only drink you could trust in the days when everything was a cheat, since a champagne cork can't be got back into the bottle. They sprawl on velvet armchairs, flushed and amiable. May scratches herself through her skirt because when the man started coming she heaved him onto her thigh and it's still wet. I take it that the man did come—that it was when he was enfeebled by release that Dora passed the roll of notes to May and let her get away while Dora hustled him into his clothes. I suppose that when the young women joined up and scampered down the street they looked joyful, the way women do when they try to hurry in long skirts. But who would have foreseen that the long run to freedom through the spring night in Edenmore would come to this—a man humiliated and furious, and two tarts, cackling with laughter?

It is a bleak enough epigraph for her new life: *It was comparatively easy after it was done.*

EVEN MUCH LATER, when May was writing her book, a thousand dollars was a lot of money. Though it was the case in 1892, when May began operating in Chicago, that the huge workforce building the White City of the Columbian Exposition and World's Fair—the biggest exhibition the world had ever seen—was unionized, and that meant that there were tens of thousands of men, temporarily in the city and living singly, who were earning good money and had time off to spend it, including spending it on dangerous women. And in 1893, when the fair opened, it was a vacation destination where visitors expected to spend a week or even two being instructed and entertained. At that time people didn't use banks and checkbooks the way they do now. Men were paid in cash and a visitor might well have a thousand dollars concealed in his clothes.

But how a sum as big as that cuts May off! What she makes—either directly in what the client pays her for sex, or indirectly in what she also steals from him—is unconnected with any measure of her own worth. How can an accidental payout be connected with worth? To make a thousand dollars between herself and Dora in less than an hour—it separates May not only from the straight people around but, in a profound way, from herself.

Is that why "immoral earnings" never seem to last? A Chicago woman reformer of the time wrote that "the majority of prostitutes have little conception of the value of money. They earn it easily, and they spend it as easily. Even among those who claim to make far more than the wages of even well-paid working girls it is not infrequent to find young women without changes of underclothing."

They did not "earn it easily." But any working girl or courtesan of the past I've read about has not managed to save her money or to use it to look after herself. She's squandered it, given it away, handed it over to pimps, lost it. May was the same. No matter how big the sum she's just made, on the next page she has nothing and she's on the prowl again. It is a very imperfect transaction—the giving of a body in exchange for money. There's no such thing as a fair price, since the sides of the equation belong to different orders of value. The prostitute gives nothing of herself, and at the same time she gives everything she has. As much as she can get in return is still not enough.

The way the money doesn't stay I take as an expression of disdain for the work, and a distancing from it. But at the same time, the lure of big money spoils a woman for anything else, like a gambler's wins.

I read the report for 1892 of a Christian society that worked to "save" Chicago prostitutes. "Very many have found homes and situations," it said. "Five have been well married, two are running a large laundry; one who was going to drown herself when rescued is carrying on a small fruit farm and often brings us fruit, butter and eggs; one is keeping a large, respectable boarding house and has several hundred dollars saved."

Several hundred. Compared to a thousand.

Some years later the city of Chicago felt obliged, as a preliminary to an effort at reform, to set up a Commission of Enquiry into Vice.

It computed the capitalized value of a local prostitute at twenty-six thousand dollars and a girl clerk at six thousand dollars.

So May starts work.

IMAGINE A YOUNG WOMAN in a wildly expensive hat moving one day through the crowds of pleasure seekers on the Midway Plaisance, the boulevard leading to the World's Fair site. On some days, 175,000 people, the largest crowd ever assembled in peacetime in all history, visit the fair, so she's in the right place to pick up a sucker.

Let us imagine that she brushed against a man in a fine cashmere overcoat but that the line for the exhibition by Little Egypt, the belly dancer, broke up at that moment and the man moved away. She paused to survey the tiny barker for the Pygmy "cannibals" from Central Africa, then cut across the path of a man coming out of the Moorish Palace—which contained a replica of the execution of Marie Antoinette, a machine for making a trip to the moon, and a display of one million dollars in gold coins—but a woman leading a child by the hand joined the man. She passed the Swiss village, staffed by natives of Switzerland, and the German village with its staff in dirndls and lederhosen, and then came to the Irish villages. Workmen were repairing one of them. The organizers of the fair tried to fend off trouble by allowing two Irish villages, in vague deference to the Irish desire to be independent of their British rulers. But Irish-American nationalists staged a protest all the same to mark their objection to the British flag being flown over "Ireland."

May would have nodded approvingly at the marks left by the patriotic demonstration.

Imagine her absorbed in the scene where an Irishwoman her own age, perched on a stool made from bog-oak, was demonstrating the fine stitches that go to make a lace runner. The stool was placed in front of what the fair's brochure called "a store such as one sees in the villages of Ireland and a public-house of the old-country style. Sods of Irish turf have been imported, and if one wishes to stand on real Irish soil he may have the satisfaction." May cast a proprietary eye over all this and over the native Irish brought from Ireland to staff the exhibit—"young girls," the brochure said, "as fresh, healthy and lithe as mountain deer, their deep blue eyes shining like the sunlit lakes of their own green land."

She studied the round tower, the harpists, the pots of potatoes, the real cattle, and the "broth of a boy" who sat on a porch in a hat and a long coat with brass buttons and every so often repeated "a tale of the old country" to a small audience. Such things as these—a harp-playing dairymaid, a one-third-size replica of a Romanesque chapel—had never been seen by Irish people. Nor had most Irish women had the leisure or the skill to engage in craft work, though here in the Chicago sun the girls lithe as mountain deer demonstrated embroidery, weaving, and lacemaking as if cottage industry thrived in their sad homeland. That was the idea the Anglo-Irish ladies on the fair committee wanted to promote—that there was or could be a female Irish peasantry that was cash-earning and self-sufficient.

Now imagine that a man with a diamond ring murmured in May's ear and, when she turned, exclaimed at the innocent prettiness of her face. He put a plump hand under her elbow and hurried her toward the terminus where a trolley for the city waited.

They passed the Women's Building of the fair, which was a sham in several ways. It was designed by a young woman architect, and the profuse detail on the façade was executed by woman sculptors selected competitively from all the states of the Union, but it was made—like most of the fair's buildings—from a hemp and plaster-of-Paris mixture, impressively white, but no more meant to last than the movie sets it prefigured. And as to its name—May is by no means included in what the Women's Building, with its demonstrations of progressive childcare, means by women. Other parts of America were more punitive; she'd have been classified in those as "a female person of a lewd nature" and been subject to arrest if she conducted herself in an improper manner within the sight or hearing of respectable

One of the Irish "villages" at the World's Columbian Exposition, Chicago, 1893

women. Here, if one of the committee ladies glimpsed May where she sat on the bus with the man's arm squeezing her waist, all she could do was turn away in disgust and complain—as many ladies did—that loose persons really must be kept off the Midway.

The fact is that May is a woman, but she is excluded from the category of women.

She is the self-sufficient and cash-earning female Irish peasant whom the ladies designed the Irish villages to promote, but no lady would ever acknowledge her existence.

And she is Irish, but an outsider among the other Irish. The Chicago Vice Commission began its work by collecting statistics, and it reported that of all arrests of Irish females in the city only 1.1 percent were for prostitution, and the Irish rated lowest of all ethnic and racial groups for "crimes against chastity."

But May is a criminal against chastity, and as such, is now an exile from every community except the ruthless community of the underworld.

PART TWO

1893 to 1900

Three

Chicago

When I was in Chicago, I stood once where the half-frozen river slid under shards of ice into the lake, dank fog rising as the winter afternoon darkened. In the 1890s, the grand ladies of this city had different stockings for morning, evening, the opera, for driving out in the carriage, for receptions. A gown of lace and supple white *satin d'orange* might be worn over corsets of the same satin made of a hundred whalebones and over six petticoats, from an outer one of imported muslin to a short white flannel "inside." But how the cold must have borne down on poor working girls! Just here at the confluence of river and lake was a district known as The Sands, where there would have been reeds and pebbles and abundant wildfowl, and out from the gray shore, small freighters puffing steam as they plied their way through shifting ice. Shack brothels made of rough boards covered The Sands a couple of decades before May came to town. The name accidentally survives of one of the women who worked there—Margaret McGuinness, a countrywoman of my own and May's, I've no doubt—who's said to have been neither sober nor out of the house for five years, and not to have had her clothes on for three. When she died—the seventh unnatural death in the place in one week—the coroner listed the cause of death as "intemperance."

In the end, the mayor led a raid on The Sands and the shacks were demolished. As the women were hunted out, bystanders poured buckets of water over them.

There's a book about nineteenth-century Chicago by Herbert Asbury, who wrote *Gangs of New York,* and he says that in Dead Man's Alley, a trash-filled passageway off Polk, half a dozen abandoned old hackney cabs were shelter for black working girls. At Peoria and Monroe, there was a terrible place called The Jungle, where a hundred or so women were kept in shacks that they could not leave unless accompanied by pimps. They were called "airwalkers" because of their peculiar bouncing gait, the result of the excessive use of encaine, a cheap substitute for cocaine. At the top end of the scale, the sex transaction was obscured by display and conspicuous consumption and overstuffed furniture—a madam called Carrie Watson, a great favorite of the police, had a house with five parlors and a billiard room and even, it was said, a bowling alley in the basement where the pins were chilled bottles of champagne. In the Everleigh Club, there was a music room, a library, an art gallery, and fountains that squirted perfume, and the girls were used on marble beds. But there was squalor at the top just as there was at the bottom. There was, for example, the constant threat of disease. Soldiers in the American army in the 1890s were ten times more likely than soldiers in the Prussian army to have chancroid, gonorrhea, or syphilis.

Picture May leading the men she picked up through a mayhem of clanging trolleys, horses jostling to get out of their way, peddlers' carts, displays of merchandise, vagrants begging, businessmen stepping outside to smoke cigars, and girls like herself with winged hats

and tiny waists above swaying, bell-shaped skirts, all mingling tumul-
tuously in the flesh smell from the stockyards, the manure smell from
the gutters, and the fumes of oil and heat from smoky engines. The
city is described as perpetually dirty with coal dust, hideous with
noise from the iron wheels of trains and trolleys and carriages, dimly
lit by yellow gas lamps, and stinking from the rat-gnawed garbage,
which included dead dogs and horses, and from the horse dung in the
streets and the rotting offal in the stockyards. But it also contained
buildings higher and more daring than any others in the world, magnificently decorated with cut stone and bas-relief and mosaics in marble and onyx and gold leaf—the buildings of the capital city of a new
empire of commerce.

THE BROTHELS of the red-light district of the First Ward were described to the Vice Commission by a police witness:

> At all hours of the day and night women could be seen at the
> doors and windows, frequently half clad, making an exhibi-
> tion of themselves and using vulgar and obscene language. At
> almost all of these places there were sliding windows, or win-
> dows that were hung on hinges and swung inside. These were
> used by the women to invite pedestrians on the street to enter
> these places and also for the purpose of exhibiting themselves.
> Extension fronts were built to many of these houses from
> which a better view could be had of the police and pedestrians.
> It was no unusual thing in those days to see from fifty to one
> hundred lounging in the doors and windows of this one block
> at one time. The habitués of this place embraced every nation-
> ality, both black and white, their ages ranging from eighteen to
> fifty years. Some were in tights, some having nothing on but a
> loose Mother Hubbard made of some flashy material which re-
> sembled a mosquito net, through which the entire form of the

woman could be seen. Others were dressed as jockeys, while others had no sleeves in their dresses. The waist was cut so low that their bosoms were entirely exposed, and some were dressed almost exclusively in the garb which nature gave them when they were born.

One madam boasted that all her harlots had been thrown out of "decent houses" for stealing and fighting, and declared that no man could imagine an act of perversion that they would not perform—and she proved it at her "circus nights." The madams procured, too. They brought very young girls to their establishments to be prepared for service by men actually paid to rape them. In 1895, one brothel-keeper brought nine girls from Cleveland and, as always, they were locked in and their clothes taken away. When four of those children climbed down on bedsheets tied together, three found a police station, but one disappeared, never to be seen again. Reformers did, however, manage to get the police to charge that madam.

White slavery wasn't imaginary. There was, as there always is, trafficking. Gangs found their victims among the underpaid domestic servants, factory girls, waitresses, and store salesgirls, thousands of whom were struggling to keep alive on inadequate wages. They were "broken in" and sold. In a single month during a reform effort in the 1890s, the police rescued 329 young girls who believed themselves to be trapped in brothels.

In the library that stands on a block of that "pleasure district," I transcribed a little letter one such girl wrote: "I wish you would come and see me and I can tell you everything then I am a White Slave for sure. Please excuse Pencle I had to write this and sneak this out."

MAY DENIES that she was a prostitute. She wants to be known as a "badger," the name for a con woman who entices a man to a bedroom where the amorous preliminaries are interrupted by an accom-

A brothel in Chicago, 1890s

A missionary pleads with a prostitute, Chicago, 1890s

plice playing a cop, or an outraged husband, or a landlord, and where in the ensuing panic she or the accomplice steals the man's valuables. She's a respectable thief, in other words. She's a skilled, not an unskilled, worker. But what did a man think the Irishwoman was going to do? For what was he savoring the black-stockinged ankle he could glimpse above the neat boot? Every gaze that rests on May thinks it rests on a prostitute. She has to live and work wherever men seek out prostitutes. If she goes anywhere outside the red-light district, it is to pick up men, using the wiles of a prostitute. She's leading him to a room that smells of sweat and sperm—because even if there wasn't penetration, there must have been various kinds of ejaculation. And though it must have taken an age to undress a woman from the lavish clothing of that time, May would not always have been able to confuse and delay her victims with net and satin and flounced underskirts and skin-smelling petticoats, and there must have been many times when she had to give what they were there to get.

It was the rare man, she boasted, *who got anything from me.* But, of course, it doesn't defend her against the stigma of selling herself to say that she didn't sell herself often.

May also worked in the "dipping houses" in Custom House Place. *They were like booths,* she wrote, *into which you took your man. If you succeeded in getting him in, the landlady soon helped you trim him. Sometimes the suckers would go to the Harrison Street Station and put up a holler. Over would come the wagon, and the police would pull everybody in the house. They would lock you up for a few hours, turn you loose, and you would hear no more of the matter.*

It is a mystery to me how the panel houses and dipping houses survived. When the sucker was struggling to spill the creamy body of someone like May from the hooks of a satin corset and a stern voice roared, "Who's in there?" why did the man panic? In a red-light district, why would a man be terrified to be caught with a prostitute? Did the man somehow believe that a woman who would take him to a room was, nevertheless, respectable? Were women literally perceived differently back then, when there were still fundamentalist categories of innocence and transgression? Was it believed, at the beginning of urban America, that a person who looked good was good?

And how did those places go on getting custom after word got out about them? Many of the customers were out-of-towners, and must have come from small places where everyone knew everything about everyone else. Can it be that they were credulous beyond our ability to imagine, when it came to believing the lies told in cities?

A cheat is what May became, and in all her long book, she makes only one reference to what she might otherwise have been.

After Dal died, she wrote, *if I had had a baby or if I could have returned to my own people the chances are that I would have gone straight.*

If I had had a baby . . . This is all she ever says about child-bearing—though I think that it is simply not possible for a woman to look back over her life and not find her thoughts snagging, again and again, on motherhood. I think women who've had children always try to imagine a life less shared, and childless women always interrogate the freedom of action that childlessness gave them. If May had had a child, her distinctive identity would have become subsumed in the terrible struggle to survive. An Italian journalist visiting Chicago at that time talked about "the smoke that blinds you, the smells which take your breath, the mountains of sacks piled up in the little court-yards, the disturbance of the rubbish dumps, the whistles and bells of a hundred interminable trains, the fury of the people." The fury came from desperation. In the year before the World's Fair opened, fifty thousand homeless men "were tramping the streets of Chicago out of work," an investigative journalist wrote, "with no place to sleep but the police stations and the corridors of City Hall and no food except what they could grab from the free-lunch counters of the saloons." And the situation was worse for women and girls, who had no personal or collective experience, then, of looking for work, and who couldn't draw on the street wisdom that eventually gave them some protection from the ruthlessness of the market. When the Board of Lady Managers advertised one hundred jobs for women at the World's Fair, they were mobbed by ten thousand applicants.

An offhand reference in a newspaper report I saw brought the process of job-seeking to painful life. The day before, it said, the writer had happened to notice

> nearly 50 girls in the women's lounge of a city department store, some as young as 14. A large number of them were continuously studying the Want Ad columns of the newspaper. Some of the girls were in groups but many were alone, and a large number spent all day without food.

If I could have returned to my own people . . . Even if May did have the abstract desire to shelter within the roles of mother or daughter, surely America was far more attractive to a young person than silent Ireland, where the Virgin Mary watched over the rain-swept landscape and the sins of the flesh were never forgiven. The Chicago underworld was cruel, but it was vital. Men poured in on the elevated railway to snatch at pleasure in the saloons and bordellos and hotels and restaurants of the First Ward, a city within the larger city, with its own government of rake-off politicians and conniving policemen. The very lightness of civic constraint made the place teem with life. Go home to Edenmore? Sometimes "returned Yanks" paid a visit to Ireland to show off how well they'd done, but hardly anybody went back to live there again. Not even the failures.

There was nothing for May to do but substitute the red-light district for the Irish village where in another destiny she would have been a leading local "character." She did just that—in her book, she reels off the names of all the crooks she knew and all the cops she knew in her part of Chicago. Presumably, she lived a village life. In Edenmore after the dawn shower sifts through the trees and the birds launch their springy songs into the day, the woman of a house opens the half-door and sunlight falls across the dirt floor. In Chicago, many hours later than that, May would have opened her eyes in whatever house she had her room, sat up slowly, shuffled down the corridor to the cold bathroom, fixed herself up at the basin of water, gone through the long business of dressing with corsets and suspenders and hooks and eyes and buttons; then, with a quick brush of her thick hair, gone out onto the street.

She'd have passed the open doors of the brothels, a maid brushing the front doorstep and sprinkling water around the hallway to keep down the dust. "In the morning just before twelve," a contemporary description of brothel life goes,

> the colored girl served cocktails to each of the women before they got up. After they dressed they took another refresher, usually absinthe. At breakfast they had wine. Then the day's work began. The girls sat in couples at the windows each keeping watch in the opposite direction. If a man passed, they would rap at the window and beckon him to come in. If a policeman appeared, the curtains would be drawn and all trace of hustling disappear, but before the officer was out of sight the girls would be there again. They went on duty fifteen minutes at a time. About four or five in the morning when they were all more or less loaded with drink, they would close the door and go to sleep. Next day it would begin again, the same dull round of drinking and hustling, debauch and drink.

Down the street May goes, greeting and being greeted. She ate breakfast, and maybe went into a bar to have a few drinks with whoever was around, to catch up on the gossip. There was in fact a gossip sheet, copies of which survive, where among the ads for a cure for the opium habit the movements of the working girls are noted amid jokes and sarcastic comments—though I don't suppose the girls, those of them who could read, thought the paper half as funny as the young men who wrote it.

That lady at 492 State Street has got some new stock at last. Lizzie Moss has got sober. Mary McCarthy has gone to the insane asylum. Big Lotta, having succeeded in bilking French Em out of sixty dollars is now stabled at Liz Allen's. They have two new strawberry blondes at Hotel de Goodrich. . . .

It is I who makes May smile and wave. She never mentions anything like that. I want to believe that there was neighborliness, at least, in the kinds of places she now lived in. When I was reading about them, I noted every reference that hinted at community. "One morning twelve inmates in flimsy costumes were seated about a parlor with five men, one a forlorn peddler who had come in to sell fruit." See? If a fruitseller could wander in and out, so could May go in and out to her pals. Or, "The odors in the old house, dirty and falling into decay, were indescribable. Through the long hours the 16 inmates sat, hot and sullen." At least the girls are all together, I thought. Or, "At the foot of the stairs which led to the bedrooms above, a man was stationed. Every time a visitor came groping his way down the stairs the businesslike and aggressive announcer would cry out, 'Next!'"

Prostitutes, I thought—the ones who worked in brothel districts, anyway—if they had been wounded long ago by men, need never have been afraid here. Even in the throes of intercourse, even buried under the bulk of a stranger, they were not alone. When a girl was selling sex, there was a girl at the same work in the next cubicle or room. And when she was working as a badger or in a panel house, it was when consummation was near that she was least alone—an accomplice, on the alert for the moment when the man would begin to lose control, would never have been more than a few feet away.

But was the presence of others community? No. Each woman must have been chilled in her very being by loneliness.

THE WOMEN exacted what revenge they could for the insult of their position. Men were made fools of when they were conned and robbed. They were punished for desire. They were punished for being able to buy what the woman had to sell. For May, the callousness was all of a piece with what she had come from. The dreary, backbreaking, repetitive farmwork of Ireland used the bodies of men, women, and children as implements. There was little pity for human beings, and none for animals. A woman of that world twisted the chicken's neck, whipped the old horse, sent the child out to the field to pick the last of the potatoes though its small hands were cracked with chilblains. People were not what mattered in Edenmore: the land was what mattered. And not because it was loved—it was too surly to be loved—but because possession of land was all there was of wealth and status. Money would have been god, except that there was no money.

People who have to scrape to stay alive and who continually experience their own powerlessness and the contempt of the powerful hardly recognize love. Women of no property, especially, are given emotional relationships to sustain with men and children, though emotion is leached from them by poverty. Marriages are arranged. Children are no sooner raised than sent away from home. What can happen over the generations but that women are alienated from their own hearts?

May does give examples of humble men to whom she was kind. But on the whole, she takes it for granted that the suckers who come her way are her prey; the heartlessness she shows to them is the same heartlessness that allows her to do her job. Some men promote the view that there's nothing much to buying a girl—it's a treat you might stand your son, a thing you might do with your friends on a night out, happy to press a few extra dollars into the whore's hand if she turns out to be a good sport. It has been in their interest to sentimentalize the transaction. But whores themselves are not sentimental. That reassuring creature, the Tart with the Heart of Gold, is not their invention. I take it that May's settled, perfectly unemotional hostility to the suckers is typical of her profession.

At this time, when she was being broken into prostitution, she was also very violent. Nothing in the quiet of Edenmore had shown her how to mark out territory—it wasn't supposed that a woman ever would have territory—so she established herself among her peers as a man would, by threat and force. When she brings the Salvation Army missionaries into a brothel she has a grudge against, and gets the slave girls—as girls working off a debt to the madam were called—to run off into the night; or when she remarks of a hotel that *I was not allowed to enter there, because I had a bad reputation for rough-housing when things did not suit me*; or when she knocks some-one's front teeth out; or when, causing mayhem *to spite a landlady and a pimp,* she heated a poker and *when it was nice and red and nasty* seared the pimp's face with it, she was in the first place securing her living. She'd get her choice of customers because the others would make way for her.

Her reputation protected her where women habitually carried ra-zors in their dresses, or revolvers, brass knuckles, knives, baseball bats. Selling themselves made the women angry, and when they weren't pacified by drink or drugs, the anger of the First Ward women spurted out in violence. The jails could hardly hold these women. One submerged a guard in water, one went on the rampage in the laundry and disfigured half a dozen other inmates with a hot iron. One woman tried twice to murder the matron at Joliet. When two prostitutes went on trial for luring men into alleys where one dragged his head back while the other threatened his throat with a blade, the justice ruled that any man who went into the Chicago red-light district deserved what he got.

Maybe the deepest source of May's anger lay further back in her history, but its flamboyant expression was made possible by where she now found herself.

Being famously bad was also, perhaps, an expression, in the only way her circumstances allowed, of an idea of herself. She was still young, after all, and that's what young people do—they pull around themselves pieces of this or that distinctive behavior, things that other people remark about them, as they construct their public personali-ties. The sheer harshness of her environment might have stunned her into alcoholism, or into seeking a powerful protector, or into taking shelter among the Irish. Instead, she came out of her corner, a tough girl. A fighter.

OF COURSE, May emphasized her violence because her readers wanted to be thrilled. But the main reason the working girls were brutal was that they were used like brutes.

The Chicago Vice Commission was a responsible and well-informed body, and it worked out, by inspecting the tallies the brothel-keepers kept, how many men, on average, each woman serviced every night. The Commission did this not to arouse sympathy, but to estimate the profits made by the operators of the sex trade. In an appendix to its very sober report, it even reproduced the ticks made in her account book by one madam as she kept track of the clients each girl took upstairs. The marks still disturb, as if they were the smudges made by slaves' hands on the walls of a holding pen.

In that sporting house, the girls were Bessie, Aline, Alice, Vere, Kitty, Mina, Edith, Florince, and Sophy. Florince over five nights serviced 130 men at fifty cents each—an average of twenty-six men a night—of which she received twenty-five cents. In one day, she serviced forty-five men. No wonder that the Commission estimated that the average professional life span of a girl in a good "house" was no more than five years. Independent women worked just as hard—two women who shared a home at that time managed about four hundred men a week between them. It seems that May made most of her money from theft and blackmail. But if and when she worked on the streets, the figure the police supplied to the Commission would have applied to her. The police estimated that the average working girl serviced fifteen men a day.

THE CHANCE of physical disease was very high, but surely mental breakdown was just as likely, given the toll on a woman's nerves, on her spirit, on her ability to like herself and other people and the world? Women and girls were penetrated hundreds and hundreds of times a night, thousands of times a week. Intercourse makes women pregnant. There was no reliable contraception in the 1890s; condoms did exist, but since when do men use condoms with women desperate enough to do anything? The chances of pregnancy were enormously high, though the girls would have used sponges soaked in vinegar— that's what the writer George Eliot used, to take a nineteenth-century woman whose contraception we know about—and they would have douched with a zinc sulfate solution, and they'd have ingested and applied all kinds of poisons to expunge the seed of life. Still, many of the women must have subjected themselves to multiple abortions. They'd have drunk ergot or iodine. Used sticks and wires and needles. Twigs. They had to abuse their bodies continually so as to go on working. They risked death to earn.

And if they did give birth, infanticide was not uncommon, nor children abandoned to the workhouse.

Books and musicals and films propose a world in which jolly, childlike tarts sing as they go about their work: *Irma La Douce, Never on Sunday, The Best Little Whorehouse in Texas*. Even in honest accounts of red-light districts, the violence is missing. And not just the violence among the women and between the women and the men, but this—the habitual, daily violence of the women toward their own fertility.

THE LAST THING I did when I was in Chicago was take the slow bus down through the Loop and past the Hyde Park district, which was the setting for various of Saul Bellow's romances about great men. The women in those books are second-rate and hysterical and try to drag the male heroes down. I was still in imagination in May's world, and the privilege on which the patriarchal sense of superiority rests

November 12. Mrs. (X1104), (X1104a) (X1104b) street. The supposed patient said she was unmarried. The midwife then agreed to perform the abortion for $25.00, but the patient must stay with her. After arguing about the price, she dropped to $20.00 and $1.00 for visits. She said it was "a great risk as the law was after them."

November 12. Mrs. (X1105), (X1105a) (X1105b) street. The woman was dirty, and the room dark and dismal. The supposed patient said she was not married. Mrs. (X1105) agreed to perform the operation for $15.00.

November 12. (X1107), (X1108) (X1108a) street. Formerly at (X1109). She agreed to perform the abortion for $25.00 but finally came down to $20.00. Said the patient would have to stay with her for two or three days. The midwife said she had a patient in the house and another one who had just had an operation was in the next room.

November 14. Mrs. (X1110), (X1112) (X1112a) street. She said she would not perform an abortion but said that a Mrs. (X1113) on (X1114) near (X1115) street would do it.

November 14. Mrs. (X1116), (X1116a) (X1116b) street. She said she would perform the abortion if she felt the patient was on "the square," or had been sent by some one she knew. She had to be careful as detectives were sent out from the City Hall to try the midwives.

November 14. (X1117), (X1118) (X1118a) street. She was afraid to deal with strangers as the people at the City Hall watched them. If she could feel sure there would be no trouble she would perform the abortion for $30.00. The patient would have to stay with her for two or three days. The flat appeared to be clean.

November 17. Mrs. (X1119), (X1120) (X1120a) avenue. She was afraid at first that the supposed patient had been sent out from the City Hall. "Of course," she said, "it is against the law, but we all do it, if any detective came to her home she would put him out of the door quick."

Mrs. (X1119) then agreed to perform the abortion for $40.00 if she had to take her into the house. She worked with a doctor, to whom she gave $10.00. She said that she has a good many young girls coming to her.

November 17. Mrs. (X1121), (X1122) (X1122a) avenue. As the investigators entered two young girls who had had treatments were leaving the house. Mrs. (X1121) then said she would perform the abortion for $30.00. She declared that a great many girls seventeen and eighteen years of age came to her, and that she was very busy all the time.

November 19. Mrs. (X1123), (X1124) (X1124a) street. Offered to sell pills for $5.00, and if they did not work would give another treatment for $25.00. She remarked that the "girls were not to blame."

November 22. Mrs. (X1125), (X1126) (X1126a) avenue. She agreed to perform the abortion for $20.00.

An extract from the report of the Vice Commission of Chicago, 1912 never struck me more forcibly. The working girls, kept going by abortionists, were part of the city. They were part of the mass on which the bourgeois achievements of Chicago, such as its educational establishments, were erected. But they were excluded from the city's opportunities. They had no hope of access to the spiritual and intellectual values that Bellow presents as gifts of personality.

The bus turns around where all that remains of the World's Fair site is a dull park of bare trees. The only building that survived the fire that destroyed the Exposition soon after it was closed was later faced with stone, so there's no remnant of the plaster that earned the fairground the name "White City." Geese stood in snow as thin as cloth in the cutting wind off Lake Michigan. There was nothing for me to see.

After the fair, everyone went away.

The Ferris wheel was dismantled and trundled off toward St. Louis.

Lady Aberdeen, the patroness who set up the Irish "villages," went away. But before she left America, she addressed her peers at a dinner.

"The forty Irish girls whom we brought out with us," she said in her speech, "go back to Ireland the pure, true, sunny maidens that came out with us, and I know that my friends on the Board of Lady Managers will rejoice that I am able to say this without fear of challenge." So the Irish maidens packed up their weaving and their lacemaking and returned to the island, where they were very likely to remain pure for the rest of their lives whether they wanted to or not.

The young woman architect of the Women's Building was removed to a psychiatric hospital, broken down by the pressures and conflicts associated with winning the commission.

The belly dancer defected from the Egyptian show and, taking her tassels, headed for a larger life in New York.

And May, in an unexpected piece of symmetry, sailed for Egypt. A man called Pat Sheedy owned a gambling club in Cairo, and she went off there to work—that is, to sell herself. There can't have been any plausible scenarios about husbands coming home or landlords wanting to know who's in there on the banks of the Nile. Off she sailed, with her red-gold hair and blue eyes and raucous laughter and tough-as-nails mannerisms and reckless energy. The voyage took a long time, and as day followed day on the ocean she must have had to think about where her run from home had brought her. She must have pondered where first love had led. But she tells us nothing. She assumes that her readers are interested in what she did—not in what she thought.

I LEFT Chicago myself and went back to Brooklyn, sick of the First Ward that was so bad and so sad.

It was a wintry night and my friend's child and I huddled up together, warm and safe, to watch a video. It happened to be *Calamity Jane,* in which Doris Day, I was startled to realize, goes from Deadwood to the Windy City in a kind of parody of May's journey from Nebraska to Chicago. The movie was like a positive version of May's negative reality. Jane makes her own decisions, whereas May moved reactively from one accident to another. Jane has an innocent flirtation that becomes romantic love, whereas Dal was gone from May's life after a year or two, and romance in a red-light district is a bitter joke. And the movie has a happy ending. *"At last my heart's an open door,"* the child and I sang along with a radiant Doris, *"and my secret love's no secret any more."* Whereas the young May, far from being free to open her heart, had learned to intimidate even savage people.

From the Brooklyn house, you can see the towers and spires of Manhattan. That's where May turned up after she'd traveled from Egypt to South America and then to England and back to America. In those days before passports, the big crooks and confidence tricksters and good-time girls were great internationalists. Somewhere, even today, May's signature may be on crumbling landing cards among the documents in the worm-eaten closets of what were once the offices of foreign harbormasters. But what names did she sign? She lived on the wrong side of the law, and so, she says, she tried not to let anyone take her photograph. And she used so many aliases that she couldn't remember them herself.

The one name she never used was Duignan—she never called herself May Duignan again after she left Edenmore. She must have had it in her to protect her family. But also, there comes a time when the emigrant stops being that and a second country becomes the homeland. That time surely came for May when she became one of the tribe of fallen women.

There was a minor justification for calling her after the city where that happened. She does often specify, even down to the cross street, the exact location in Chicago of some event she describes, as if—the opposite of the exiled James Joyce mapping Dublin so as to go on possessing it—when she arrived in her first city, she mapped it so as to possess it.

But that's not the main reason why her nickname is correct for her. Crooks, in those days, were named not after where they really came from but after where, in vast, hardly knowable America, they seemed to come from. They had names like Bitter Creek Newcomb, Texas Jack, Klondyke Flo. And May's adult identity was forged on the desperate streets of the First Ward. She never lived in Chicago again and scarcely even visited it, but it is perfectly appropriate that she was known for the rest of her life as Chicago May.

Four

The Tenderloin
of Manhattan

In *The Great Gatsby*, there's a hot day when the narrator finds himself having lunch in a 42nd Street cellar with Gatsby and the man who fixed the World Series. The man tells an anecdote about the night when his friend Rosy Rosenthal was called out of the old Metropole restaurant across the street, and "they shot him three times in his full belly and drove away."

"Four of them were electrocuted," the narrator says, remembering.

"Five, with Becker," the man says.

Becker was Detective Charles Becker, who was a very famous cop in the Tenderloin—the vice and entertainment district—of Manhattan in the last decade of the nineteenth century and the first of the twentieth. He was big and handsome and charming, but he was also outstandingly corrupt even among the corrupt lot who, protected by the political establishment in Tammany Hall, exploited the Manhattan

Charles Becker of the N.Y.P.D. and his wife, Helen

underworld. Becker's fortunes rose and fell with the struggle in the city between corruption and reform, but eventually he ran a lucrative protection racket, taking a percentage of their earnings off street-walkers, sneak thieves, burglars, pickpockets, and the operators of pool rooms, brothels, and most lucratively, gambling dens, such as the one Rosy Rosenthal ran. Becker was the only serving policeman ever to die in the electric chair; he was executed in Sing Sing for his part in murdering Rosenthal.

In 1896, he was "a formidable-looking man with huge arms and a fierce visage, picturesque as a wolf"—that was how Stephen Crane, then a young journalist and the celebrated author of *The Red Badge of Courage,* described him. Becker and Crane crossed paths once in the Tenderloin. Crane was out late in the company of women friends—

he said as part of his research into the nightlife of Manhattan—when he saw Becker order a junior cop to arrest a girl called Dora for soliciting. Dora was, in fact, a prostitute, but there were no other people around at the time and she wasn't working—Becker got her taken in and charged just as an exercise in power. Crane was outraged, and he stayed up all night to testify, in morning court, to Dora's innocence— which was a brave thing to do, because the police of the time were dangerous enemies. They'd smeared the names of various reformers and they were, in fact, to smear Crane about this—some of the sensational newspapers picked up the hint that he had been in the Tenderloin looking for sex himself, and this episode was one of the things that made Crane leave New York and begin to travel, and may have, therefore, played a part in his early death.

I came across the story of Becker and Crane in an essay that appeared in 1962 in *Studia Neophilologica,* the journal of Germanic and Romance Language and Literature of the University of Uppsala.

There, of all places, I got my first independent sighting of May Duignan, late of Edenmore. She's a person in the background of the scene where these famous people are in the foreground, but she's there—she's as much a historical figure as they are.

SHE WAS a witness at the court hearing, the morning after Becker got Dora arrested. "One of the legendary prostitutes of the 'nineties," a newspaper report said, "Big Chicago May, was one of a stream of witnesses the police had called from the night world of the Tenderloin." We happen to know that May's height was five-foot-six, which was tall at a time when people were in general shorter than they are today, but the new adjective is surely as much a tribute to her personality as a description. She's not auburn-haired anymore—she's a blonde. And she hasn't become a heroine. She is not a witness for Crane. She is not a witness for Dora. She has turned up on Becker's side. She stood in court and testified sanctimoniously that Dora had offered her twenty-five dollars to tell a lie but that she, May, could not but tell the truth—she, personally, had seen Dora soliciting. And she threw in, according to newspaper reports, that Stephen Crane was often in the company of crooks and prostitutes.

May wasn't perjuring herself just to stay in the good books of the most powerful policeman around. She was friendly with Becker; he once had hidden her when she was in trouble, and she once gave him a ring she'd stolen that he admired. And May's friend Pauline *who was married to a dip was crazy about Becker. She had a private opium lay-out. As I did not smoke, Becker, a newspaper man and myself used to drink her champagne.*

May didn't get away with it. She was asked what her occupation was and she said she was a typist—a typewriter, the job was called then—but it turned out on cross-examination that she didn't know anything about the machine she was supposed to type on, or any other aspect of office work. Dora was cleared. But Becker appealed, and later, he in turn was cleared, and the Dora episode was not the one that was to bring him down. May stuck with him. During the appeal hearing she turned up again, this time in a brawl outside the courtroom with a prostitute appearing for Crane's side.

At this point—1896—May has been in the States for only six years and in Manhattan for two or three. Another report of the Crane case says,

> She was as familiar a sight on Sixth and Twenty-third Street after dark as is the Masonic temple. She was a big Irish girl with fair hair whose diamond rings were as big as hickory nuts. She was famous for her method of biting the stones out of men's scarf-pins while she amorously pretended to bury her face against their chests.

So she has become something of an urban legend—the tart who could bite diamonds out of tie-pins was a creature in Manhattan myth long after May was dead—which was an achievement in a soci-

Part of the coverage of the Dora Clark affair

ety monstrously deformed by an oversupply of women with nothing but their bodies to sell, whose desperation was intensified by cheap drink and an abundance of every kind of drug. Walt Whitman once walked around lower Manhattan appalled at "the women half exposed at the cellar doors as you pass, their faces flushed and pimpled." By the time May came to town, the bottom of the ladder was more, not less, crowded. Underground people, near-animals, lived in the cellars and basements of what were once handsome houses down near the waterfront, now warrens of dives for diseased and drunken men and women. "In the East River Hotel," a reformer wrote,

> where two big policemen in full uniform are propping up the bar, at the back of the dirt-floored room where the bar is stained yellow by thousands of quarts of tobacco juice squirted from their mouths by customers, there is a partitioned-off space about twelve feet square. No chairs or tables were in the room. The women customers of the place and the depraved men they lured to it were accustomed to stand up and drink until their senses gave way. Then they were at liberty to fall down on the filthy floor and sleep their intoxication off. We walked into the room where there stood the most disreputable-looking lot of women I think I ever saw. Women were there, once of the East Side middle-class world, but now hopelessly lost. Dirty; I never saw such dirt. It was caked and crusted on hands and faces. Hair tangled and matted around bloated, rum-flushed faces. Clothing scant, soiled, ragged and ill-smelling, half covering gaunt bodies. Eyes gleaming with the madness of delirium tremens, or faded from potent drugs, masqueraded in alcohol as liquor. Women lost to everything in the world.

No book or illustration or film has fully captured the horror of this city, a city into which people poured—in the decade after 1890, its population increased by 127 percent—only to find that they could not get jobs. Women especially were caught in a phase in which the factory work of the early industrial revolution had disappeared or passed to men, but jobs in the clerical sector had not yet opened up. The "pleasure district" where May operated was tricked out in light and music, but beneath the appearance of entertainment lay a world more cruel than we can easily imagine. Police photographs some-times capture its physical misery—there are eloquent ones in Luc Sante's brilliant book *Low Life*—but the only written work that feels true to it, to me, is, in fact, Stephen Crane's *Maggie: A Girl of the Streets*. This is a melodrama about a pure girl who because she has no home and no job is driven to sell her body, and about how the cult of female purity has such power even in the lower depths that her own kind condemn her. I think the book is faithful to the vicious and repetitive cruelty of the life of the drunken poor in their tenement slums, which Crane had certainly witnessed.

There were women for sale everywhere—standing in windows barely dressed, behind the curtains in cigar stores, in barbershops, bathhouses, massage parlors, behind lunchrooms, in soda-water restaurants, beer halls, cafés, pastry shops, and delis. The Raines Law, which was intended to regulate saloons, said that a bar had to have bedrooms to keep serving liquor; the bedrooms were let for sex. Re-porters recount being stopped on one block, ten times, thirteen times, by streetwalkers in cutthroat competition. Women harassed men going in and coming out of the Metropolitan Opera, then on 42nd Street. Women snatched the hats off men, forcing them to run into hallways after them. They shoved and jostled and called. "They even called to respectable women," one reporter said. "They yell like a set of wild Indians for young girls to come in."

I always wondered what words they used and eventually I saw them quoted: "Come up?" they called. "Got a dollar and a half? O how sweet. Want to come by and have a good time?"

THE CITY of block after block of brothels was obsessed with female "purity." Streetwalkers dressed themselves as the schoolgirls their clients desired. Evelyn Nesbit dressed like a very young girl when she gave evidence at the trial of her husband for shooting Stanford White. Innocent society women were ostracized if they were involved in divorce cases, as if they had been polluted by their husbands' adultery. And conception was such a fetish that the legislation enacted under the influence of the extremist "purity" reformer, Anthony Comstock, made even withdrawal, in sexual intercourse, an offense; in Connecticut, a married couple could go to jail for a year for using birth control. The family size of native-born Americans was shrinking at the same time as immigrants were gaining political power, and the elite sensed the possibility of losing their superior position unless their white, Protestant women had as many children as the Irish, the Italians, and the Jews. So contraception was demonized under the guise of a crusade against vice.

The people who could least afford it, of course, continued to have large families, though it was impossible to keep a poor home adequately warm in the winter or cool in the summer. In one baking hot week in the summer of 1893, 607 children under the age of twelve died in Manhattan tenements. The infant in Crane's *Maggie* dies, but nobody cares.

HOW WERE WOMEN to live? Compete for work as a domestic servant for a few dollars a week? Join the mass of needlewomen whose bent, exploited forms could be seen from the 2nd Avenue El, "a gangway through a vast workroom where multitudes were forever laboring, morning, noon and night"? What if there were children? A now forgotten playwright called Bayard Veiller left in his memoirs a mention of the Irishwomen who squatted with their infants and goats in Central Park. "Their shacks were made of vagrant pieces of wood and discarded tin cans opened and flattened out. Every family had a goat and a couple of dogs and God knows how many children."

The women of the underworld were responsive to the contempt in which their culture held them. They thought nothing of harming themselves—slowly, through drugs, or quickly, through suicide. Drugs were everywhere. The police themselves used to take visitors, for a fee, on tours of the underworld, and one of the stops was an

Irish squatters in Central Park in the 1880s

opium den in Chinatown—a real one. Cocaine was widely used, and its cheap substitutes. There was even a drink, a mixture of wine and coca, called Vin Mariani, which was endorsed by the respectable figures of Thomas Edison and William McKinley. A British visitor wrote an account of the drugs he saw used in Manhattan:

> Opium, laudanum, morphine, chlorodyne, chloral, chloroform, hashish, quinine, anti-pyrin, anti-fibrin, bromide, cocaine, the injection under the skin, the sugared pilule, the drops from a phial, the tiny opium cigarette—all these measures beguile the American citizen to sleep, relieve pain, or tranquilize the nerves, and make them ask for more and more and more.

A "hot punch" for six cents consisted of whisky, hot rum, camphor, benzine, and sweepings of cocaine. Women overdosed on the opiates they took for contraceptive effect—the drugs stopped or interfered with the menstrual cycle. They shot themselves or swallowed arsenic or chloral. There was a saloon known as McGurk's Suicide Hall, where—Luc Sante says in his book—the waiters were instructed to form a flying wedge and hustle the presumably half-crazed woman to the door at the first sign of a suicide attempt. There were seven attempts there one year and six deaths, including that of Blonde Madge. Her partner Big Mame drank carbolic acid with her, but spilled most of it on her face. "The disfiguration," Sante says, "resulted only in getting her permanently barred from the place."

I came across the suicide note left by one young prostitute.

"Please bury me in my silk dress and bracelets," was all it said. She didn't even bother to explain why she did it.

FRAGMENTS—some reported by May, some invented—can be pieced together to make a picture of twenty-four hours in her life in the Tenderloin.

And unexpectedly, the day begins with a little scene that has such a rare tenderness to it that I walked up and down Park Row once, in lower Manhattan, hoping to see the faded lettering or old fascia board that might be a vestige of the drugstore where it took place. May allows a rare glimpse of her private life when she makes a passing reference to a sweetheart she had at this time—a newspaperman—in an anecdote about something else. *I was down in Park Row, after I had closed my creep joint for the night. I usually went there when business had been good. I would meet Harry, we would get breakfast, and we would then go home together.* According to old street directories the drugstore was on the corner at Broadway, and the corner building is long gone. But I could still imagine a tired young woman, seductress makeup half worn off, slumped companionably beside a young man. The pleasure of it—people coming cheerily in; coffee and eggs; then a cab home to sleep deliciously half the day.

But for all the talk of diamonds, May was a scavenger, and never secure. The places she lived in would have been nothing much. Sometimes, if you're looking for someone in the warren of old rooms and offices above a Midtown store, you glimpse from the battered stairs what might have been the apartment of a prostitute back then—a board floor, a small, cast-iron fireplace, the brick of the walls showing through discolored wallpaper. A discolored toilet and basin on the bend of the stairs outside. Drip-drop of cold water.

She'd have woken in the afternoon in a wide bed where—I imagine—a ratty old fur coat served as an extra blanket and where the curtains were tacked across, not hung from, the windows. I suppose that she might hear the cry of a man below hawking fuel from a cart and he might carry a bag of coal up the stairs and—maybe there was a servant around who built up the fire and balanced a pan of coffee on it—that she huddled into the heat as soon as the fire burned red. She lifts her cup of coffee with a jumpy hand, picks something to wear out of the chaos of clothes, cools her hot face with splash after splash of cold water from a tin basin. Then straight to the wooden bench or the bentwood chair of her usual spot in whatever saloon was for the time being her crowd's headquarters. A first drink. The place, ready for the evening, would be quiet—the wooden floor, soft with age, swept; the glasses and bottles and metal dispensers shined and ready; the few customers keeping themselves to themselves behind partitions of embossed glass. The May I imagine is an initiate of the drinking life, not a mere drinker. She sits calmly, looking at nothing, breathing perfectly easily, her mind rambling from rumination to rumination as she sips.

She comes and goes from the saloon during the evening, I suppose, going out to look for a sucker every now and then. May is not, now, the wild woman she was in Chicago, but she must often have crashed back in through the swing doors because some furious man was in pursuit. For purposes of blackmail, for instance—she tells us this— she concealed cameras in the ceilings of the bedrooms she used, though the flare and hiss of those early cameras must have infuriated the victim who was there in the room with her. She once stole a man's gold and—she mentions in passing—went out and bought a bottle of whisky and *came back*.

Another time *I was walking down 14th St on a snowy day, shortly before Christmas. I had been shopping in Macy's store. A young fellow in a beautiful sleigh drove past, smiling. He stopped, and asked me if I would like to take a ride and I of course said "yes." I was asked what I did for a living and I said I worked in Macy's and that I lived in 45th St.*

They drove up through Harlem and away out into the country, stopping at roadhouses here and there. In the last place, they went up to a room and she stole the young fellow's money there. Of course he found out—he was certain to find out. They tussle all the way back to the city, and the man gets May charged and she ends up in court. I accept that the jingle of sleighbells, the Currier and Ives setting, the country inns by candlelight, the flanks of the horse gleaming in the starlight in the dark stretches between villages meant nothing to her. But what was the point of the theft if she was certainly going to be attacked and half-throttled by her furious victim?

At some point late at night, I suppose, she stopped working and relaxed with her pals—May calling for champagne and paying for it with bills peeled from the stash in her garter. That's a detail in a strange story she tells.

One evening she was with a pal called Nick, a wealthy young man who liked to party and who squired her around because, she says, *I was some looker, and it tickled him to be seen with me.* She sat on Nick's knee while they were drinking and so did another woman, a *wonderfully good thief* called Net Manning. Later, it transpired that a valuable stone was missing from Nick's scarf and he accused May of taking it.

When I arrived home I was drunk and depressed, May writes. *I did not mind the loss of the money so much as to be accused of snitching the diamond. Nick was too good for me to even think of robbing him. I drank some stuff in the bathroom which was kept there for the purpose of killing roaches. It sickened me—that was all! They got a doctor who pumped out my stomach. I speedily recovered, and started working again as if nothing had happened.*

The end of the story puzzles me.

My friend, Net Manning, sold the big diamond to one of the payoff boys for three hundred and fifty dollars. I got my half, although I did not deserve it. I had been a fool to stay at the party. I tried to see Nick to square things but he would have nothing to do with me. I couldn't squawk on Net, and I had my loot.

If she didn't steal the diamond and self-righteously wouldn't steal it, how come she takes half the profit when it is stolen?

And what of the suicide attempt? How capricious is she? Is it really all the same to her whether she lives or dies?

THAT HER MEANINGS are at an angle from ours is even more obvious in another story.

The forgotten playwright Bayard Veiller, in his memoir of the

1890s, tells a story about May that he claims to have heard directly from her.

She "picked up a man on the street," Veiller wrote, "and took him home with her. She was rather attracted to him. He woke the next morning raging with typhoid fever. May wouldn't let them move him. In some queer way, she felt the man was her guest."

That's Edenmore coming out in her, I thought, that's an obligation that would have been felt there.

"He didn't amount to much," Veiller wrote, "a telegraph operator, but this big Irish girl tramped the streets at night and spent the money she earned on this man."

The telegraph operator got better and left.

But a few days later he came back to May, and whether because he felt he owed it to her or because he'd fallen in love with her, he asked her to marry him.

Veiller told the story because he thought the end of it was amusing.

"I wish I could put in print her language as she described the scene to me later," he writes, "but she was a big, husky Irish woman, strong as a man, and she picked this suitor up by the seat of his pants and the back of his neck and threw him down two flights of stairs."

Maybe she was angry at the man for misconstruing her kindness. Maybe—if his earning power was much lower than hers—she was insulted by the proposal. Maybe she was so threatened by anything that spoke of hope and the future that she had to dash the man away. Maybe she became gauche when people were soft with her, as the man must have been when he stood on the stairs and proposed; the words that propose a partnership, after all, are full of power. Maybe she was treating the man badly to protect herself from believing him.

The idea of handing herself over to be cared for must have seemed to her almost surreal. But caring for another person is different. It was the nurturing part of her being that had been called on to look after the telegraph operator, and perhaps she was feeling pressure from that unrealized part of her potential. Any woman can be lightly and subtly haunted by the role of mother, with its promise of turning the dry self into an abundant fountain of protective love. She is pitiable, in any case, when she throws him down the stairs.

Detective Becker, for all that he was greedy and brutal, was an eloquent man, and he adored the woman—a schoolteacher—who was his third wife. The day before he died in the electric chair he wrote her a letter which begins:

> My heart's blood, my heart cries out for you, for your love and for your caresses. There is no way in which I can tell you all you are and have been to me. You are simply the flower of my life, the guiding star of my hopes and my comfort in my anguish of soul.

It signifies May's fiercely restricted opportunities and her gross lack of privilege that however free she seemed to be, it is not imaginable that she would be spoken to like that. Nor could she speak like that. She couldn't speak at all, when the telegraph operator stumbled out whatever it was he said, standing there in front of her.

SHE'S TWENTY-SIX, NOW. She's lasted as long as women lasted in her line of work. But sick and tired of it as she must be, how can she escape? Her sweetheart, the newspaperman, is lazy, she says, compared to a hard worker like herself, and she's afraid he's taking advantage of her, and once he pawned all her jewelry for gambling money. Marriage isn't mentioned in connection with him, anyway; a newspaperman—even if this one isn't married already—may be a bohemian, but he belongs to the straight world. He wouldn't marry a whore. But I think May liked him very much, because there's an uncharacteristic note of affection when she writes, *I never knowingly harmed a newspaperman. I always had a warm spot for them, poor, reckless, happy-go-lucky spendthrifts. Considering the quality of their work and the nervous strain they were under at times they were the worst paid and most generous people as a class I ever had the pleasure of meeting. They knew all about everything but their own affairs.*

Marriage was, then, how a young woman transformed her situation. If May had been a common streetwalker, it would have been impossible for her to move in that direction. But she was a con artist, too. She even, as a badger, feigning first a sexy welcome for the sucker and then terror at a returning husband, was, in her way, a practitioner in the outer reaches of show business.

In that, she was a creature of her time and place. The Tenderloin during its *belle époque* must have been very like London at the time of the first Queen Elizabeth—alive with experiment, a seething hive of fraudsters and grifters and con women and snake-oil salesmen, its crooks setting up every kind of scam as much out of the vitality that comes from new opportunity as out of greed. The characters in Ben Jonson's *Volpone* or *The Alchemist* would fit perfectly into the world May knew. Come this way, sir, and I'll turn your dross into gold. For a small purse, sir, that beautiful girl will bed you. May was involved in confidence tricks that were above all elaborate. An accomplice of hers, for example, dressed up as a bishop and rented a lavish apartment, and May was "nurse" to his "invalid wife." The bishop and the "wife" in a wheelchair visited a jewelry store. The wife "became faint," so the bishop begged to be excused from buying anything that day. Of course the jeweler offered to come to the apartment when the wife was feeling a little better, and of course when he did, and sent the selection into the invalid's bedroom, the crooks decamped through a back door.

When a scam like that succeeded it was surely because, in that phase of the formation of a city, there was very little collective experience of cities. City dwellers were not expert at the meanings of appearance and manner. While they were learning, they were vulnerable to crooks like May.

Or they would have been, if the crooks' whole heart had been in it. But the striking thing about the bishop-and-his-invalid-wife caper is that it is a rare example of ingenuity being used to profitable effect. Jonson's crooks are full of energy and point—they'd get away with their schemes if they weren't outconned by smarter adversaries. But the scams May describes were curiously perfunctory, and often collapsed through carelessness. An addressed envelope would be left behind or the crooks would hang around the bar nearest to the crime or a rifled jewel case would be thrown away where it could be traced back to a gang member. Or someone would snitch. It was as if in May's transition era thieves earned their core living as thieves always do—by mugging people, or picking their pockets, or stealing objects of worth left unguarded—and the tricks were more vestiges of the commedia dell'arte than crime.

MAY WAS at ease with impersonation. So when she heard that they were looking for girls for the chorus of the hit musical show *Belle of New York,* she wouldn't have had a moment's worry about applying for the job, though I don't suppose she had ever set foot on a stage in her life, much less learned to dance or sing. Smart young men about town did court and sometimes marry actresses and showgirls and girls from the chorus.

The innocence of her blue eyes and cupid's-bow lips paid off again. The brawling prostitute of the Crane affair is not a year later wearing the costume of a Salvation Army girl in the chorus of *Belle*— though someone who saw her dance described her later in a newspaper article as "a spirited, longlegged Irish girl," which suggests that she made up in enthusiasm what she lacked in finesse. She was lucky in her timing. Not long before, the girls in burlesque were picked for their size—they were "husky ladies of forbidding bulk," I read, who wore tights and sateen shorts; she was curvaceous but she wasn't hefty. A little later she wouldn't have suited the prevailing taste either, because the ideal was the sporty girl next door. But in 1897, she looked right.

She hadn't raised herself quite off the street. Showgirls were part of the demimonde, and even when she was on the stage May went on picking up suckers and robbing them—*it used to make me laugh*, she wrote, *when I drew my wages from the show and compared them with what I made on the side. However, the stage life was a relaxation for me, and enabled me to catch johns more easily.* But those are new words for her—"laugh" and "relax." Where she was now was far, far above the women of the red-light district. And she was one of a troupe now, with gossip and laughter backstage and supper afterward. And the theater is a place of ancient skill on one side of the lights and enjoyment on the other. May was at last at play. When she dresses in a girly costume and silk stockings and tap shoes and struts her body across the stage while below, in a spill of light, the eyes of the men in the audience gleam with desire, she's doing essentially what she did in doorways and on street corners. But this time the men are not urgent, and she's not looking for their money.

Her new life renewed my eyes, too. I seemed to make out the traces of an entertainment district in parts of Manhattan where the store-front shutters are covered with graffiti and small cafés close down overnight, leaving nothing but bluebottles drying into dust behind smeared windows. I'd see a fragment of decorative plasterwork up on the corner of an alley and I'd imagine the whole façade of a theater. Inside some big space—a catering equipment showroom on the Bowery, maybe—I'd imagine that behind the plywood sheeting there'd be an old wall covering softened by the excited hands of girls as they made their way sideways along a narrow passageway between the dressing room and the stage. Hands that had known the grainy surface of sods of turf and the bite the wire handle of a bucket makes in

May wore Salvation Army costume in the chorus of Belle of New York.

the palm and the feel of varnish on the sloping top of a pitch-pine school desk, now pink with greasepaint, fingered the wall.

I imagined May walking to work across Midtown, peeping into a cool bar a step down from the street, or into a paneled saloon or a mosaic-floored beer hall, or waving across the red velvet barriers of restaurants at the waiters sprucing the tables with damask and tall glasses for the evening. She knew, now, the viscous smoothness of stage paint, the sensuous touch of a feather powder puff, the lightness of the body in a *crêpe de chine* shift and kid shoes. She'd known tallow candles at home, and the flickering oil lamp, and stately wax candles in Ballinamuck Church, but now she knew the perfect whiteness that flared up into their faces as the girls followed one another out onto the stage, each one momentarily blinded, cheered by the raucous men in the pit of the theater. May danced in, and the footlights made her flesh-colored stockings look like bare flesh. In Edenmore, there was music in every house and, on Sunday nights, dances in the kitchens when the chairs were pushed back. There was music and dancing after the annual digging of the potatoes, where the flute entwined with an old woman's concertina. At the dances for people leaving for America, an old man played the fiddle, and when the melodeons of the twin sisters from Drumlish joined in, the roof nearly came off Reilly's barn. But this was new—the syncopation of brass and drums as she high-kicked along the footlights to "At ze Naughty Folies-Bergère"!

The men roared and they stretched out their arms as if it were possible to reach across the musicians in the sunken pit and touch skirt or leg. The tired eyes of the musicians rested on the girls. The air was thick and warm. A surge of appetite rose to where the girls threw glittering, oblique glances left and right, mock-bashful, twirling parasols as if to hide like fawns from the men's swelling gaze. The girls' belts bit into their waists like handcuffs to make more extreme the spring of ribcage into bosom just covered by a gauzy blouse, and the curve of the other roundness under tight skirts. But the girls were coy.

There was nothing outrageous here, no hootchy-cootchy. The star of the show was the prettiest little lady in all of America, and even a girl who had come to the chorus from the horrible world of the streets was bathed in her sweetness.

Maybe the mantle of the gas lamp in the dressing room was broken, so the girls had the light on all the time, levered down to half-strength. Not girls so much as women on vacation from their destinies, more childlike than they had ever been as children. They hung long loops of fake pearls from the hooks on the picture rail beside the hangers with their good gray skirts—high-waisted, smooth, neatly hooked at the back to tighten over their hips before falling exactly to the point where the ankle in the little boot would show and then be hidden, playing peekaboo to any man who followed them in the street. Everyone who danced smelled of sweat, but May and the girls hardly ever noticed, and when they did, they sprayed around the cut-glass bottle of cheap perfume. When the show was over and they bounced out into the night, they were some sight. Yellow satin bows on their boater hats. High-necked blouses tight as skin over high, puffed-out pigeon breasts. Boots click-clacking. Their restless fingers brown with nicotine under clean white gloves.

That is how I imagine May's best hour.

THERE IS HARDLY a life but knows some rest and beauty. There's a description, for example, in a nineteenth-century Irish song-collectors' book, of a scene witnessed by the writer on a turf bog very like the one beside May's childhood home.

"It was a fair, summer day," he wrote,

> and the whole village had traveled out to the bog by donkey
> and cart to stack peat sods to dry in the warm wind. After their
> morning's work they were relaxing, lying companionably on
> the soft grass of the causeway, white cloths spread with bottles

of buttermilk and floury potatoes and salt herring. Then a girl, famed in the district for her voice, began to sing an old Irish love song, and all present fell silent.

"*Pósfainn thú gan bó gan punt gan aireamh spré a searc mo chléibh . . .*"
I'd wed you without herds, without money, or rich array,
And I'd wed you on a dewy morning at day-dawn gray;
My bitter woe is, love, that we are not far away
In Cashel town, though the bare deal board were our marriage bed this day. . . .

May has lost all that—the natural world, the link with tradition, the intricate, formal beauty of the song and the song's language, the respect for passionate love, the ease of community. But look, she might say, at what she'd gained! Strong, the blood high in her cheeks, the young men of Manhattan agape at her feet, a wealth of shining hair on her head, her long legs supple.

In the tenements all around a mass of humanity huddled and sighed and ached with desire for what May now possesses.

Light. Warmth. Food. Money. Laughter. Admiration. Camaraderie.

The knowledge that she has not been beaten by the odds.

MAY MARRIED.

The star of *Belle of New York* left her first husband, a one-hour cycle champion, to marry the heir to a copper fortune, and young men from the audience unhitched the horses and pulled her in her carriage to the Ritz after her final appearance. May's own nuptials were at the opposite end of the upwardly mobile scale. Because her admirer, Jim Sharp, though the son of a widow who presided over a successful metal-shelving business, was the spectacularly black sheep of the family. The business had premises down near City Hall, in the same area as the newspaperman's office and the jail and the courts, where May must have long known every tavern. Jim, to put it mildly, was a drinker. Their marriage sounds very like a plan that first came to them in a bar.

May went up in the world when she got into the chorus, but she still picked up suckers and she still stole, and around now she made the big mistake of stealing a Lutheran minister's pocketbook. The minister pressed charges. This had never happened to her before— she had often been taken in by the cops, but no sucker had ever braved the publicity of taking her to court and the cops always let her go. But times were changing; the N.Y.P.D. had been somewhat reformed since Theodore Roosevelt became commissioner, and around now there was a push against street crime. Up to this, May had no criminal record, either in Chicago or in New York. No matter what might be said of her or said to her parents at home about her, the fact was that she had never even been charged with a crime, much less gone to jail. But now, she faced jail.

James Montgomery Sharpe, the son of a well-to-do family, went to the D.A. and told him he would marry me and take me out of the life I was leading if I was released. I had known Sharpe as a man-about-town, a regular fellow, dashing and handsome. He was always decent and liberal with me when we had parties, but that was as far as it went. I was released all right, so I had to carry out my part of the bargain.

The added *e* in "Sharpe" must have been May's idea of the genteel.

The ceremony took place in 1899 at the Little Church of the Transfiguration in Manhattan. And God alone knows what was in the minds of the couple as they knelt before the priest.

The information given by May on the marriage certificate is comprehensively fraudulent. Her name is not and never was May Vivian Lettimer. Her mother was not called Isabelle Richardson; women called Isabelle were unheard of in Edenmore. Her nationality is not English. She is not twenty-four—she's twenty-eight.

I'm sure many marriages in the America of those pre-bureaucratic days were similarly insouciant about age and name. But what about legal status? A question that had to be answered was, Previous Marriages? Dal Churchill from Nebraska and the marriage in Salt Lake City are forgotten or denied or never existed.

None, May wrote.

There was no reason for Jim Sharp to lie. He's an American, his home address is North Arlington, New Jersey—he's still living in his mother's house, as a matter of fact.

He has acquired Chicago May as his bride but he's a kid; he's twenty-two.

MAY SAYS in her book, *I had visions of escaping from the life I was leading.* So there was hope behind what she did. *I had the desire to lead a good, if comfortable life, among refined people,* she wrote, and those were extremely powerful motives. But after the ceremony—she tells us this as if it were perfectly normal—Jim went back to his mother's house and she went back to an apartment she and the newspaperman shared. *My sweetheart did not know I was married,* she writes, *until I flashed the certificate on him, one morning at our breakfast table. He was furious, but cooled off, apparently, when I told him it was none of his business. I owed him nothing; and he had nothing on me.*

I was in bed, pretty drunk and sick when the colored maid brought in a man who wanted to see my face. . . .

The man who wanted to see her face had come to check on the rumor that the newspaperman had been spreading around town—that May had married Jim Sharp and immediately committed suicide. If this is a practical joke, it is such an angry one that it makes me suspect that the newspaperman never expected May to leave him, and that she bided her time to tell him when it would most infuriate him. Did she go through with getting married to spite her sweetheart?

Sharp and I then decided to make one more night of it, she writes, *and settle down and live together at his mother's home in New Jersey. We visited all the resorts, good and bad, mostly bad, and I went home alone to my apartment, from which my lover had vamoosed. The next day we went to his house.*

The sequence of events doesn't say much for May's enthusiasm.

But in and around the Tenderloin there was an end-of-century desperation. Half-starved women were giving "acrobatic" displays for a living. Women were lying on men's laps wheedling. Women in tights were parading themselves. Very young girls in cigar shops "who can speak five languages" were coyly explaining that their half-nakedness was due to shortage of funds. Women were drinking up at the bar with men. Women in the theaters were wandering among the men, making lewd suggestions and then going back onstage to sing sentimental ballads. "For 5 dollars in a Tenderloin brothel, a police officer watched six prostitutes stripped to their stockings. Then one placed a portion of a lighted segar in the private parts of another." Black girls danced "lasciviously" with white men, white girls with black men, girls were doing a gymnastic exhibition called "the dance of nature," girls were dancing the cancan in private boxes in saloons, they did it as an exhibition, fanning each others' crotches with handkerchiefs.

Who wouldn't flee across the bright waves of the Hudson to try some other life?

And as the carriage jogged along the leafy lanes to Belleville, May must have been sincerely optimistic. It's true that she said in her book that she thought when she married Jim that she married money—that she hadn't known his mother kept him on a strict and very small allowance. But I don't believe that the hope of money was the only reason she married; she could get money herself. In the culture she grew up in, gold-digging was admirable but idealism was not, so there were things she would not say. She would never have revealed whatever delicate hopes she privately harbored, or whatever earnestness she was bringing to this new beginning. A peasant doesn't want to be accused of acting for any other reason but material advantage.

SOCIALLY, she hadn't been as daring since, in her brand-new gown, she walked into the first-class dining room of the steamer from England to America. What did she know about domesticity—she who had known only the extreme environments of simple Edenmore or "pleasure district" America? What did she know about the challenge of moderation? *But we were received into the family as if nothing serious had happened, May wrote. I suppose they decided to make the best of a bad bargain. The horse and carriage was ours for the asking.*

I think Jim's mother must have known that it would take someone as formidable as May to straighten Jim out, and so she made her welcome, whatever suspicions she may have entertained about her chorus-girl daughter-in-law. And surely only the lure of being mothered could have kept as genuinely independent a person as May in a bourgeois drawing room. She speaks of Mrs. Sharp with respect; there's a glimpse of the powerful matriarch May might have been herself, if her fate had been otherwise. May never makes the slightest effort to win the reader's sympathy in *Her Story*. She probably didn't appreciate how sad some of the things she says are.

I am sure that the dear old mother felt that I would do right if given half a chance. Probably she knew me better than any of them and appreciated me for what I wanted to be.

"What I wanted to be."

By the time she was writing about it, May was able to see her marriage as a rather grim comedy. Jim was the problem. *I did my best to go straight, out of gratitude to Jim and the family. But Jim was a bad egg, and I wasn't the one to reform him.*

Only a reprobate or a most exceptionally perceptive man would have offered himself as the husband of the infamous Chicago May. There

are well-known examples of men marrying women of the streets—
the English novelist of the turn of the century, George Gissing, married an alcoholic prostitute who might have been a character from
one of his chronicles of hopeless lives. Stephen Crane's short life was
made happier by a partner who is said to have run a brothel. But on
the whole, the feminist Emma Goldman, a contemporary of May's,
was surely right when she remarked that even the "meanest, most de-
praved and decrepit man still considers himself too good to take as
his wife the woman whose grace he was quite willing to buy."

Jim was not only a reprobate, he seems to have been as mad as a
hatter. It was the bitter truth that a man mad enough to marry a notorious whore was very likely a madman.

At one point, May says, Jim's "fool actions" were so trying on her
nerves that she had to go back to the city to get drunk with her
friends for a week—no drink was allowed, need I say, in Mrs. Sharp's
house. The "fool actions" she mentions include Jim forging his
mother's name on checks. Jim buying poison to murder his brother
with—the cook hustled him out of the kitchen before he could get it
into his brother's coffee. Jim trying to kill the same brother by waiting in the rain to shoot him as he was being driven home—the
brother, fortunately, had missed the ferry from Manhattan. Jim, also,
trying to steal the savings of the hired men who worked on his
mother's grounds.

The only bad deed May was complicit in was cheating Christmas
gifts from a store where the Sharps had credit. To steal from the family so as to give gifts to the family may seem merely childish, but it betrays a wider desperation. Giving gifts involves parity—being able to
match the other person in conferring an obligation—and stealing to
give Christmas gifts suggests how hard it was on May to be a dependent. Not many wives at that time would have been accustomed to
earning money of their own before marriage, but she was.

She seems, in fact, to have taken trips away from the Belleville
house from time to time to do some of her old work. What was there

to do, after all, in New Jersey? Why was a new wife kept in comfort, fed and watered, pampered like a prize beast? Why was the married woman taken up from her toiling sisters and put to idleness? Wasn't it because she was there to be bred from—to become a mother? It may beggar belief to suggest that May, even with her capacity for trying anything, was trying to have a baby, but that's what I think she must have been doing. She knew, surely, that getting married is the beginning of a job, not the end of one. If she and Jim were to remain dependents of his mother, they had to do something to deserve it, and what skills did May have that she could contribute to the Sharp household? What had she ever had but her body?

Mrs. Sharp senior might have had the not unreasonable hope that if he became a father, fatherhood would calm Jim down. So I imagine the warm, orderly house, the tick-tock of grandfather clocks, the soft boom of the gong that marks the times of meals, the drives out to take fresh air, the teas served on the lawn. I imagine the newlyweds' luxurious bed. Sheets and pillowcases of lace and linen ironed impeccably by the laundry maid, throws of alpaca and fur, the bed itself a low divan on a carpet like velvet beside floor-length windows framed in thick drapes of embroidered muslin. I imagine May's pale form materializing in the mirror of the armoire opposite the bed as she sits up to her breakfast tray, like a nymph emerging from a dark thicket. Could she catch glimpses of herself everywhere she moved: out to the bathroom, over to the dressing table to look at her impassive face, across—doubled by the mirrors of the pier glass and the armoire—to the dressing room to contemplate the day's clothes? Pearly fleshed. Upright. Long hair gone back to its native reddish-gold. Perhaps she even tolerated without much impatience Jim coming to press against her. She was in the prime of life and well fed and rested, and she had no occupation, and she had to keep him pacified. A woman who wanted true lovemaking might turn away and stare at the wall with desolate eyes. But May was expert at deploying her body without involving any part of her feeling self.

So she waited it out, though she wasn't a prisoner and the carriage would take her to the ferry terminal, and once there she wasn't twenty minutes from her old haunts in the Tenderloin.

But all the waiting came to nothing.

If I had been different, she wrote, *perhaps I could have made a change in the man. I tried and failed. He never tried. When I left, I think the family was sincerely sorry to see me go.*

She left a picture of her husband and herself—companionable in their way—written in the sardonic tone of voice which is the stoic's rebuke to self-pity.

One day, she writes, *Jim and I were sitting in the library before an open fire. Hanging on the wall was a painting of one of the Sharpe grand-uncles, a very fine man, dressed in Colonial style. My better half told me the history of this picture. The old codger was killed by a barrel of plaster of Paris falling on him. That wasn't very interesting to me. It seemed, however, that this gentleman had said, just before the accident, that he hoped God would strike him dead if something wasn't so. The English, generally, are in the habit of making this appeal to the Almighty. I do not believe in preaching, but I took this relative's fate as a text, and preached a sermon to my husband.*

After she preached her sermon *my husband promised me solemnly that night before we went to bed that he would not try to kill his brother.*

Having accomplished this much good, if good it was, I left.

HOW LONG do you suppose May stuck it out with the crazy young man in the teetotal house? A month? Two months? Three months?

No. She made a much longer effort than that.

There was a census taken in New Jersey in 1900, and she was at home that night. There she is, counted by the enumerator among the household of the Sharps in North Arlington, New Jersey. Mrs. James Sharp, daughter-in-law. Place of birth, England.

Children? None.

It's just about a year since her wedding, so she stuck it out for that at least.

But she left. And Jim went off to enlist in the Spanish-American War and never came back. *My husband is still "missing,"* May wrote more than a quarter of a century later, *probably dead. I hope he did not suffer when he died, if he did die; but I hope he does not come back to me if he is alive.*

And *the mother is dead now, God rest her soul.*

PART THREE

1900 to 1907

Five

The Paris Heist

There are no photographs that are definitely of May during her working life. She avoided photographers, she says, so as not to give the cops the advantage of knowing what she looked like. Some images have survived that have her name on them, but they might not be of her at all. One of them, an idealized portrait of a girl with a Kewpie-doll face and a little pout of a mouth, has bobbed, waved hair. The girl is about twenty years old, but by the time that hairstyle came in, May was in her fifties. In one the woman does look Irish, but that may be because someone has touched the picture up with black marker and the eyebrows have been thickened. If this is May, I can see how she misled so many men—she looks too cozy to be dangerous.

Another has a lively eye and an expectant mouth, and it is possible that it is of May and from around this time.

Pictures said to be of May

She took off for London, like a lot of the other American crooks did at the very beginning of the twentieth century. The cops in Manhattan were in a reform phase and the Pinkerton detectives were becoming more effective, so the Tenderloin was harder to make a living in, and the World's Fair of 1901, with all its opportunities for crime, was on in Paris. Her crowd, anyway, always drifted from country to country. One of things that gives a period flavor to May's life is that she and her like think nothing of working in any of the countries of Europe or in Scandinavia or Egypt or South America or South Africa. These weren't crooks of any renown—in fact, they seem to have been barely competent—yet they could all manage immensely long voyages on boats and trains, and hotels, and foreign languages, without giving it a thought.

May started off in London with the traveling company of *Belle of New York,* but soon, with her friend Pauline, she was haunting hotels like the Langham and the Russell, and they were up to their old tricks.

Pauline and I trimmed an Irish absentee landlord one evening. We went to a wine room in Shaftesbury Avenue and had supper. If you pay ten shillings extra you are not bothered there. Pauline was sitting in the boob's lap. He had his vest open. She pulled his pocketbook and handed it to me. I emptied it, stuffed a napkin into it, and handed it back. It was replaced.

I hope his tenants did not suffer, the daughter of an Edenmore tenant says about the landlord.

They got away with the pocketbook; though, later, not knowing London, they accidentally got on the same bus as their victim.

Then we went to the Continental, where the girls used to go and sit in evening dress, to catch men. It was called the Cow Shed. You pay so much for your reservation. When a gent comes in he is ushered to your table. We were wearing shirtwaists, serge skirts, collars and neckties, the American style at that time. That Gibson girl look must have been as outrageous in its day as the first blue jeans *because the waiter would not let us sit down, we looked so much like bums, though we had enough dough to have bought the joint, almost. We had to go to a private room. After ordering wine and supper, we had a twenty-pound note changed.*

The detail May gives is one of the rewards of her book. How the Cow Shed operated. What response the two American bad girls got to their state-of-the-art clothes. They must have looked delightful with their midcalf A-line skirts and black-stockinged legs and boaters perched on their manes of tumbling hair.

MAY WAS DOING WELL. But if she'd been lucky, she would never have met Eddie Guerin.

That's what anyone would say at the end, when there was nothing left of their relationship but a trail of destruction. But physical attraction has more authenticity than anything else. And May must have needed to abandon herself to something like attraction, after the long effort at self-discipline in New Jersey. She needed to forget her *visions of escaping from the life I was leading.* The marriage had been a very significant defeat.

In the photo of Eddie from around the time the two of them met, he's half-smiling—which must have to do with refusing to be intimidated, because it was taken by some police force for some Rogues'

Eddie Guerin

Gallery. But otherwise his face is austere, with dark red hair and hazel eyes. He's about May's age, and he's five-foot-ten to her five-foot-six—crooks leave behind in their arrest records, if nothing else, their vital statistics. I think of him as slender and remote, and her as bosomy and apparently—though not really—sociable. The differences between them, I'm supposing, were part of the attraction.

Much later in their lives both of them wrote, or helped to write, their own stories, within the highly stylized genre of memoirs from the underworld. Hers was *Her Story . . . by "The Queen of Crooks."* His—brought out in the same year, no doubt to capitalize on her publicity—was called *I Was a Bandit,* in straightforward appeal to the men's adventure market. With both books there's the problem of disentangling what really happened from what the author says happened—Eddie had a special obligation to astonish and thrill his readers, and the most sensational passages in his book are, without question, inventions. There's the problem, too, that by the time these books were written, their authors were looking back a long way, and Eddie, at least, was still settling scores. Yet it is extraordinary to have any, never mind two, would-be memoirs from a milieu as erratic and transient as theirs.

Eddie seems never to have been as interested in the detail of experience as May, and therefore he doesn't remember as well as she. He says that in London in 1901, he often saw her patrolling for clients near the big hotels and that when they were introduced by a burglar called Kid McManus, she was "about 28 or 30, and painted up to the eyes, with peroxided hair, pretty enough in a way and no doubt quite fascinating in the manner she spoke to you. At any rate, I fell for her, so nothing more need be said about her charms." He says the Kid warned him, "You leave that dame alone. She's dangerous."

The grudging note is sounded early. But later in the book he says, as if he couldn't keep it from bursting out, "I could not leave her alone. Her beauty held me spellbound—as it had held many another in years gone by."

May prefaces her account of their meeting with a description of the funeral at Finchley Cemetery of a well-connected Irish-Jewish fence. *Thugs,* May wrote, *strong-arm men, sneaks, second-story workers, dips, moll-buzzers, confidence-men, safe-crackers, beggars and people who looked like the Lord's anointed to say nothing of the women and girls, made up that burying crew.* The London police and detectives were at the funeral, too, to take note of who was around. Criminals and cops *occasionally intermingled,* May says, *just as I have seen a fox and a hound act friendly towards each other before a hunt.* I wonder about that comparison. I'm sure it is hers—ghostwriters don't bother with metaphors—but she cannot, when she was a little girl, have seen a young fox skitter out in front of a yelping pack of hounds, because the terrain around Edenmore is too wet for that kind of hunting. Had she read about foxhunting in novelettes about the English aristocracy, and if so, is this one of her absentminded gestures in the direction of a high-class background for herself? Does it occur to her at this point because she thought that Eddie was, in his way and all things considered, classy? Was that what made him attractive to her? She certainly describes their getting together as if it were an alliance between crowned heads. *Both of us were successful, prosperous thieves,* she wrote. *Eddie was a gang-burglar and safe-cracker, at the head of his branch of the criminal profession. I was an independant badger, at the head of mine. Both of us were good-looking, healthy, vigorous, well-dressed specimens of our respective sexes.*

They wouldn't have met earlier because Eddie had just returned from France after serving ten years in the jail of Riom for a bank robbery, but he was from Chicago, so both of them knew the underworld there and both were friendly with the club owner Pat Sheedy, in whose gambling den in Cairo May had worked.

Eddie was one of the neglected children of an impoverished Irish-American widow in the old Chicago, the wooden one of before the fire—in fact, the household got its milk from the same Mrs. O'Leary whose cow kicking over a lantern, the legend says, started the Great Fire. He was a bellboy on a steamer on Lake Michigan and then a callboy in a theater and then a cashboy in the Marshall Field's store and then a Western Union telegraph boy, and he stole whenever he could so as to play pool and gamble. At the age of fifteen, he was put into the House of Correction for the theft of a box of cutlery. "I went numb with horror," he wrote, "at the sights I saw. There were blacks and whites of all ages and sizes and the place stunk like a sewer. Men were lying about the floors smoking, spitting, cursing, idling away the time till they were dealt with." But repeated incarceration did nothing to stop him settling into a life of crime. "People now," he wrote in *I Was a Bandit,*

> can have little conception of the wild criminal life which existed in the United States of America for a good many years after the war between the North and the South. Cold-blooded murder was looked upon as an almost everyday occurrence, while such comparatively trifling offenses as robbery under arms, "sticking-up" banks, dynamiting safes and other forms of getting money easily were regarded with a tolerant eye.

Eddie's schools were the crime academies of unreformed American jails—the state penitentiary of Ohio, the Tombs, the Allegheny State, and many more.

He took from those prisons what nourishment he could. He remembers the peace in one place of "the niggers singing their plantation songs to the strumming of the banjos and the twanging of guitars played by the foreigners." In another place, visitors who came to gape at the prisoners were charged twenty-five cents apiece, and the money went for library books; he read some books, and a daily newspaper. But he hardly knew normality. From the window of the punishment cell in the jail in France, he'd seen one day "a crowd of people following behind a curious contraption which chug-chugged its way across the square riotously cheered by the excited country folk. It was the first motorcar." The little anecdote brings home the fact that since he was a boy, he had been in touch with the history of his own time only occasionally. He had lived for longer outside the ordinary world than in it.

He could see the motorcar because he was in the punishment cell. In every jail he'd ever been in, he'd spent time in the punishment cells—for trying to escape, and for fighting. The first joint on two of the fingers of each of his hands was missing, I suppose from some episode involving violence. I said their differences may have attracted May and Eddie, but there was this, too—that they were both at home with aggression, especially when threatened. It would have been a miracle if Eddie had known how to love himself or another person.

He was a man's man. He was one of the boys—a handful of Chicago men who had known each other all their lives, some of whom were law-abiding and some not, but who still looked out for each other. Because of that, there's a source of information about Eddie (which includes some information on May) that neither of them ever knew existed.

IT OCCURRED TO ME one day that if the Pinkerton agents followed crooks around, they surely wrote reports on the crooks they followed. And, yes—there is a Pinkerton archive, and it can be consulted in the Library of Congress in Washington, D.C. And in its files, in the company of Dillinger and the plot to steal Lincoln's body and the Homestead Strike and Jesse James, is the obscure Guerin, Edward. Eddie's dossier is more like a child's attempt at a dossier than anything else—those were early days in the surveillance business. But the reason he's in the archive at all is because he was from Chicago. The agency itself was founded in Chicago, and for a long time the Chicago branch was run by one of the Pinkerton brothers, Billy. And Billy was one of the boys, too. Loyalty was a major factor in his attitude to crooks from his hometown. His attitude toward Eddie, in fact, though he tried to conceal it from the brother who ran the New York branch of Pinkerton, was richly fraternal—even protective.

Eddie never knew that fragments of information about his life were being filed by Billy. We know things that Eddie thought he'd prevented anyone from knowing. For example, we know that only three weeks before he and May got together, he'd married his wife.

We only know the fact as noted by Billy. We can't be sure that it means what it seems to mean—that Eddie was completely overwhelmed by meeting May.

DID MAY KNOW he'd just been married? If she did, did it make any difference? Did she have any idea, however vague, of where their affair might go? She had a very distinctive personality, which must have interacted with the accidents of her life in a way that created patterns. But does that amount to making a way through life? Did she have goals? Or was she completely a creature of circumstance?

Someone said to me once, idly, "Would May have known Jane Austen's novels?" *Jane Austen?* Jane Austen's world is the exact opposite of the world of Eddie and May. Jane Austen's people know exactly the communal structure that personal relationships exist to uphold. In that perspective, May and Eddie are social flotsam, people dangerously dependent on the meshing of obscure inner needs and desires to give meaning to their being together.

Had May read Jane Austen? I stumbled off into an answer. Of course, I began, there might have been an Austen novel in Longford town, fourteen miles from Edenmore, but it would have been in whatever private circulating library served the wives of the high bourgeoisie—the doctor, the solicitor, the army barracks' top brass. It was unthinkable that May—a country girl, a peasant—could journey to town to borrow novels, or that she would have been allowed time to read in the dark and crowded dwelling that was her home. Or that she would have been physically able to read there, even if a few issues of something like a Dickens weekly or a nationalist journal did survive the animals and the children and discoloration by damp. Just seeing the print, for example, could be a problem. The smoke of the fire made eyes sore—that's the reason for the eye cures offered by so many of the miracle-working wells that dot the landscape of Ireland. And though magnifying spectacles cost the same as a stone of potatoes or a barrel of porter when May was growing up, so they were not prohibitively expensive, candles and lamp-oil were, and turf doesn't flame like other fuels—you can't make out small print by the light of a turf fire. May could read perfectly well—anyone who went to a national school for six years, as she did, could read. She would have committed many poems to memory when she was at school. But reading a book is a different matter. It is both an action and a reflection, and reflectiveness was not May's strong point.

But the question illuminates one of the dimensions of underprivilege. Privileges like leisure, like literacy, like access to light and heat, were retained by the few and denied to the many well into the twentieth century. But also, a society where serious fiction isn't available, such as the one May grew up in and billions of people did and do grow up in, contains as many people who have imaginative needs as anywhere else. May had hungry dreams—that's why she ran away,

that's why she made something of a legend out of herself. That's why she was delighted with Eddie Guerin. People lead lives of consequence whether they read books or not, and people don't need to hear morality discussed to be moral. But what else besides fiction finds words for the incoherence of consciousness, and encapsulates memory, illuminating through comparisons of before and after the principle of development in individuals and situations?

How well able to imagine was she? Of course she would have been perfectly familiar with stories—from the rich oral tradition of her culture, from the parables used in Catholic teaching, from dime novels and light magazines passed around, perhaps, between working girls as they waited for clients. But Jane Austen's novels connect the events of a life with character. They do more than tell a story; they do what Henry James said novels do: they help us to *know*. Knowing never stopped anyone—including, perhaps, Jane Austen and Henry James—from emotional suffering. But May—what resource of reflectiveness, her own or imagined, was she able to bring to the liaison with Eddie Guerin?

What beliefs did she have, for example, about what lovers owe each other? This is a question on which a pivotal action of May's life is going to turn.

But in the meantime, May's lack of self-consciousness pays a wonderful dividend. It is a negative quality to the biographer, whom it condemns to incessant speculation. But how positive it must have been when she fell for a man. She wouldn't have had any reservations. Imagine all her vitality, unchecked by reflection, turned, at last, to happiness!

THE HEIST was their honeymoon.

Leicester Square in London is uneven and a little sloped, like the Elizabethan garden it once was, and Wordsworth wrote a sonnet about looking at the night sky through a telescope from there, so

until late in the nineteenth century it must have been a little
apart from the light and noise
of the city. But by 1901, the
Hotel de Provence in the
square was specifically not re-
commended to respectable travelers. "It is conducted in the
Continental style," Murray's
Handbook says. "There are
many disreputable houses in
this neighborhood, therefore
travelers should be cautious not
to resort to any without some
reliable recommendation." Eddie was living in rooms with May
and her maid, a woman called
Emily Skinner, in Bloomsbury,

"Dutch Gus" Miller

not ten minutes' walk from the Hotel de Provence. There he found
"dozens of Americans," he said, "kindred spirits most of them, ready to
take on anything."

One of them was a man known as "Dutch Gus," "a highly-
educated German-American," according to Eddie in *I Was a Bandit,*
"tall, fair and handsome."

"He was the possessor of a refinement of manner which often
made me wonder what had induced him to take to robbery," Eddie
wrote. "The thousands of little banks and post offices that were scat-
tered all over the States used to use safes that were easy to an expert
like Gus. However, the Pinkertons got him in time and Gus came over
to Europe to make a fresh start."

By "a fresh start" Eddie meant at robbing banks. And Gus had a
job in mind. He'd been in Paris, sizing up the American Express office
in the Rue Scribe. He'd had letters sent to him there so as to become

acquainted with the staff, and he'd befriended the young black man who was employed as the security guard there and slept on the premises—the office was not more substantially protected because the safe was state-of-the-art impregnable. It would be a really big job to rob that safe, and Gus needed colleagues. He invited Kid McManus—"Irish-American by birth, safebreaker by trade, and desperado by nature," a man who once, when he overheard someone saying the Kid would rob a red-hot stove if there was nothing else to rob, immediately stole a red-hot stove—to join him in a burglary of the American Express office. And he asked Eddie to join him. Gus wanted Eddie because, after the ten years in jail in France, Eddie could speak French. That was the very reason why Eddie should have had nothing to do with the plan—if he was caught for anything in France again, he'd get an extra-heavy sentence. But Eddie told May that he cherished a hatred for every last French *flic* and *juge*. He *wanted to best the frog-eaters*; that's what she says he told her.

She says she was in on the whole thing from the start, and I'm sure she was—can anyone believe that while her man was hanging out at the Provence she stayed at home? Can anyone imagine that she didn't make the hotel her headquarters, too? Yet Eddie says, "I told May nothing at all about the real object of the trip. Never having seen Paris, she was delighted with the idea of going. 'Sufficient unto the day' was always May's motto. Dutch Gus didn't mind her accompanying me; I fancy he was rather sweet on her himself and probably thought he might work me out."

It is a big thing to lie about, but when it comes to sharing the limelight with May, Eddie's book does lie.

At the time, however, with the lovers still in the first weeks of being together, everything about the preparations for Paris must have sparkled with excitement. If ever May knew what it was like to go about practical matters with a lilt—like a bride doing her chores on the night before her wedding—it must have been as she packed to leave London. It wasn't even necessary that she be crazy about Eddie—even without that, the American Express job transformed her situation. To have left the streets and the brothels behind, to be associated with prestigious colleagues, to be plotting against a company as big as American Express—this was her graduation day. She had walked as tall as anyone could in the world of drunk, half-naked suckers, but she was out in the fresh air of commercial crime now, unimpeded by her own flesh or the flesh-and-blood of her victims. And to be the consort of a man who'd been solicited to do a job as big as this—how she must have melted toward Eddie each time it came back to her! If she broke off from rolling a silk stocking onto her foot and tumbled him down among the half-packed bags on the bed—her lacy corset biting into her flesh—it was to give him what she was expert at giving even in whatever few minutes there might have been before Emily came back from fetching a cab.

Surely, new connections were possible between spirit and flesh now? Leaving sex aside, I take it as very significant that once she was off the streets May stopped being violent. She was still well capable of anger and roughness, but it looks as if the violence she used to provoke wasn't intrinsic to her—it was a response to circumstances.

So maybe she was able to enjoy her own body, too.

I WISH I KNEW what words the three of them used in farewell, the night Eddie and May said goodbye to Emily Skinner. Were the crooks of that time a bit like theater people—did they deliberately wish each other bad luck so as to keep it away? Or were they laconic? Was there just the wave of gloved fingers from May in the cab and a peck on the cheek from Eddie? And then—I imagine—a jingling hansom to the night train, and waiting in shadow in the flare and clang of Victoria Station until, when there was a gap between patrolling policemen, the pair could dart onto the train. And at midnight in Dover, in the swaying light of the windy quayside, the train shunting onto the boat for Calais and sliding out of there, puffing and belching and taking on speed as it ran toward Paris.

At some point, knowledge of how a crook wished another good luck died out, like the last of a species in the depths of the jungle. An enormous amount of what the world once contained is lost. That's why it seems to me marvelous that we do know about Eddie and May. Millions of people have come through the Gare du Nord and are quite forgotten. But this pair came in April, on the night train from London that arrived in the calm of early morning, just as the city began to wake up. They swung out into Paris bent on stealing a lot of money. That atom of history has not, at least, been lost.

HOW PLAUSIBLE is it that for the three weeks the gang kept the American Express office under observation, May never asked what was going on? Eddie says that while he and the other two men kept vigil, "May blissfully enjoyed herself. I took her around to all the stock sights of Paris, the Bois de Boulogne, the Louvre, even the Morgue." Some details are too unexpected to be invented, and I'm sure that whatever else, they did visit the Morgue. I'm sure they went to the Louvre, too—they were staying very near it. A novelist—Henry James, for example, in *The American*—can play with the relationship between art, Paris, and the ignorant visitor. But real life is more mysterious. Who can imagine the conversation between May and Eddie as they strolled from Old Master to Old Master? I think they must have been confined to asking themselves what art was for, or what art was like—not what art was. Eddie had been a street urchin, and the school curriculum of May's time didn't attempt to make sense to the children, even if it had included painting and sculpture. I assume that many people assimilate art objects to their own experience by thinking of them as decor, but neither Eddie nor May had lived in a home of their own since they were young, and those were very poor homes.

So I am not able to imagine where—in what part of their experience—they could put the act of looking at the pictures in the Louvre. But I think that like honeymoon couples similarly contemplating the beauty spots and cathedrals and prehistoric tombs and geological curiosities they have been instructed to admire, there'd have been an intimacy to being out of their depth together, as well as the satisfaction of doing something generally considered worthy.

It shows the big idea they had of themselves that they visited a gallery at all—an idea that, if it had ever been tempered by education, might have made them as robust in their dealings with culture as they were in their dealings with other aspects of the world.

Breakfast in a Parisian hotel would have been the same then as now—what could have changed? A bowl of milky coffee, fresh bread, butter. I like to think of a sleepy May in a wrapper rising from the low bed to eat with a country woman's appetite, and not just from sentimentality, but because I know what she does not; I know the gang is being watched.

The undercover detective branch of the Paris police was called the Sûreté. Billy Pinkerton, back in Chicago, had professional acquaintances in the Sûreté, and in the Pinkerton archive there's a hint that there was advance knowledge that a big heist was planned in Paris. The Pinkerton files are full of information gained from snitches; snitching was part of the bleakness of the criminal world.

But even if no one had tipped them off, Eddie and Dutch Gus and the Kid had attracted the attention of the authorities. As burglars, they were very advanced—they had the technology, for instance, to blow a safe in a way that wouldn't damage its contents—but they were otherwise not smart. They bought rope to tie up the security guard on the night, and they bought it in a store very near the American Express building and—of all things—paid for it with counterfeit money. They also hung around the American Drexel bank for so long that the people there got worried and asked the Sûreté to put them under observation. So the Sûreté followed the gang, though they never figured out who the men were or what they were planning. But, by the way, they reported that they saw the men eating with a woman in restaurants in the Rue d'Amsterdam and the Rue d'Ulm. That woman was surely May, and she was surely part of the gang.

ON THE NIGHT of the robbery itself, Eddie claimed, he had left her in the hotel "blind drunk. I wanted her to be sound asleep all night long so that if I were arrested she could truthfully declare that I had been with her at ten o'clock and had not left her all night. When I left her about a quarter to twelve she was speechless; I had no fear of her waking up for at least another eight hours."

Apart from any other improbabilities, May had based a whole career on not getting as drunk as the men she rolled.

What she says is that she was a full member of the gang and that in the American Express office none of the staff noticed her slip away at closing time and hide under a counter. *I had to wait, crouching, a couple of hours before the negro went upstairs to attend to his watching business. When he did, I shifted a large inkstand near one of the windows (the agreed-upon signal). Then I drew back the bolts of the designated door. In came my confederates. They, too, had to wait for the negro. He took a long time to come downstairs to attend to his watching business. Finally he came, like a good fellow, and was trussed up proper. It took a couple of hours to drill and charge the two safes.*

Then, she says, *I went on the lookout beat outside.* And I believe her about that. The three men had their work cut out inside, and they needed someone to keep watch. A woman of the streets, like May, was ideal—she could stand in the Rue Scribe without attracting suspicion.

Eddie's description of what they did inside the office is probably perfectly accurate. They tied up the security guard. "If you don't keep

The American Express building, Paris, 1903

quiet," the Kid threatened the boy, "I'll throttle the life out of you. This ain't no game, nigger. Shut your mouth and you'll be alright."

Dutch Gus worked at getting the dynamite charge exact. The noise it made would be the danger point and would bring the cops or not.

"After ages," Eddie wrote, "there came a tremendous explosion which rocked the whole building. I stopped upstairs, expecting at any minute to hear the police rushing in."

The three burglars froze in position.

And outside, May tells us in her book, she, too, heard the sound of the muffled explosion, and waited.

She'd been standing in the golden glow of the Théâtre de l'Opéra, and I suppose that her face was shadowed by the brim of her wide hat, though no one would have paid much attention to her in the profusion of drivers' warning shouts and klaxons from motorcars and the bustle in and out of cafés and the carriages lining up for the ladies in jeweled slippers and with bare, powdered backs who came down the side steps of the opera house on the arms of men in silk hats.

The hat she was wearing is not imagined. It was "a very large hat of black and white lace decorated by several pink roses." A boa of black feathers is thrown around her neck. She wears "a beige robe covered with ornamental lace amidst which can be seen ribbons of blue." These are clothes of hers we know about.

That district on the Right Bank of the Seine has hardly changed in a century—it is still a *belle époque* experience to stroll past the glowing façade of the Opéra and along the sidewalk past the elegance of the Café de la Paix and around the corner to where, between wide streets full of evening strollers, the American Express building stands. About a mile away Proust, that particular week, was trying to work on his Ruskin translation and to spend what time he allowed himself away from that task with his ailing mother and not with the Comte de Montesquiou, who wanted him to attend his lecture on Victor Hugo.

His life by now, Proust said, had accustomed him "to do without nearly everything, and to replace people with their images and life by thought."

What the bandits were doing as they breathlessly attached sticks of dynamite to the wheel of the safe was the exact opposite. What they could touch was their only reality.

MAY MENTIONS in her autobiography that a cop she was once trying to avoid came up behind her and said, "No use hiding your pretty face, May—I'd know that straight back anywhere." So I see her stand in the Rue Scribe in the upright way of her countrywomen, who were well able to brace their shoulders to two buckets of water. I see her watching the street as at ease on her feet as if she were standing at her own gate, watching the road for her children coming from school.

On this night, if she weighs herself against what she might have been if she'd stayed at home, she must surely believe that she has made the better choice. In Edenmore, at the beginning of the twentieth century, there was an even chance that her husband, if she had had one, would have been at least ten years her senior. A woman with the dowry she'd have brought him would have had the minding of whatever number of children "God sent," and of three or four cows, ten young cattle, fifty or sixty hens and cockerels, half a dozen ducks and a drake, a gander and maybe two geese and their goslings—geese do a lot of foraging and cattle won't come where they've been, but in Edenmore, the rough ground at the edge of the bog is ideal for geese. There'd have been the horse that drew the cart, and a pony, if they had a pony, and trap as well. And twice a year she and her husband would have killed one of the two fat pigs. Her dark kitchen with its dirt floor would have had flitches of bacon hung to smoke from its rafters. She would have labored day and night at bringing in water, planting and digging up potatoes, milking the cows, feeding calves, preparing feed for the pigs, for the hens, for the family, for the baby, for the mother-in-law above in the room. The dog, at least, would have looked after itself.

There was also washing, scrubbing, smoothing, peeling, blowing ashy turf fires into flame, mashing, dividing, putting the bowls on the table, taking the infant by the hand to the table and showing him the spoon and the bread-and-milk and how to use his fat little hand to eat. And helping the children with their schoolwork, as not all mothers could—in 1901, in spite of compulsory primary education, ten percent of brides in Ireland signed the register with an X. And there'd have been praying. And talking. And kneeling on the doorstep to scrape out the burnt pot with a bit of flint, her limbs wound round with rags, maybe, under a heavy worsted skirt. Unless she was expecting again, and another child, to be raised for emigration, was on its way.

So if, in the mild Paris night, May smiled as she stood outside the

American Express office—her senses tingling with alertness, her mind focused but vague—she had reason for it. She had only to smell the Parisian night and taste her own excitement and be aware at the same time of the shape—like an iceberg—of the life of brute labor that crushed the life out of a woman.

EVERY SINGLE ACCOUNT of the robbery gives a different figure for how much they stole. Whatever the sum was, a large part of it was in the form of drafts and checks that would be very difficult for the gang to turn into cash. An article about Eddie in the *Chicago Tribune* some years later, which is accurate in other respects, says that their haul was six thousand dollars, the equivalent of six hundred thousand dollars today. Whatever it was, the men divided it into three equal parts. Then they slipped away from the building to make their separate ways out of France.

"When I got back to my hotel near the Madeleine in the early hours of the morning," Eddie wrote, "I had a fortune in my pockets. Chicago May's peroxided head peacefully reposed on the pillow. I was busily shaving myself when she woke up, blissfully ignorant of what had been happening."

I doubt that.

What she says is that soon after the sound of the explosion, *I went home to bed. Little sleeping was done by me, the balance of that night. I got up early, so as to be at the door when the maid came with coffee. This was to prevent her from noticing that my "husband," Eddie, was not in bed as usual.*

That's possible.

But about what happened next I am confident.

There was a hotel room and May was waiting in it—they agree on that. Eddie had just pulled off a really high-class burglary under the noses of the French police he hated, and he was free, now, to tell her about it and to show her the money. Of course, when he came in, he threw his coat with its heavy pockets onto the chair and in electric silence looked down on her bright face. They were in their prime, the pair of them, and they hadn't known each other long enough for the first attraction to wear off and they had to do something to express their relief after the suspense of the night. Of course their celebration was a thing that heaved and licked and sucked and slapped skin against skin.

They had what Proust could not have: no thought, just life.

THERE'S a contemporary internal American Express report on the robbery in the Pinkerton file, sent from one of the Paris managers to headquarters. It includes this detail—remember that Dutch Gus Miller had prepared for the heist by getting to know the office staff.

> On the day after the robbery many of our young men at 11 Rue Scribe were on duty straightening up matters in connection therewith and four of them adjourned to a restaurant for luncheon at about one o'clock on Sunday afternoon. Mr Dodsworth, Asst Cashier, was the last to hang up his coat and proceed towards the table when in passing a table midway the man Miller rose up, extended his hand and made some jocular remark in regard to the fact that the office had been robbed. The woman with Miller quickly asked, "Who is this?" and Miller in a nonchalant way said, "Oh one of the boys from the American Express Company's office." The woman then relapsed into silence.
>
> This same woman was seen at the train.

What was the little crew of Americans doing? Why were they back, like daring children, at the scene of the crime? Was Dutch Gus showing off to May? Were they all showing off to each other, heedless of the risk they took?

Over and over I'm checked by what seems to me the strangeness of the crooks of May's time.

In her Manhattan days, May's grifter pals put all their energy into the setting up of a scam and were relatively indifferent as to whether the scam worked, in the sense of yielding a profit. They were so careless about covering their tracks that they seemed not to care, at heart, whether they were caught or not. Was the passivity a kind of despair? Were crooks, then, not so much antisocial as unsocialized or socially incompetent? I always took it for granted that they couldn't feel for other people. But the story of how the American Express gang was caught makes me wonder whether they also couldn't feel for themselves. Only Kid McManus took any pains to get away—he headed for Italy and was never caught for this robbery, though he was for others. Eddie and May simply headed for the boat train to England, though they must have known that the cops would, of course, be watching this of all trains.

As the cops were. They recognized Dutch Gus when he turned up at the Gare du Nord. They took him in for questioning, and when they opened his suitcase, they found some of the stolen dollars there and—even more unbelievably—some of the rope.

And yet Gus had put sustained work into setting up the robbery; from the technical point of view, it had been brilliantly done.

May and Eddie did at least catch the train. She was carrying his share of the loot when it pulled out—their two accounts agree on that.

Everything might have gone well, May wrote, *if it had not been for Eddie's infernal conceit. He was very proud of his ability at slinging French. The French dicks happened to ask him, in broken English, where they could find the dining-car. We had been posing as English travelers, but what does the chump do but answer the detectives in French that would do justice to an educated native. At that, the sans-culottes did not know who they had in their clutches. They thought he was a French criminal they were on the lookout for.*

Once they had him, the fat was in the fire. It took half-a-dozen men to overpower him. I went on alone, not appearing to know the man who had been arrested.

Whether or not it had to do with his speaking French, we know, from a report in the Pinkerton archive, that there was nothing heroic about the scene when Eddie was hustled off the train at Amiens, halfway to the English Channel and the boat for England. He broke away and ran, long-legged and desperate, into the station, and eventually locked himself in a toilet from which he kept calling that he wanted to see his ambassador. Nobody realized that May had been with him.

I imagine the train beginning to pull slowly out along the sun-washed backs of old houses that had weeds growing between the slates of their uneven roofs. She says she threw most of the drafts away. Perhaps she did it this way—as the train rolled out from under the canopy of glass and iron and everyone ran to the right-hand windows to crane back at the station, May, at a left-hand window, tipped an envelope stuffed with checks and drafts into the oily water of the deep, littered bay between tracks. Perhaps, of course, she did nothing of the kind.

Five or six weeks went by, and they moved Eddie to La Santé prison in Paris, where he was kept in solitary confinement. Meanwhile, the police were putting together his dossier "in which is written," Eddie wrote, "everything that is known about you. Your past is sifted out from your childhood upwards. It is set out when, how, where and why you were born, what you have done for a living, and what your habits are." In London, May was being watched, too. But there was no evidence against her. Her name had never been mentioned, and she had managed to stow the stolen cash away. As much to annoy the watchers as anything else, she went about her usual life. We don't have to rely just on May's own account to believe this—it is one of the solid facts to emerge from the profusion of information and misinformation and supposition about the American Express robbery that survived to be filed in the Pinkerton archive.

For the first time, we hear her in her own contemporaneous words.

She wrote to Eddie, and the police intercepted the letter, and it was read out, translated into French, at Eddie's trial. Translated back into English, it says,

Dear Eddie, What can I do for your defense? I've run around all day. And you must defend yourself! We'll do all we can—tell us what we must do. Write me a letter. Say what you want me to do about your underwear. Why don't you prove your alibi? You know that you didn't go out that night. Do you want me to go to the hotel in the Rue Vignon? Say yes or no.

These aren't private words, of course—she's trying to prompt him to say that she was with him in the hotel all night. She's offering her help.

She is, in fact, offering to go back to Paris.

SHE DID GO BACK TO PARIS. And I see that as one of the cardinal actions of her life, as important in its way as stealing the family money or as the choice she made, whenever and however she made it, to become an outlaw. She went back on impulse, unreflecting, to the jurisdiction where the robbery had taken place and where the interrogation of Dutch Gus and Eddie was continuing. Of course she did it because Eddie was her man and she knew, as every woman ever born knows, what it is expected a woman will do for her man. But I think she was the prisoner of another code as well—the code of the underworld, a male code, a simplifying one. I think because she had no general beliefs about right behavior between people, she obeyed the specific guide to proper behavior between crooks.

And I think she believed, somehow, that she'd get away with it. Her return, at bottom, was based on her belief in herself.

I went to Paris, she wrote, *and slipped five hundred dollars to Eddie while he was in the Palais de Justice awaiting trial, so that he would have some ready money to use to the best advantage. Then I went to the American Consul and gave him a line of talk about my*

bad brother being in jail, the result of association with evil compan-
ions. His poor old mother, of a very respectable family, was supposed
to be breaking her heart.

May promised the consul that if he got Eddie out, she would bring
him back to their mother and he'd never get into trouble again, and
I'm sure there were tears of sincerity in her eyes when she pitched her
story. And what eyes! She had huge experience in looking out from
those eyes while she told tall stories to men, and of men falling for the
stories.

But confidence tricksters do keep raising the bar, and this time she
had raised it too far. *I was not as smart as I thought I was,* she wrote,
or the breaks went against me. The consul called the police. She was
arrested. A newspaper report begins, *"Des agents de la Sûreté ont ar-*
rêté hier la maîtresse d'Eddy Guerin"—undercover agents arrested
the mistress of Eddie Guerin yesterday. *"Cette femme, une demi-*
mondaine très élégante, a déclaré se nommer Cennonwill et avoir
27 ans. Elle est, toutefois, imprisonnée." This elegant woman of the
underworld said that she was called Cennonwill and that she was
twenty-seven.

Another false name. Another lie about her age.

And now she, too, is sent to prison, while an investigating judge
oversees the preparation of a case against her.

THERE IS NOTHING attractive in what Eddie said in *I Was a Bandit*
about May's return to Paris. He calls her act "maudlin generosity."
He says "she was drunk most of the time or she wouldn't have been
so insane as to go over to Paris to see me." But the bitterness came
afterward. In 1901, in Paris, he and May were still a couple.

"The months slipped by," he wrote.

May was shut up in the woman's prison of La Roquelle, and I
only saw her about three times in nine months. I felt a bit

afraid, not knowing what she would do. Dutch Gus had already snitched but unless May did the same, I had a good fighting chance. To keep her square, I got a friend outside to engage
a barrister for her, but nevertheless it was an anxious time
looking forward to the day when we would be brought up at
the Seine Assizes.

I had retained Henri Robert, one of the greatest French bar-
risters of his time, and another lawyer who spoke English well.
This man came to me one day and said: "What is the use of going on with the case? Why don't you plead guilty and throw
yourself on the mercy of the court?"

"I'm not going to plead guilty for what I haven't done,"
I replied.

"Chicago May wants to plead guilty."

"She can do what she likes. They've got nothing against me
except that I am supposed to have given May the money."

I imagine Eddie going back to his cell after an interview like that.
He resumed his work, I suppose—it was sorting ostrich feathers for
use on women's luxury hats—and took off the mask which outside
their cells, all the prisoners had to wear. Presumably, self-satisfaction
was keeping him going, but the position he had taken up was foolish,
and cruel to May. The charge against her was receiving monies knowing them to be stolen. She couldn't plead guilty and get it all over with
because to do that, as long as he was pleading not guilty, she'd have to
turn against him.

I suppose one of them was sent to the other in a closed van, hand-
cuffed, on the three occasions they met. We can never know how they
held themselves as they walked into the room, or whether they were
allowed to embrace, and if so, whether there was warmth to it. But
May's heart must have been getting cold to Eddie, since she wanted to
plead guilty and he wouldn't allow her. And Eddie was moving away
from May, to judge by an outburst of his made during one of the in-

vestigating judge's interrogations. When his trial began, it was read into the record.

"I was born to be an honest man," Eddie declared,

> but without a fortune it is difficult to be honest if your tastes are not modest. I detest manual labor, which besides, you can hardly make a living at. After ten years in prison in France I went back to Chicago and I set myself up in the hire-car business but no money came in. I went to England and I got married in Birmingham. My little reserve was soon spent, and I started stealing again. And here I am. What will become of my poor wife?

Not a word about what will become of poor May.

SHE ENDURED a year on remand in various Paris prisons, which were hardly less punitive than if she'd already been found guilty. For a while she was in the prison of Saint Lazare, where so many women were piled in together that there was no space in the dormitories to move between the beds. Then she was in Fresnes, a place that had five hundred absolutely identical cells, each containing one chained chair, a toilet, a table, and a pallet bed—an environment so stark that a modern artist who wrote a text to old photos of the place called it "an empty hall, a factory where no work is carried out, a hospital that does not cure, a sort of frozen hell, divided into compartments, silent and pale." The day there began at five in the morning with compulsory polishing, without actual polish, of the floor of the cell. If the floor was not made as glassy as a mirror, the prisoner was put on bread and water or deprived of reading on Sundays, or was threatened with being put in irons.

Then she was in Clairmont prison, run by nuns—a cold place where May was always hungry, and where she fell very ill with something resembling tuberculosis. And she was dirty; washing was almost impossible. May and another girl identified a weakness in security—a breach in the wall of the section of the jail that was kept for Protestant prisoners. They claimed to be Protestants, and were eventually moved to that section and began to plot their escape. But it was too late; the wall had been built up.

The nuns did not allow the women to wear underwear. *The French,* as May wrote tersely, *are very refined in their cruelty.*

Once when I was walking at nightfall across a quadrangle in the complex of law courts beside the Sainte Chapelle in Paris, a door somewhere opened and a group of lawyers hurried toward me down the steps, men in the ballooning black gowns and white neckbands of the antique dress that *avocats* wear in court in France. They swooped past like harsh, intent birds. For the first time I felt a twinge of the fear May must have felt when she stood in the dock at the Assizes. She didn't speak French. She'd been in court before, but that was the raucous Manhattan night court where she'd have known most of the cops and judges and defendants. Now she was an outsider in every way. She couldn't deploy her personality to effect because it was hidden behind the language barrier, and without it she had no power. And the past year spent in prisons, in constant suspense about the future, must have damaged even her exceptional confidence.

The trial of Dutch Gus Miller and Eddie Guerin on charges of burglary with violence, and of May for receiving stolen money, was reported by the *Gazette des Tribunaux*.

"The three accused were all tall, and obviously Anglo-Saxon," the report begins. "The two men, well-groomed and elegantly dressed, have the correct and effortless look of perfect gentlemen. The woman is carefully dressed"—and then it describes the black and white hat and the beige gown that I borrowed to dress her in on the night her destiny still hung in the balance, when she stood guard outside the American Express office.

But if the *Gazette* liked her clothes, it didn't like her face. "The chic of the outfit shows up the ordinariness of her face," it sniffed, "and her numerous freckles."

The freckles, on the other hand, make me feel for her. She was a young Irishwoman, not a person in a book.

In French trials, the accused are invited to address the court, before being cross-examined, to make what general points in their defense they can. According to the newspaper report of the trial, all May asked was that the judge not reveal the name of the family she came from. She had always lied about her birthplace, her name, and her age, but this is the first evidence that she did it to protect the Duignans of Edenmore.

"The only defense I could put forward was that of an alibi," Eddie said in his book.

> I went into the witness box and swore that I was at an hotel with Chicago May and had not left my room all night. I added that Dutch Gus had tried to implicate me in the crime owing to jealousy and that he was an old and experienced bank robber who had been guilty of many similar crimes in the past. Chicago May went into the box and told exactly the same story, saying I had been in her company at the time the robbery took place and furthermore that I had not given her the large sum of money I was alleged to have received.

They must have made their statements slowly, each listening critically as the other spoke, each looking more or less imploringly at the jury, each searching the judge's face for reaction as the translators passed on what they had said. Now is the time to remember that they had known each other in freedom for only about six weeks. They can't have meant to be as dependent on each other as this. It was a fling they were having—not a relationship.

May made no attempt to defend herself. The French police had learned a lot about her career in America and England, but she said this must be a case of mistaken identity—the person that information was about, Chicago May, wasn't her. She knew nothing about the robbery. This defense is so astonishingly limp that I wonder whether it isn't another example of that caving in to punishment I seem to keep encountering in the criminal behavior of the time. Little wonder, as the *Gazette* reported, that during the rest of the proceedings May "laughed nervously from time to time, and crushed in her hand a handkerchief which she sometimes raised to her eyes or her forehead."

No prison worse than the ones she had already endured was waiting for her. But for Eddie there was the prospect of the awful penal colony in South America known as Devil's Island. It had become infamous during the recent exile there of Captain Dreyfus, an army captain framed for treason in a plot orchestrated by anti-Semitic elements in the French High Command. During his years in solitary confinement, before the retrial that began the process of clearing his name, even those who hated Dreyfus had learned enough about the regime in the penal colony to shudder at its name. It was far away across the Atlantic in South America, on the mangrove-jungle coast of French Guiana, hot and humid and insect-ridden beyond description, and abandoned to a most brutal prison culture. To be sent there was known as "the dry guillotine," because such a huge proportion of the convicts died.

Yet Eddie had nothing to say except that he didn't do it and that Dutch Gus, who had pleaded guilty, was lying because he was jealous of Eddie's relationship with *"la femme Scharp,"* as some of the French newspapers called May—I don't suppose that respectable Mrs. Sharp in New Jersey knew that her surname was being bandied around a Paris court. But when the concierge from Eddie's hotel was called, he said that Eddie had gone out and had come in late.

Eddie's lawyer "made a passionate speech to the jury," Eddie wrote,

> pointing out how terrible it was that a man should be betrayed
> by another so that he could escape the full consequences of his

misdeeds. Chicago May's lawyer pleaded want of guilty knowledge on her behalf. The President of the Court summed up and the jury went out. We were being taken below when I made a jump at Dutch Gus and landed him a smash on the jaw which sent him staggering down the steps. Three or four gendarmes jumped on me to prevent further mischief but at any rate I got the satisfaction of giving him something he would remember for a week or two.

Half an hour elapsed before we were brought back into court. I am no coward, but my heart was thumping badly when the jury returned and delivered their verdict.

Half an hour! The jury had hardly hesitated.

Eddie Guerin got transportation to Devil's Island for life.

Gus Miller, even though he had cooperated with the prosecution, got the same.

May got penal servitude—hard labor—for five years.

When the verdict was read out, Eddie tried again to jump across the courtroom to throttle Miller. Only then, when the warders had hustled Gus away, did he remember to embrace May. A paper called the *Gazette du Palais* noted that at the last, *"Guerin et la femme Sharp se sont jetés dans les bras l'un de l'autre"*—they threw themselves into each other's arms.

IN HER STORY, this is the lowest point May's life has so far reached. Even decades later not a detail is forgotten.

Soon after the trial, she was marched in a convoy of women from all the prisons of Paris to the train to the south of France—she was to serve her sentence in Montpellier prison.

We were a sight, she writes, *going through the streets of Paris. Each of us carried a bundle on her shoulder and had a blue handkerchief round her head. I wore sabots. They were tough sledding.*

The French girls opened their bundles and put on their high-heeled shoes. They were the limit; prison clothes, kerchiefed heads—no hair was allowed to show—and the high heels. The guards, as usual, carried drawn swords.

The train on which we journeyed to southern France was composed of voitures cellulaires. They were boxcars with cells. We were stuck into little cages where it was impossible to sit down. Some people wouldn't treat brute animals like that, but then we were only criminals. When we would come to some jerk-water town, we were taken to the local jail and allowed to sleep in the jailyard. There were not cells enough in such a place to accommodate us. They had to halt the caravan for rest and sleep, or some of the women would have died on their hands. When it came time to eat, the guards would chuck a hunk of bread, a piece of cheese, and a can of water into the carcells. The train was stopped in order to feed the animals. If anyone wanted to go to the toilet, the door would be opened by the guard who stood right beside the woman occupying it

When we passed slowly through the small towns, the crowds would yell, "voleuses," "coquins," "cochons."

ON THE American Express internal website, there's an informative "This Day in the Company's History" feature. On April 27 every year, the event commemorated is the raid on the Rue Scribe. From the company's point of view, the raiders themselves are not of interest— Gus and May aren't even mentioned. What the company finds worthy of comment is that "The raid tested the efficiency of the traveler's cheque system."

I see the same event, of course, from my perspective, which is perhaps just as partial. I see the night of the raid as the night when May's boat capsized. I think of how young she still is—she's twenty-nine or thirty—and of how her patience has never yet been tested, and how five years of hard labor may ask more of her spirit than she has to give. I wonder whether being a jailbird will be a watershed in her view of herself. Up to now she could say to herself that she'd become Chicago May half for adventure and half because she didn't know any other way to make an independent living. She could almost deny that she'd ever done anything bad. There had been nothing on paper to say she was bad. But this was on paper. She's a convict, now.

ONCE, in an iron-cold Paris, I left the warmth of my hotel room and found my way to the street where May and Eddie stayed on the night of the American Express job. Places I could share with May were very important to me. The getting to them and the being there were certainties, not open to too many interpretations, as words often are. I'd already strolled around the American Express building at midnight for no better reason than that standing where she'd stood was a mime it was obscurely useful to me to perform. Her physical path through the world marked out actual ground. I could escape from the transaction of reading her words and then turning to my own experience for a response.

I searched out the hotel, too, for the same reason I'd looked for the drugstore in Manhattan where May and her newspaperman boyfriend used to have breakfast. Her book puts so much emphasis on the rough, tough, public figure that I value the moments when she was close to another person and well and happy. I know what it's like to have a tired and companionable breakfast with a lover and I know about rooms in Parisian hotels that have flowered wallpaper and an enamel bidet on a little stand and a wide bed made for love.

There's still only one hotel in the Rue Vignon, a narrow backstreet near the Madeleine—a humble street where men deliver sacks of vegetables to restaurants, and children with schoolbags hop across the stream of water rushing down the gutter, and the clerk from the hotel—a building four or five stories high and a single room and a steep staircase wide—stands in his doorway peacefully watching the scene. I stood and looked up while everyone around me went about their business, paying my respects to the celebration the building must have known when Eddie got back with the money from the American Express job.

In my head I allowed the pair every license. Because how many people ever know that this time is the last time? Eddie wasn't to know that after this there'd be no more triumph, nothing but arrest, jail, trial, and consignment across the ocean to Devil's Island. May wasn't to know that her body, superb on the rumpled bed, would be confined to a cell for years and years.

She pulled her fate down onto herself, it might be said, when she returned to Paris to help Eddie of her own free will. But how free was her will? The freedoms women gain when they are young and have money and are not yet in interaction with the traditional women's roles are superficial and temporary. In reality, what they will do is circumscribed by what other people, and they themselves, think they should do. May would have been some kind of awesome super-creature—not one of us—if she had contemplated Eddie's fate and left him to languish in French jails and decamped with the money.

And therefore she made the journey to Montpellier on the slow train for criminals, the curses in a language she didn't know ringing in her ears, the boxcars crawling slowly across grade-crossings, the women in prison clothing bowing their kerchiefed heads behind the wire of their cages as the respectable women shouted at them, "Thieves!" "Whores!" "Pigs!"

Six

Escapes and
Homecomings

The non-convict population of French Guiana—native peoples and Indian shopkeepers and a few colonists from France—tried to keep prison camps away from Cayenne, the capital, but there was one on the coast beside it, one deep in the jungle, and a huge one on the river that divided French from Dutch Guiana to the north. The whole country and its offshore islands were essentially the penal colony known as Devil's Island. In Cayenne, prisoners on work detail were marched through the languid streets of a town enervated both by the climate and by the local alcohol, home-distilled from sugar cane, where ex-prisoners, Eddie Guerin wrote in *I Was a Bandit,*

were wandering about, practically starving. They were pathetically glad to receive the odds and ends of food thrown to them by prisoners marched out to work. In Cayenne town itself there

were hundreds of discharged prisoners wandering about unable to keep body and soul together.

This was the most awful thing about being sentenced to life on
Devil's Island, as Eddie and Dutch Gus had been. A man might be released after twenty years. But he would never be allowed to leave the
colony. Lifers never returned to France.

Captain Dreyfus had spent years in strict isolation—never spoken
to, yet kept under surveillance at every minute of the night and day
for fear of a raid to release him. But no one had ever been rescued or
escaped from the islands. It was simply impossible without a very
good boat to get across the water to the mainland. Many men did try,
but all any would-be escaper got was years more added to his sentence and to "go about," Eddie wrote, "for the next six months or
more, with a fourteen-pound chain riveted to his legs." In any case,
many of the prisoners were too enfeebled by TB or malaria or scurvy,
and by the heat and humidity and the stinging insects by day and
mosquitoes by night to exert themselves. "The guards leaned on their
rifles dozing," Eddie wrote. "Nobody had sufficient energy to lift a
hand beyond what was absolutely necessary."

After a year on one of the islands, Eddie managed to get himself
to a camp on the mainland. There, languid men crawled on their
knees on the ground around the stone cellblocks, picking up individual leaves—and if they were sane they did what they were told because a convict who spoke insolently to a warder might get five, eight,
maybe ten years in isolation. They worked in clouds of mosquitoes
attracted by their sweat. At night they were locked in and the warders
went to their own houses and left them alone till morning. In a convict's primitive drawing from inside a barracks, one shaven-headed
man has a possessive arm around the waist of another; the policy of
the prison administration, I read, "encouraged homosexuality." Eddie wrote years later about the nights and how, "when there was nothing to do but lie in your hammock trying to get your tortured brain to

sleep, the Italians would get together and sing songs from the grand operas." Singing! Against the nocturnal howling of the monkeys. Until the equatorial sun rolled up out of the hot sea again and another day could not be prevented from beginning.

Hatred of Dutch Gus, who was in another camp, kept Eddie going. And the hope of *"la belle"*—the beautiful thing—escape. If a man could get away, he had an outside chance of survival, though the people who lived in the mangrove swamps were just as likely to murder an escapee as to help him, and the terrain was so hostile that escapees who had taken off together were known to have descended to cannibalism. And even if, somehow, a fugitive did get past the alligators in the wide river and make it to Dutch Guiana, he was likely to be returned to the French colony by bounty hunters.

A man with money could at least try. The difficulty was in holding on to money while waiting for a chance to use it. The stronger convicts stole everything from the less strong, and most men hid what money they had in a tube in their guts. When a man dropped dead— and about 40 percent of the prisoners sent to French Guiana did die—the others jumped on his stomach to expel the tube.

But there was another side to the Devil's Island regime, as I discovered when I found, in the Pinkerton archive in the Library of Congress, a copy of a letter Eddie wrote from Guiana. I hadn't imagined that the French postal system extended to the penal colony and that, considering the brutality of other aspects of the place, a convict could make use of it. I didn't know the men could get magazines sent to them and even get money sent—in the letter Eddie is fairly openly asking for money for bribes.

The letter was written about three years into his sentence.

May, at this point, is still in Montpellier prison, back in France.

The letter was not sent to May.

It was sent to "Dearest Em," who is Emily Skinner, the maid May had in London. A woman in May's line of work has a different relationship with her maid than a housewife does—the maid is an accomplice rather than a servant. But all the same, the "dearest" in Eddie's greeting comes as a shock.

It would have been a thrill at any time to come upon this letter, which may well be the first personal account of Devil's Island in the English language. But it also introduces the speaking voice of the man for whom May, in the prime of life, has lost her liberty.

"I met an old friend and he manages to get me food and buze which is absolutely necessary here as the food is horrible," Eddie writes.

O'Brien tried to get away and had not the necessary things, in fact he made a boat out of thick hammocks but was immediately caught and was tried, he was given 2 years to carry a double chain attached to his leg; the prosecuting Attorney appealed the case against him as he wanted him to be sent to solitary confinement for 3 to 5 years for stealing the hammocks and if he is sent there it is slow death. . . . Dutch Gus has hard work and is despised by all, the few English won't speak or look at him not even give him a pipe of tobacco, and he is exiled on the Island the same as I and he will die here, I have no doubt. . . .

There is a chance to crush, only I will need stuff and have a screw right. The necessary must be sent from England or America. If it is manufactured in the USA it is the only way— this screw cannot be righted for short of a hundred quid.

"Crush" must mean escape and "stuff" money and "screw" a prison guard. He wants Emily to get in touch with—where else?— Chicago. He's appealing for money. "Send this over to Sheedy and tell him to send it to Paddy"—Paddy is Eddie's brother and Sheedy the rich and well-connected gentleman gambler in whose club in Cairo the young May plied her trade. When Eddie was arrested for the American Express robbery, a reporter door-stepped Sheedy for a comment and he said, "I don't know Guerin, a bank robber. I know a little chap that was my schoolmate."

And Billy Pinkerton was another of the circle. The letter—or rather, a typed copy of the letter made somewhere along the line—ended up in the Pinkerton archive, presumably because Sheedy sent it on to Billy. The Pinkerton firm was actually employed in a security capacity by American Express; on the other hand, Billy must have felt, Eddie was one of Chicago's own.

"Drop me a line," his letter ends,

> and let me know how May is, and if her conduct has always been good where she is, and what the prospects are. Give her my fondest love. Say I am well, but not strong, and I have not hard work. Say I think of her always and always with affection and I hope some day to see you both. You are my brave true little friend, who have been so kind and so true, as true as steel to May; she appreciates it, I know she does, and so do I, and some day you will see and know I do.

One big surprise here is how explicit Eddie dares to be, though I suppose he could rely on the local censors not being able to read English. But another is the glimpse of his private self. Was this his tone to May, and if so, was this what thrilled her in him—this fatherly sentimentality?

May says very little about her own time in jail. The difficult, fearless person is in eclipse during the years in Montpellier. She says, *I had to work, but I was sick most of the time. I had to go to school, of which I thoroughly approved. The French,* she impressively remarks, *had begun to separate church and state. We had regular matrons instead of Sisters. The nuns in Clairmont used to make us dress and undress under blankets. If you exposed yourself in the slightest you were reported and punished. In Montpellier the matrons laughed and*

*said "Girls, dress and undress like human beings!" We all felt more
clubby, in consequence.*

But sickness would have cut her off from the life of the institution
and so, of course, would not knowing a word of French. Usually the
reader can rely on May to respond to new situations—and imprisonment was altogether new—and to look around her, and even many
years later to be able to recall the details that struck her. But it is as if
she refused to look when she was in Montpellier. She devotes only a
few paragraphs of her book to the nearly three years there.

Her energy, like Eddie's, was concentrated on getting out, though
all she could do was try to interest a network of American and French
philanthropic ladies in her case—which she represented, of course, as
a miscarriage of justice. She played the innocence card and, for good
measure, the health card; she was so unwell, she wrote, that *the good
prison doctor said it was absolutely necessary for me to have fresh
air, sunshine and proper food or I would kick out.* Years later, Eddie
said in his book that May seduced this doctor and then promised to
marry him if he got her an early release. Nothing Eddie says about
May is to be trusted, but I daresay that if May made up her mind to
seduce any man, she had a good chance of succeeding. She was in her
early thirties, an age when many women blossom. She was living, for
the first time, in a benign climate. She was off the streets and out of
the bars. Perhaps she looked very well—not that I think her power
rested on looks. I think she was both unconsciously charming and
knew how to charm.

She got on very well with women, always. A network of ladies
who took an interest in prisoners did exist—we don't have to take her
word for it—and through it, May pulled off a coup she'd never have
dared invent. In 1905, a president of France was leaving office. It was
the custom for outgoing presidents to assert their symbolic power by
granting pardons. *The old dear probably did not know who I was but
others did.* May's ladies managed to get her name included in President Emile Loubet's list—a unique distinction, I do not doubt, for a

native of Edenmore, and a far more impressive way of getting out of jail than merely seducing a doctor.

Vivacity returns to her book as soon as she is a free woman.

She was escorted to the ferryboat to England, she wrote, by *a semi-official lady who was a go-between for wronged society and criminals. She talked to me all the way, without ceasing, gesticulating vehemently, and preaching to me to be a good woman. On the train, an English boy asked me who was my companion in black.*

I whispered, "She's my maid."

May went back to London. *The lawyers, court costs and prison officials had used up most of my money.* There doesn't seem to be any left from the American Express job; in Eddie's letter from Devil's Island he doesn't even mention it. But money was never May's problem. She worked at what she calls *the old game,* and also went to Cairo *to meet Pat Sheedy and arrange to raise money to spring Guerin. During my stay in Cairo I stole about five thousand dollars, most of which I got by fainting in a man's arms at Shepheard's Hotel. I slid to the stairs when he let go of me to get help, and cached the bills under the stair-runner. When I "recovered," the next day, I got the money.*

She also acquired a new boyfriend by the name of Baby Thompson, and when he gave her five thousand pounds to buy a little love nest for their assignations, she contributed that, too, she says, to the Eddie escape fund. And although she must be exaggerating the amount, Eddie himself says that money was sent to him "from Chicago and from London." Years later, he denied that May did anything to help him, but it was surely she who was the London contributor.

THE AFFAIR with Baby Thompson—*a first-class confidence-man and a crook dealing only in finesse,* she says—was not, according to May, a *disloyalty on my part. Eddie and I had got drunk, once, before the Paris affair, and I had told him I no longer loved him.*

There's always a mystery when someone says to someone else that they no longer love them. What did the love depend on, then, that has now so suddenly disappeared? But if you read May's life as a struggle for something there were no words for in her time—a struggle to stay true to her authentic self—then the break away from Eddie is perhaps more important than her falling for him in the first place. It returned her to an essentially unpartnered self. It also lends, by the way, a certain nobility to her return to Paris to help him.

But why did she have to apologize for being with Baby? Was the criminal world even more patriarchal than the straight, though men and women were in some ways colleagues there? Was May expected to be Eddie Guerin's woman forever, even though the likelihood was that he would never be free, except, perhaps, as a derelict ex-con on the streets of Cayenne? It is now the end of 1905 or the beginning of 1906; he and she were last together in April 1901, and at that point they had been a couple for only about a month. May has just served more than four years in various French jails because of Eddie, yet nothing could be further from apology than his lordly manner in the letter to Emily Skinner. It patronizes May in its condescending inquiry after her conduct and in his speaking for her. But the important detail here is that May had to be drunk—had even, perhaps, to get drunk—to tell Eddie she no longer loved him. May, as reckless a woman as ever lived? May, who used to go around practically looking for a fight? The Eddie who grew up in penitentiaries and spent years in punishment cells—the Eddie with the finger joints missing—was certainly a violent man. But this is the first hint that May was afraid of him.

SHE HAD BEEN very much alone in recent years. The noise and event and speed of her life had stopped, abruptly, when she plummeted into the silence of a jail cell. In prison in France she was not only not a legend, she was barely a person. She was convict number such-and-such.

She must have had to draw on every memory of what she was before, to muster her forces against her dehumanizing surroundings.

Everything around her was strange. She was used to rain, not sun; to butter, not olive oil. She was used to the sound of wind, not the shrill hum of cicadas on long, stifling nights. How everything must have conspired to make her long for home! Wasn't she the finest girl in the parish of Edenmore once? Wasn't she May Duignan? And wasn't she loved when she was a little girl? Love is not only about who you know, but who knows you—whose knowledge of you is part of them. By that measure, no one had ever loved her, except her family. How it must have crept up on her—the thought of being in Ireland, on grass, under lark song, amid ways of talking and behaving she knew so well that she was supple in them. She must have seen in her mind's eye the leafy lane that led to the farmyard and the dog racing forward and the faces she knew since, when they bent over her, they had been everything she could see.

The longing overcame common sense.

There was the money she'd stolen from her family. There was the scandalous way she'd lived. May was Irish herself—she was well aware that people with links to Edenmore, living now in America, would have repeated every rumor about her in their letters home and would have greatly enjoyed doing it. She knew that her parents knew about her. Yet, as soon as she'd done her bit for Eddie, she began to get ready. *As soon as I raised the money for Guerin,* she wrote, *I got me extra nice fine linen and filled my purse to overflowing.*

Then I went home.

ON THE OTHER SIDE of the world, Eddie tried to do the same thing. He, too, set out for home.

About five years after he landed in Devil's Island, his chance presented itself. He had been working as a tailor of prison clothes on the porch of one of the buildings of the camp of Maroni and he'd often dropped his thimble, and the guards were accustomed to giving him permission to go down to retrieve it. One day he dropped it, jumped down to look for it, and didn't come back. In the jungle, the Belgian he'd picked to escape with was waiting—a country man whose country skills were needed in terrain full of leeches and rats and terrible insects and stinking undergrowth and the threat of hunger. Now, the money Eddie had collected over the years came into its own. He bribed their way across the wide and dangerous river where the ferrymen usually turned escapees in.

They reached Dutch Guiana, where

for the better part of a fortnight we slogged our way through the marshes and creeks that abounded there. Our clothing was torn to tatters as we struggled across the rough country, daily we got soaked from head to foot fording waterlogged wastes. At night-time, under the shelter of a bivouac made by the Belgian, we would lie awake in a state of fear while the wild animals of the forest came sniffing around. Gigantic snakes struck at us as we fought our way through dense patches of undergrowth. Unkempt and unshaven, our feet a mass of blisters, starving but for the tropical fruit we could pick, it was nothing short of a miracle that we ever found our way at all.

After many lurid adventures, Eddie got to the outskirts of Paramaribo, the capital of Dutch Guiana. A kindly Scotsman helped by procuring him a suit of white duck and, dressed in it, Eddie was able to mix with the people on the streets. But now what? There was a boat to New York from British Guiana, the next country to the north, but how was he to get there?

He had to take a chance on confronting officialdom. So, "lean, hungry-looking, pitted all over with mosquito bites, and no doubt appearing an all-out desperado," he set off to ask for help from the consul for the United States.

The dangers Eddie had faced and the difficulties he still faced were all exterior to him. Whereas when May set out for home, though the journey was perfectly easy to accomplish, she was risking her inner self. If I had met her on the ferry to Ireland—and stray women did confide in each other during the night on the boat between countries—I'd have perceived that she had blurred her imagination to what was likely to happen. I'd have said, "Oh, be careful! If it doesn't work out you'll be much worse off than you are now! You're asking for too much!" But how many people are reasonable when it comes to finding their parents again?

THE RAILWAY STATION in Longford is not very different now from what it was a hundred years ago, except that then there would have been great clangs and exhalations and piston noises when the train from Dublin came in. The filigree of notes that birds in station yards make would have been more noticeable, so distinct was the silence after the steam locomotive pulled away. May would have walked up the street to the Longford Arms. I don't doubt that passersby stopped, awestruck, to watch her pass. The first years of the twentieth century were a time of tiny waists and ankles and big hats and bosoms—Joyce set *Ulysses* and the lushness of Molly Bloom in 1904, and this was a year or two later—and in that era of womanly women, May can have had few matches. And she wouldn't have stinted on the finery. Returned Yanks, as they were always called, never did. If they had a diamond or a fur stole or a pair of fancy boots or a hunter watch or a hat with feathers and plush roses, out they came to display the emigrant's success. May wasn't young anymore, but it was exactly her peers that she'd have been most in contrast with, bowed by work as they must have been. Conversation, on the main street of Longford, would have ceased as the splendid woman passed.

Small-town Ireland has unrivaled intelligence networks. Before she even got to the hotel, the whole place would have known who she was. And while she was negotiating a rate with the jarvey driver and having a pot of tea or a stiff drink—depending on how nervous she was—the news of her arrival would have reached even to the small house on the edge of the bog. The family would somehow have been informed that May—May, of all people!—had come off the train. It doesn't take much to imagine the confusion of gasps and prayers and the faces suddenly red with tension and the rush to tidy the kitchen and, at the same time, the urge to bar the door.

The countryside would have looked much the same as when she ran through the darkening evening fifteen years before. Nothing had happened in Ireland since then to halt the advance of rush and briar— if anything, drained of life by the continuing emigration of its people, it would have been more obviously an abandoned landscape. But once around the base of Edenmore Hill, the trap would have jogged along a lane that is a tunnel of bright leaves between slopes of emerald-green fields. She'd have walked across the dirt of the yard in her wonderful clothes against a backdrop of near trees and distant, purple bog. Her family would have been clustered at the door. It was up to her father to step forward to welcome her home, but he, like everyone else in Edenmore, had never before been in the presence of a woman steeped in sex and crime. It was a terrible situation for all of them.

No one can have known what tone to strike. The teenage girl, who was the baby born the night May ran away, looked at last at her sister; her sister looked at last at her. The brothers—three men now—would have been made shy and furtive by the crisis. The mother, even with tears leaking from her eyes, would have been painfully aware that every detail of the family's reception of this daughter would be reported by May's driver to an avid audience, and that whatever the family did would be judged to be wrong. The father, on whom the burden of greeting rested, was obliged to find something to say. But when he spoke he would have been quiet, in the way of old-style Irish men. Whereas May in reply—and it was their accent that the people

A rural Irish scene

at home always picked to sneer at—would have sent up a smoke screen of slangy American speech. Both to impress, like her clothes. And to hide behind.

Because if her return was hard on everyone, it was hardest on her. It was she who had had the dream that brought her back. From the perspective of a jail in France, a golden penumbra had surrounded this place and these people. They had seemed to be waiting, immobilized, where she had left them years before. And now—there was only this little tongue-tied group. A gray-haired father and mother—rain starting, perhaps; the dog refusing to come forward to be petted; the neighbor's children watching in the bushes. Nostalgia should never have to bear such a weight.

WHEN I WAS A CHILD, the person who came home, exotic as a king-fisher, was my mother's young sister, Maureen. I was always waiting for her. When she'd come out to see us where we lived in the middle of dull fields, hurrying toward us, tall and thin in her red peep-toe sandals, with hair that rippled down the back of her tweed suits and her legs dyed orange with suntan makeup, she was the nearest thing I could imagine to a film star. We resented having to polish the floor for our mother, but Maureen tied cloths to our feet and danced with us and the old boards shone. She took out her coral lipstick and drew generous lips around our pursed mouths. She'd pick us up and swoop with us; "Waltztime in Vienna, hearts were gay there, dreams came true. . . ."

I didn't realize that she was beginning to have a drinking problem. My grandfather feared for her, so he told her to marry the most constant of her admirers. She tried to run. Her fiancé was an Irishman who worked here and there in oil fields abroad. He sent the money for her ticket and she drank it, but that only meant she had to go the second time he sent the money. We saw her off at the start of her journey to join him in Venezuela, our hearts breaking at saying goodbye. She waved down from the deck of the old ferryboat and the whole quayside was heaving with tears, the streetlamps along the North Wall cried themselves in the drizzle and darkness, and the boat pulled away onto the black river with a long-drawn-out sound like a groan of sorrow.

I see May when I remember Maureen back on a visit, sitting up in bed, long-limbed and brown in a nightgown of a cotton so fine that I can feel its silkiness still, lighting cigarettes with long fingers that shook. They were American cigarettes that she kept in a handbag of real crocodile. Her skin became thick and slightly pockmarked, but her hair was always lovely.

Her mother had died when she was a girl and her big, gruff father was her only compass point. She used to tiptoe up the stairs, trying to be steady, because he lay awake waiting to hear her come safely in. Why she beat her way home was to be near him.

I remember it as the central truth about Maureen that above her mouth where the lipstick was often smeared, her eyes were bewildered. Her self-destructiveness seemed to have nothing to do with the child who looked out through those eyes.

Did May's family see in her eyes the girl she had once been?

"IT WAS YEARS before she came back and we were glad to see her"— that's what her mother said in the one interview she ever gave about her notorious daughter, the interview in the local newspaper. "But we were troubled over her dress and fine jewellery and the talk of the money she had spent."

The mother wouldn't have minded making the point that May Duignan came home loaded with wealth. But there was no way to express the complicated truth—that May was their eldest child, their daughter, even if she was a prodigal daughter. They couldn't not welcome her, although she was more than embarrassing: she was a disgrace.

Only the teenage girl would have reveled in the situation. Local legend has it that May broke with the custom of sleeping at home and stayed instead in the hotel in Longford, and it seems very likely to me that she would have taken the girl to sleep in the hotel with her, as Maureen would have done with me. I imagine May striding toward her sister that first day, already more at ease with her than with any of the others, already holding her away by the shoulders to measure her with a squinting eye for some of the fancy clothes in the traveling bag. Impressing the girl would have been something to do. Besides, in the hotel every drink she had would be noted and reported, and she couldn't even think of picking up a man—it wouldn't do to have even a convivial chat with the commercial travelers who played cards all evening in the Residents' Lounge. She didn't dare steal, not if there were sheaves of banknotes sticking out of a sucker's pocket. All the long, provincial evening, she had to be on her best behavior—a state she hadn't known since her attempt to be Mrs. Sharp of New Jersey.

As well as the satisfaction of giving her yearning sister a treat,

May needed her to talk to. The returned ones need confidantes, to try to make the whole of themselves, fractured between different countries, known.

What were the people of Edenmore to do? It was the custom until recently that when one of their own came back from America, all work was suspended and a meadow was mowed and a platform of boards put up and half-barrels of porter were tapped and musicians came from everywhere and the dancing party lasted for days. In the parish history, there are touching photos of occasions like that from later decades—the men in open-necked white shirts and dark suits, the women in print frocks, sitting on hay bales in sunlit fields. But May—May was profoundly estranged from the community. That was the reality, underneath all the fascination with her. The people of Edenmore really were devout. They really did believe in sin and that she was a sinner, and that that was the most terrible thing you could be. They really did believe that she had hurt God—that she had chosen the side of the devil. There are cultures, even Roman Catholic ones, where all the uses of flesh are accepted and working girls are part of society; in the alleyways of Genoa, for instance, in Italy, I've seen the prostitutes sit out on kitchen chairs among children and stallholders and slinking cats and neighbors calling out to one another and pizza ovens being stoked for the evening. But May's Ireland hated and feared sexuality. That's what she should have allowed herself to remember.

Her return had its utility. Irish history, in the popular mind, is composed of rebellion and politics, but May's trajectory through Edenmore was politics, too. It forced the community to a first conscious, collective exercise in ambiguity. Who knows what she led people to think? If she went to Mass, for instance, nodding and smiling at the tight-faced neighbors, she was the first female ever seen to flout the rules and sanctions of the men who ran the place, and not just survive, but—apparently—thrive. Though May must also have seemed, to an extent we will never recapture, not quite real. Many of the people who gaped at her in church and counted every tiny, patent-leather button on her boots and every stone in the bangles she wore over her long gloves had never seen such a figure as she cut. But then, they'd never seen a color print or a moving image or heard recorded sound. She wasn't only bad in a virtuous place; she was modern in an antique world.

But—did she go to Mass? I heard a very interesting thing when I was in Edenmore myself. It was that May set off for the church, but then turned back. If we knew why she did that, we'd know a great deal about her. Was she succumbing to the pleas of her family to not, for God's sake, make a show of them? If so, did she do it out of affection for them? Or had her own nerve—usually as steady as a trapeze artist's—been damaged by the years in Montpellier? Were the people of Edenmore the one tribunal that intimidated her? Was she afraid the priest would denounce her from the altar—that she'd have to stand up from her seat and walk down the aisle between the silent ranks of the congregation and go out the high door, alone?

For the sake of the respected Duignan family, she wasn't run out of the parish. But neither could she be welcomed. Usually, the returned Yank was made available beside the fire in the home kitchen to sit and be looked at and answer questions while neighbors dropped in and friends passed by, and the family served tea and whisky. Or the Yank went visiting. But if May tried to drop in on a neighbor, was the woman of the house to wipe her hands and get the good china cups out of the press and take down the tin with the sweet cake kept from Christmas, or was she to flee down the yard with the children, and wait there with bated breath till the visitor turned and went away?

And if May didn't go visiting, what was the family to do with her all day? They had the work of the place to get through, they couldn't be always sitting with her. I suppose they found some kind of middle ground, and that though silence surely fell between herself and her father, May and her mother could gossip about who married whom and who'd left Edenmore and how they'd done abroad and the problems with everyone's health and the difference between homemade bread and store bread and where the speckled hen might be hiding her eggs. Did May sit beside the fire while her mother bustled around, or did she stand at the table like a good daughter and roll up her sleeves to mix mash for the calves? Did she fetch water? Did she take the spade and go out and lift a bucketful of potatoes? Or did she hang around the doorway in boots too light for the place, staring desolately at Edenmore Hill? She had to guard her tongue. What could she contribute as a conversational topic? That the food in a prison in the south of France isn't so bad? That if she didn't have as much money as she'd like to lavish around, it was because a lover of hers halfway across the world needed it to escape from a brutal penitential regime?

Disappointment is itself a dry experience. The words you find for it—even in the privacy of your own head—are no more than perfunctory. "Was the house always as small as this?" May might have thought.

EDDIE'S ESCAPE turned into quite a community affair, too.

The American Consul in Paramaribo was very kind. And Eddie wrote to Pat Sheedy in Chicago for help—Sheedy's reach appears to have been global. Sheedy wrote in turn to Billy Pinkerton to check that that was all right with him—all the letters are in the archive. There must have been a limit to Billy Pinkerton's indulgence of Eddie, but it had not been reached. Billy wrote to his brother, the head of the New York branch, to tell him that Sheedy had made the inquiry and that Billy had "told him that we had no personal interest in Guerin other than that we had known him all his life."

The big Chicago boys, in other words, allowed Eddie's escape to go ahead. But the interesting thing is that it was touch and go. It might have been decided to let Eddie Guerin founder.

On the letterhead of the Dutch Guyana Leasing Company, not long afterward, a businessman in Paramaribo also "took the liberty"

of writing to Pat Sheedy. He wanted him to know that "the US con-
sular agent here has done out of the fulness of his heart a very kind
turn to one Eddie Guerin, keeping him at the same hotel where he
lived and giving him a cot in his private office at night." As I read,
I imagined the setting something out of Graham Greene or Conrad.
In Paramaribo, I remember hearing once, miniature jungle plants
grow overnight on the electric wires, so humid is the hot air. I see the
businessman, the consul, and Eddie on the dark verandah in the
seething night.

But the letter isn't, in fact, at all exotic. The businessman wants
Sheedy to send fifty dollars,

it being the amount the doctor has disbursed for Eddie, not
counting the clothes, shoes and other necessities which he gave
him from his own. Eddie left this morning for Georgetown,
British Guiana, the doctor paying his passage and giving him a
few dollars, and an address there which he can fall back on for
a job.

In Georgetown, Eddie says, he

vainly tried to obtain employment, with nothing but a franc or
two in my pocket. I gave up the idea and went aboard the *City
of Quebec.* My steerage ticket took me into the company of
niggers and coolies, who easily decided I was poor white trash,
worthy of nothing but contempt. I shouldn't have had any false
pride but it cut me to the quick, herded down below with black
men while up above in the saloon were my own race going
about in lordly ease.

This may be true, or it may be what the ghostwriter thinks Eddie's
readers want to hear—there would have been a frisson, back when
I Was a Bandit came out, at the thought of a white person sharing the

experience of black people. But Eddie's account of things isn't necessarily reliable. There's a further letter in the archive, from Billy Pinkerton to his brother, commenting in disgust on a particularly lurid account of Eddie's escape in some magazine. "Characteristically," Billy writes, "and true to his low standards, Eddie Guerin omits entirely any reference to the financial and other assistance known to have been rendered to him by the American Consul at Georgetown."

So he was helped twice by officials—quite as if he were a tourist who'd lost his wallet.

Still, it was a tremendous achievement to get himself out of Devil's Island—to stay well enough to do it, to be patient in planning it, to be tough enough to survive the jungle, to be able to present himself so sympathetically that men from the legitimate world helped him. Eddie's was one of the great escapes. One day in 1905, he disembarked in Brooklyn, "paid five cents to cross the bridge, another five cents to reach Broadway—and there I was in the city I had not seen for over twenty years, penniless, homeless, but full of a joy that made me jump about like a little child."

And then he did what May had done; he headed for where he grew up. He should have done it quietly—he was a fugitive, after all, and French pride was at stake in getting him back to Guiana to serve his sentence. But instead, he went home to Chicago in a blaze of publicity. So the homecoming omens were not good for him, any more than for her.

WHEN I WAS SEVENTEEN and I'd just got out of boarding school, Maureen and I stayed for a while in a house in a seaside village on the east coast of Ireland where the tide went out so far across the level sand that the sea was only a silver line on the horizon. It was the beginning of summer, but still cold, and it got dark quite early. We had very little money. The landlady—who loved her—used to lend Maureen enough to buy a naggin of whisky at the sliding window in the back corridor of a pub, and we'd go along the silent main street to the front and down the steps to where there was a breakwater of big rocks under the seawall, and we'd sit among the rocks, cozily huddled together in our heavy coats, facing the sea that was not there. And she'd drink her whisky and talk to me, a lonely woman telling me about the big world.

I imagine the girl who was May's young sister carefully rolling up the ribbons May discarded, and smoothing with her fingernail until it was translucent the tissue paper so carelessly thrown away. If she was watching her sister as voraciously as I watched my aunt, then she, too, in the warm bedroom in the Longford Arms—May a vision in her satin corselet dabbing the roots of her hair with bleach—saw through May's bravura.

There was a ballad current at that time—James Joyce's hero, the tenor John McCormack, recorded it later—called "The Old House." It begins, "Lonely I wander through scenes of my childhood. . . ." It ends, "Why stand I here, like a ghost, like a shadow? 'Tis time I was moving. 'Tis time I passed on." The material for making her experience conscious to herself did exist. But May denied the complexities of her return to Edenmore. She gives only a few sentences to the visit in her autobiography.

But they're sentences to pause at.

We were perfectly happy together for a few weeks, she blandly says. That simply cannot be true. She adds, *Then we separated, never to see each other again.*

Her mother, in that one interview she gave, was more precise. "She stayed at home some little time and then all at once she disappeared again," is what she said.

And I think that that must have been what happened—that May just up and went, not spelling out to herself that she was disappointed in the visit home because that would be to admit that there was something she had hoped for from it. She knew that the family could not press her to come back again. By leaving, she rejected them before they rejected her. Perhaps, in her own mind, she did not run away; she just left. But she must have known that she left diminished. She had exhausted, now, the promise of healing implicit in homesickness.

But if I blame her for her folly in going back to Edenmore, I am being less tender toward her than I am to myself. She went home because memories collect in us and form aquifers of meaning below the surface of our lives. When May led me back to the Maureen I had hidden away, I found that I could hardly think about her without tears. Women in Ireland often paid for fitting in—for having huge families in utter dependence on their husbands. But how hard Ireland was, too, on the women who could not fit in—the wild ones, the ones who had to get out, seeming emigrants, but actual exiles. And how the wound of exile never heals! There is guilt as well as loss in it. The sensory experiences of childhood, Proust said, remain persistent and faithful, poised a long time like souls, remembering, waiting, hoping, amid the ruins of all the rest. Ireland could not be put away, however sad this visit. It would have persisted for May in the feel of a rough bedsheet, or a pond gleaming through rushes, or the wind breathing on a window, or tea that tasted of tannin because it had stood too long in the pot.

Once, in a tropical country as night fell fast, I saw egrets flock to their roosting trees down the silvery water of a lagoon, the air thick with them, the branches of the trees swaying with their gabbling until it got dark and they fell into silence. It was the few last stragglers coming in through the dark and circling and circling as they tried to find space for themselves that awoke the fear of being barred from home. How can it ever be natural to have no home to go to? Late in her book—late in her life—May says almost as a passing remark that she hopes her parents have forgotten her—

As, she says, *I have tried to forget them.*

EDDIE WAS EXPELLED from home, too.

In Chicago, the French consul came to Billy Pinkerton's office.

France very much wanted to extradite Eddie, he said, and a warrant for his arrest was, in fact, in the hands of the Chicago police. But, he said, he was afraid that the police out of local loyalty were doing nothing to find Eddie. So the consul, who had read an article about Eddie's sister in the newspaper, wanted the Pinkertons to shadow her until she led them to Eddie. (A detail the gossipy Billy recounts is that "the article gave the street address of the sister, and her husband was so angry that he did not come home for some days and it nearly wrecked the home.") But—and what modern researcher would think of this?—the consul's office hadn't got the funds to pay the Pinkertons to shadow anybody. It had been allotted only fifty dollars to catch Eddie.

What's more, the consul was applying to the wrong man. Billy Pinkerton was inclined to shield Eddie. He wrote to his brother in the New York office to say that he was afraid the U.S. government would return Eddie to France.

"President Roosevelt is one of those men who would turn him over as a matter of courtesy to the French government if they made the request," he says crossly.

So Billy privately advises Eddie that it would be wise to get out of the United States. And Eddie does.

He'd gone home, like May. Like her, he could not stay. I take it that going back to a home you left long ago, where you know in your heart you are no longer welcome, is a last try at belonging. And that you're profoundly at a loss afterward.

WHAT EDDIE SAYS is that he met May again by accident. He says he went back to London, and in a pub in Great Portland Street one day, there she was. It would have been a pub—that I do believe. The two of them weren't people who made homes, so where else would their reunion have taken place but in one of those high, half-empty drinking halls with their false luxuriousness of panel and tile and gleaming brass?

"She wore an expensive dress. Her hair was peroxided as brilliantly as of old, in fact she looked to me like a well-groomed bird. The last time I had seen her, of course, was in the dock in France. Here she was, drinking in a London public-house, apparently as young as ever."

He boasts that as soon as they met, she more or less asked him to look after her. He reports her as saying, "'You're clever, Eddie. You know how to manage women,' thus with a languorous look telling me as plainly as a woman could tell that she loved me as well as ever." He presents their reunion as something decided upon by him. "Once more under the influence of booze I did something I afterwards bitterly regretted," he wrote. "I again took May to live with me."

Soon they went off on a jaunt to Aix-la-Chapelle—a spa town on the border of Belgium and Germany—presumably to exercise their respective criminal skills. But he got angry with her there, for picking up a man. "Her idea of a good time," he wrote, "was to have half a dozen men fighting for her favors, and I might as well admit that I didn't think enough of them to get into any trouble. So we had words, most of which won't bear repeating." May came back on her own to London. Then, according to Eddie's book, Emily Skinner, the former maid, came to Eddie and showed him a letter in which May said that "after I got hold of money she, May, was going to play me up in London, and suggested that she and Emily should get me drunk, rob me of all my money, and then inform Scotland Yard that the man who had escaped from French Guiana was back in London."

I don't believe much of this. Maybe May did flatter Eddie, but if she did, it was out of nervousness. As for the conspiracy, for one thing, Eddie had no money, and for another, May didn't need Emily to help her rob him, and for another, since they all drank in the Hotel de Provence there wasn't the slightest need for May to put anything in writing. She had only to go into the ladies' room to talk to Emily.

But it turns out that Emily—"dearest Em"—wants to take May's place with Eddie.

And next, Emily lures May to her apartment, where Eddie is hiding.

Eddie locked May in.

"Take off that sealskin coat," I yelled at her. "Take off that dress you are wearing and tell your thieving friends or anyone else you like that the fellow who gave you these things is taking them away again because you are a dirty damned traitress of the worst type." I didn't wait for her to take them off. I tore them from her body, gave her a thrashing which I wager she still remembers, and then flung her outside the door.

"Now," I shouted after I had finished with her, "you can go and tell the police all about me."

That's what Eddie says happened.

I don't know why whatever affection and desire he once had for May has come to this. I don't know what she's supposed to have done to deserve being called a "damned traitress." Picked up a man in Aix? Prostitutes do pick up men.

Billy Pinkerton always thought that Eddie had been deranged by his experiences on Devil's Island and during the escape from it. I do think that a person who has been brutally treated looks around in turn for someone to treat brutally. His mad jealousy is an expression, I think, of Eddie's need to punish someone for the punishment he'd endured.

For the first time, we have a source besides her book for May's version of events. Some time later, three letters written by her were printed in a newspaper. I believe they're genuine letters, not least because she tweaks her story in each of them to better appeal to the recipient. But the speaking voice is unmistakable, and what it is repeating is that she was terrified of Eddie.

The first one begins by throwing a whole new light on her years in jail for the American Express robbery. It reminded me that Eddie's attorney told him, when he was awaiting trial in Paris, that "Chicago May wants to plead guilty."

May is obviously writing to someone who hasn't had news of her for a long time.

I waited trial in Paris for one year, her letter says. *He would not let me confess to the truth or as much as I knew. After that they would have tried me alone and got me off with a light sentence. No, he made me go with them, and I got five years' hard labor with expulsion. Of course I had a pardon but no thanks to him or his friends; so when I came out I had no friends or no money. I could not go back to my husband's family. My husband got a commission in the American army of the Philippines and has never come home. My mother-in-law don't want to receive me after what happened. I lived here with a man who was kind to me. I was completely wrecked both in mind and body. Then Eddy Guerin escapes from South America and comes back here and tries to find me. . . . When I was in Ireland to visit my people, Guerin returned to England. Seeing a newspaper ad that I would learn something to my advantage if I went to a certain place in Newton Street, Holborn, London, I answered it and dropped into Guerin's hands. I fell for it because I thought, maybe, mother-in-law Sharp had willed me some money. I was never able to get away from him. I was always in fear of him, even when we were friends. . . .*

I was so afraid of the man that I became his slave, until I could make my escape without fear of immediate punishment. He sent my maid Skinner for my clothes and took me to the Ivanhoe Hotel. I was too afraid to yell for help and it was against the crook code to squeal.

I was a virtual prisoner, and had to go with Eddie to Germany and Italy where both of us worked, but not very successfully.

He had my trunks packed by Skinner and took me to Aix-la-Chapelle. Before we left for that place, we went out in public, eating;

but I dared not try to escape. My former maid, Emily Skinner, helped Guerin watch me.

On one occasion when we were dining at Thatcher's he drew a gun and said he was going to shoot me, but changed his mind when I reminded him that I saved his life by raising money to spring him from the Devil's Island settlement.

At least the two of them agree that they went to Aix—lending a new realism to the great spa, which I had imagined as a place where frail beauties like the deceitful heroine of *The Good Soldier* walked slowly along graveled paths past white orangeries and graceful fountains with men who looked like the heroes of Russian novels. There were backstreets in spas, too. The likes of porters and and swimming attendants and seamstresses had to stay somewhere, too. And crooks.

We put up at the Hotel Monopole in Jacobstrasse, May says in her book. *I took the baths. The carnival was in full swing. Eddie tried to rob a jewelry store and failed. Then he went on to Italy. I was told to stay put and that I would get a fur coat and be taken to Norway, as a reward. He wanted to keep me away from Baby Thompson.*

The Hotel Monopole is gone, but there is a Jacobstrasse on the map and it is, as I'd guessed, near the railway station. I furnished May with a dim foyer to walk across beside a spruce and terrifying Eddie, a heavy wooden door into a musty bedroom, a lace curtain over a street loud with trams, an eiderdown with a cut-out circle in the middle, a fretwork tray with a clothes brush and a shoehorn hanging from a little hook—the physical detail of a world that is gone. I imagined Eddie and May, their heads swirling with hostility, drinking in silence in beer halls, while in magnificent *salles* the rich, on whom these two were parasites, took dinner.

THE SECOND of the three letters takes up the story at this point. This one was, perhaps, written to one of the charitable ladies who helped May get out of Montpellier.

This man Guerin has been the ruin of my life. When I heard he escaped I tried my best to hide from him. Finally he found me and forced me to go to Aix-la-Chapelle with him, me paying the expenses of the trip. He was like a skeleton. He could not do anything in England and was afraid on the Continent. Plainly speaking he had lost his nerve, he had suffered so much in getting away. While he was in Milan, I came back to London and was very glad to be rid of him. Then he sent me a telegram asking for ten pounds to be sent through Cook's, which I did not send.

I am going into a home "bon volontaire" as I want to learn how to work—also to be patient. Then I will be able to make a start and I will put myself out of reach of people like Guerin. I know in my heart what he would do and I am sure he will never rest until he does for me. Guerin was making threats that he was going to disfigure me, so that my face would never lure another man. I was to be made hideous to look at.

I should have gone away in the first place and would have if I had any idea he ever would get out.

"*I want to learn how to work—also to be patient.*" These aspirations put a stop for a moment to the whirl of May's life. Who would have thought it? Who would have guessed that May knew herself well enough to know exactly what she needed to do?

These are the first private letters of May's that I saw (the one she sent to Eddie after he was arrested in France, that figured in his trial, she wrote knowing it would be read). They confirmed what her book often suggested—that she could be eloquent in a way that was available even to people of little education when culture was oral, before the mass media contracted and simplified and homogenized ordinary speech.

"*I was always in fear of him, even when we were friends.*"

But of course, what she should do, such as learn to work and be patient, and what she did do are two separate things. Sometime in

1906, she borrowed the money for a ticket to South America from Baby Thompson. She disguised herself as a nurse, and she kept the disguise on until the ship was clear of England.

She wanted—she needed—to be out of town.

I do not believe her when she says that she was in Argentina when she discovered what happened next to Eddie Guerin.

She says that she was in a beer garden with a manfriend when she opened a copy of a *News of the World* newspaper that had come from England. Her eye fell on a cartoon that had two pictures.

The headlines of this yellow journal read, "Betrayed by a Woman."

It showed Eddie Guerin in a cage, with the caption, "The Fate Which Awaits Guerin If the British Court Decides Against Him."

The other picture showed me.

Someone had ratted on Eddie. Someone had told the London police where he could be found. He had been arrested and was now in Brixton prison while the authorities waited for an extradition warrant to come from France. Once it did, it had only to be reviewed by a British court and Eddie would be returned to Devil's Island. This time, what waited for him there was unspeakable. As an "incorrigible" he would work naked and tethered to a log of wood by a cable, alone for twenty-three hours out of every twenty-four, his skin covered in blue and purple bruises, his teeth falling out from scurvy. It would be a life to make a man long for early death.

Did May do this terrible thing to him, as *The News of the World* evidently believed that she did? As *he* believed that she did?

He said that on the night he beat her up, May must have

> got some clothes from somewhere and hurriedly made her way to Tottenham Court Road police station. . . . In the course of our fight she had screamed out that she would send me back to Devil's Island to die like a dog while I, no doubt, had told her a few other choice things about herself which must have

bitten deep even into the treacherous nature of a double-dyed harlot.

She denied it and never ceased to deny it, all her life. But I believe she did it, and that she arranged with the police to get away to South America before they picked Eddie up. I believe it, even though I know that someone else might have done it—that the Pinkerton archive shows that most of those big international crooks spied on and betrayed each other almost as a matter of course, for all that squealing was supposed to be against the code. I think that betraying Eddie was May's animal reaction to his encroachment on her freedom. It was intolerable to her to be controlled by him. He was waiting, she was convinced, to disfigure or kill her if she did not obey him, and there's a response, when someone threatens our survival, that is all but mindless. "I never loved you," people say; or "I'm not allowing access to the children"; or "I've had that dog of yours put down." It takes training not to slash out at a tormentor with a savage stroke, and where would May have got that training?

People who have been intimate punish each other with the same fluency they once knew in pleasure. They hold moderation in abeyance, as once they did in the act of love. May was habitually unrestrained by calculation. She would never have been one for minimal revenge, and this particular revenge was to hand. When she moved against Eddie's harassment, she pulled the sky down on him.

THE THIRD of the three letters from this time was evidently written after the South American trip. It begins, *When I left you in Lincoln, I came back to Boston and joined the . . . company in* Swell Miss Fitzwell . . . *I joined* The Belle of New York Co., *but only stopped three weeks with them.* So it was addressed to someone she knew when she was on the stage.

She runs through all the countries she's visited since then in quite a breezy manner, but her tone becomes ominous toward the end.

I wish now, she writes, *I had stopped in Brazil.*

If I pull out of this affair I am going into a home, because I am in mortal fear of Guerin.

Will I ever be safe from him?

England was safe enough at the moment, anyway, since Eddie couldn't get out of Brixton. But when May landed *at Catherine Street Dock in London, prepared to defend my stool-pigeon charge, I was crying while waiting to get off the ship. The captain asked me if anybody had insulted me. I said no, I just felt depressed. He said something about it being no wonder, just coming to a climate such as England, with its gloomy fogs.*

May hardly ever cried. But children do start crying, preemptively, when they know they're about to be found out in having done something bad.

THEY CRY, too, when the party's over. And the roller-coaster of May's life had hit a peak at this time, before tipping onto the downward slide. May had one of the great nights—maybe, if she'd been asked to nominate one, the greatest of her life—in Rio de Janeiro.

The major diplomatic and political event called the Pan-American Conference—an early version of a U.N. Assembly—was held in Rio in 1906. Every hotel and rooming house in the city was packed with delegates from the Americas and all over the world, including many heads of state. The SS *Charleston* was moored in the bay with the secretary of state for the United States, Elihu Root, on board. One of the luminaries at the very grand formal ball that opened the conference was His Britannic Majesty's consul-general in Argentina, His Excellency Sir Sidney Hamilton Gore, nephew of the Earl of Arran, near relative of the Bishop of Oxford.

He must have been a troubled man—gay, perhaps, or alcoholic, or in some other way a dissident—because he had recently come across May hard at work, no doubt, seducing and robbing the local men—and he invited her to be his partner at the ball. This was an act of breathtaking aggression against his class, his country, his family, his colleagues, and the country to which he was accredited. And against his own future. When he arrived at the ball, the lush-figured, bright-haired, splendidly dressed woman on his arm was May Churchill Sharp, once known in the north Longford area as May Duignan from Edenmore. No one could possibly have mistaken her for a respectable woman. That, after all, was the consul's point.

This was a dream come true for May. She had always been an innocent social snob, looking up to English aristocrats as if they were figures of fascinating glamour, there being no Irish aristocracy. To be taken up by a titled man, to be brought by him into the highest circles, to be transformed—she, a jailbird, a woman who not long before had been flung naked and battered into a London street—into the belle of the ball! No wonder she gushes about it as she does about nothing else in her whole life.

How well I remember that seductive, tropical night, the flowers and music! she wrote. *And how our names were called out—mine linked with Gore's. The eyebrows of the wife of the American ambassador went up in the air when we took precedence of her crowd. I noticed that the real ladies among the British guests did not bat an eyelash, though they had the same eyefull and earfull. I don't want to throw bouquets at myself, but I knew, and the papers said the next morning, that I was the best-gowned woman at the show. What is more, I had life, strength and vigor, what few women have in the climate of the big South American republic. These attributes were some of the reasons why the virile Sir Sidney was so fond of me. He was that kind himself.*

Virile he may have been, but it is not the action of a normal diplomat to bring a whore to the ball of the decade.

May really did, for what seem to have been a blissfully happy few days, lose touch with reality. She and Sir Sidney took off on a bender during which it was somehow decided that he wanted to marry her. *But I told him to wait, both for his sake and mine. In time, we could have lived down everything.* One afternoon they provoked a scene in a bar in the Rua dos Ouvidores. May seems to have claimed that a native officer had insulted her by speaking to her, and Sir Sidney took offense on her behalf. That's a minuet I've seen danced in public by other couples; she, sensing that she's despised, becomes drunkenly self-important and calls on her man's equally drunken and ready chivalry.

I don't suppose the fracas was going to do Sir Sidney any good with the Foreign Office, though he was obviously far gone, anyway, in alienation.

He left May at her door that evening and she told him that he should go home and take a sleep.

He said, she wrote, *"Nobody cares about me but Boozer."* Boozer was his dog.

I laughed and said, "Oh yes, somebody does."

He replied, "I know you do, but you can't help much now."

He turned away and that was the last I saw or heard of him in this world.

That night about 11 o'clock, the poor fellow shot himself through the head with a shotgun. The barking of the dog attracted the man in the next room.

Later in her life this tragedy became part of the legend of Chicago May, when it was said about her that she drove a titled gentleman to suicide. But I believe every word of the pathetic exchange recalled here. It rings absolutely true to me. And the person I'm sorry for is May. Sir Sidney provided the social high point of her life, and I wish he could have been glorious in her memory. But ever afterward, when she thought about her triumph at the ball, she must have had to think, too, about what became of him and to realize again that their brief liaison and the talk about marriage had been nothing but despairing babble. It was absurd of her, of course, to offer herself to him. But still—she did mean it. And there is no rejection as absolute as suicide.

THERE WAS one more twist to the night in Rio.

It seems that in spite of everything that had happened between them, May wasn't able to resist showing off to Eddie. Maybe she was even taunting him: he had taken up with her maid; she was the consort of a titled diplomat. She sent cuttings about the Pan-American Ball from the *Rio News* and the *Correio da Manhã* back to London, and she sent them to Emily Skinner, which was much the same as sending them to Eddie himself.

Who is to say whether she did it to hurt him? Or—as if he wasn't dangerous enough—to provoke him? She didn't know herself why she did it—she just says she sent the cuttings and leaves it at that.

But this is a time in her life when she has been experiencing extremes of loneliness. She sat in those prisons in France cut off by the language from knowing what anyone was saying. She sat in Edenmore cut off from family and community by her very self—by the self she had made out of opportunities that presented themselves and opportunities that did not—and she might as well not have spoken the language of her homeplace for all anyone wanted to talk to her or listen to her. In London, she'd lost what had briefly been, in the rooms in Bloomsbury, her household. Eddie had reappeared, but as a parody of his former self—a bully, not a protector; crazy with possessiveness, not love. And as for Emily—she sent the cuttings to Emily Skinner, but Emily had chosen Eddie over her.

The truth was that May had no one to boast to. She sent her enemies the press cuttings because she had no one else to send them to. And that shows up what the restlessness of her life usually obscured—that she could hardly be more alone. She's as alone as if she lived in a hut in the middle of an island—an island that looks attractive but that's barren and scorched with heat, and where sharks slink beside the rocky shores.

Seven

London

In those days before the First World War, when national and international bureaucracies had not yet perfected their systems, people could call themselves whatever they liked. No one in this story, I think, ever knew the real identity of the young American who said his name was Charley or Charlie Smith or Smyth. He turned up on remand in Brixton prison, in London, when Eddie was in there waiting to be extradited, and he confided to Eddie that his name was really Cubine Jackson. Perhaps it was. But he was also known as Clarence Caldwell and as Robert Considine. Sometimes, even, when using one alias he absentmindedly slipped into another.

Charley had been in South Africa for the last four years or so—since he was about twenty. He said he'd served in the British cavalry during the Boer War and stayed on to run a gambling joint, but the South African authorities said that he was a burglar, and deported him for housebreaking. When the ship on which he was being returned to his native United States called at Southampton, in England, he somehow got ashore, attempted another burglary, was caught and sent to Brixton until his trial came up.

At that trial, a newspaper reported the following intriguing passage:

> The judge said he would look into the prisoner's past before sentencing him, whereupon the prisoner sent a document to the judge and asked him to read it. The judge, having read the document, said he would assume that the burglary was the prisoner's first offense in this country and would set him at liberty on his entering into recognizances.
>
> Later, in explaining his action, the judge said: "In the document handed to me the prisoner begged that his identity not be disclosed and that his family should not know of his downfall. I respected his wishes, and the document was destroyed. He comes of a good family and I thoroughly believe that everything stated in the document was true."

That was all that Charley would ever say about his American past—that he was from a good family.

Charley and Eddie Guerin became friendly in prison. "I told him more frankly than I had ever told anyone except my lawyers," Eddie wrote in *I Was a Bandit*, "exactly what had happened with Chicago May—I daresay I added, without any unnecessary disguise of words, that if ever I got out of prison alive I would surely kill her. I knew by that time who had played the traitor—Emily Skinner continually visited me in prison and kept me fully posted as to what was transpiring outside." Charley Smith understood that May had transgressed against the code of the underworld and must be punished. Whether explicitly or by hinting, Eddie commissioned him—because Eddie couldn't get out himself—to find May as soon as he was freed and punish her extremely severely. Charley took to heart what his friend asked him to do, and when he was released he did set about looking for May, with the idea of disfiguring her.

IT WOULD BE many more months before Eddie's extradition hearing came up. In the normal course of events it would have been quickly disposed of, because he wasn't important and he had no funds. He certainly wasn't in the running for top-class legal representation. But Captain Dreyfus touched many lives, and Eddie's was among them. Attention was drawn by Dreyfus's ordeal to the conditions in which France kept its prisoners on Devil's Island, and one prestigious London barrister felt obliged on humanitarian grounds to do what he could to prevent anyone being dispatched to such a place.

"The actual fee on his brief," Sir Richard Muir's biographer wrote, "was fifteen guineas and if I say that the Guerin case dragged on for fourteen months it will give some idea of the work Sir Richard must have done to try to save a man who many people might have thought not worth saving."

Muir was intent on proving that Eddie's father, and therefore Eddie, was a British subject, because under certain sections of the Extradition Act, British nationals were not extraditable. The senior Mr. Guerin, born in Knockany, County Limerick, emigrated to Chicago in the 1850s, in the aftermath of the Famine. He never voted in America and he never became a naturalized American, but the difficulty lay in proving this, since what relevant records there had been were destroyed in the great Chicago fire of 1871. Nevertheless, in a long and expensive process, Muir gathered what evidence he could, and the day came when he argued before three judges of the High Court that "the prisoner's father having been a natural-born British subject, the onus is on the Crown to show that he had changed his nationality."

"Never, I beg of any boy thinking of committing a crime," Eddie wrote in *I Was a Bandit*, "expose yourself to that awful ordeal of waiting in a court not knowing whether you are going to lifelong imprisonment or whether you will ever be free again. Want of courage I never had, but I will confess to dying a thousand deaths that day."

But so, somewhere in the city of London outside, was May dying of suspense. I'm sure the thought had never crossed her mind when she informed on Eddie that there would be a day when legal proceedings ended, and that on that day there was a chance he'd get off and come looking for her for vengeance. And she was a different May now from the distracted person she'd been when she was hanging around London after she came back from Edenmore. Then, not only was she running this way and that trying to escape Eddie, but she had nowhere in the world to go where she might be loved. But this May, waiting to hear what the High Court decided, was a woman with something to live for.

She says that when she met Charley Smith—*the D'Artagnan of crooks,* she called him—he had already decided not to harm her, *being a gentleman from Virginia, not a product of the Chicago stockyards.* I don't know where they first saw each other. I only know that I always believed that opera is as true to life as the most cautious realism—that quiet lives and theatrical lives are made of the same basic material. People are betrayed, alliances are formed, misunderstandings thrive, and villains and heroes abound. Things happen in the most improbable ways and places. And sometimes the hero has only to set eyes on the heroine to fall instantly in love.

And that's what happened to Charley Smith. He met May and he fell for her at once.

She had been a hard-living woman for a long time. Eddie remarks—not, of course, that any opinion of his wasn't influenced by what she did to him—that she had become "a bit coarse and blowsy." But there was some charm she had, something that was hers that attracted both men and women to her, and it was not dependent on her appearance. I imagine that she kept some of the qualities of youth—some of its vitality and zest and openness—even though youth itself had gone.

She also had a sense of humor. And she had always been carelessly confident of her womanliness—I'm sure that when she made an effort, she could still look magnificent.

And I'm sure the age difference between them helped. Charley, aged twenty-five, can't have known a woman like her. As for her— well, May was about thirty-six and she hadn't been loved by a man for many years, if she ever really was. Above all, she'd had nobody to love. She fell for Charley, too, though the words she uses don't do very much to communicate what she saw in him—she was never good at describing men she admired. He was *a high-grade prowler,* she says— she introduced Eddie, too, and Baby Thompson, by stressing that they were distinguished crooks, not just ordinary crooks. He was *of a good family*; that would certainly appeal to the snob in her. *There was a brave man!* she exclaims. *Where there was work or danger, him for the frontline trenches.* She had a very clear idea, evidently, of what a man should be, and physical fearlessness was part of it. Charley *was not the kind to lean on a woman,* she says. *He was a gentleman, and reminded me of my first husband*—by whom she means Dal Churchill, back in Nebraska—*who forded rivers,* in her description of him, *where fords there were none.* Who can blame her, in the difficulty and loneliness of her life, for yearning for a knight errant? Even a woman as emphatically resistant as she was to any kind of control may dream of a protector.

It is touching to see her open, still, to romance. And there was a symmetry to this relationship. She had something to give to Charley. He must have been out of his home very young, however upper-class it was, to have stacked up a substantial criminal record and still be only twenty-five, and May was of an age to be motherly if he still needed mothering. And once, when he was asked by an arresting officer for his name and address, he replied—and you can see why he might be happy to find shelter with someone powerful—"Mister Nobody from Nowhere." The very excess of personality in May might have complemented a void in him.

It is a pleasure to imagine her with Charley. Since it was, in sober fact, a matter of life and death that they not be discovered, I imagine them finding a home at a distance from the criminal haunts of the West End. I picture to myself the front and back street-level rooms of a bow-fronted house in a quiet terrace somewhere like Camberwell or Islington, and May going to work in new places, picking up men at the shows in the Agricultural Hall or in the promenade bars of the Hackney Empire or on the forecourt of Liverpool Street Station. I imagine her doing a few hours' work in alleyways and doorways, then jumping gladly into a cab for home. Her young man would be waiting for her there. Perhaps he even had some domestic skills— former soldiers do. Perhaps he had the fire bright for her, and bread and cheese and a jug of beer under a cloth on a little round table beside the fire. Let us suppose that their bed was in the back room, on the other side of the connecting door from the parlor, and that he wrapped heated bricks in her flannelette nightgown every night and pushed the bundle down into the well of the bed.

It was winter still—we know because we know they were together for about four months and their idyll ended in the month of June. It was very cold in English houses in those days, a penetrating, damp cold. When she came in at night and warmed herself at the fire, her legs and face would become blotchy with heat, but her back would still have been cold, though Charley nailed curtains as thick as blankets across the window and stuffed a draft excluder under the door. They'd have put off going into the cold bedroom. The chamberpot would have been kept under the bed so that they didn't have to go down the hallway to the icy toilet, and once they dared the sheets and shivered for a while in each other's arms, warming their feet on each other's, they didn't get cold again. There would have been heavy rain against the window night after night, and hail, and silent, hard frost, and at the beginning, in the morning, when Charley pulled the curtain before shuddering back against the warmth of May, there might have been the minute rustle of gray sleet against the glass of the window. Soon he'd bring her her tea in bed. A big hunk of bread toasted on the embers of the parlor fire. Both of them had known luxury, of course. But had they ever, before this, known everyday solace?

Spring came. The first fat bee buzzing against the glass of the window. Summer began. But in the third week of June there was an end to it.

Eddie's fancy lawyer pulled it off.

"I FELT I had never done so much for a man in all my life when I saw the change in Guerin's face," Sir Richard Muir is said to have remarked when the court decided that it would not grant France's request for Eddie's extradition. "It lit up with the most unspeakable relief I have ever seen."

He wouldn't shake Eddie's hand when Eddie offered his. But that minor humiliation was all there was to mar Eddie's joy. He walked, a free man, from the courtroom.

Free to go looking for his betrayer. And it was only about twenty-four hours—much of which Eddie spent drinking with Emily Skinner—before there was an encounter with May and Charley.

It all ended in a trial in the Central Criminal Court. It could have been either of them, in my opinion. Eddie was just as likely to try to harm May as she was to harm him—more likely, in fact. How things fell out was half accidental.

But *The Times* of June 27, 1907, reported:

Edward Guerin, who escaped from Devil's Island and successfully resisted his extradition to France, was shot at and injured early yesterday morning.

He and a woman were near Russell Square on their way home, when a cab drove up. Several revolver shots came from the cab, and one of the bullets caught Guerin's foot and brought him to the ground. There were several people about, and the occupants of the cab, a man and a woman, were arrested after a struggle and taken to Hunter-Street Police-Station. Guerin was taken to the Royal Free Hospital where it was found that a bullet had entered his foot. The bullet has been extracted and Guerin is making a good recovery.

May and Charley on trial

And soon *The Times* reported further:

Charles Smith, a tinsmith, and May Vivienne Churchill, 31, an artist, were indicted for shooting at Edward Guerin with intent to murder him and for wounding him with the same intent.

They pleaded "Not guilty."

In July, the trial of May and Charley opened at the New Bailey. It was something of a celebrity trial, and the feature writers were there as well as the reporters. One paper reported:

Churchill presented a sharp contrast to her companion. Attired in a smart, white, lace blouse with a highly effective touch in the shape of black lace mittens, and with her wealth of auburn hair piled up artistically she made a most attractive figure. She stood almost a head taller than Smith, and smiled pleasantly at the court at the opening of the proceedings.

There was something attractively audacious in the woman as she faced the court with easy dignity. She looked every inch the bold, handsome adventurer, did this majestic Irishwoman, with her dusky eyes flashing fire and her saucy mouth tinged with rouge. He looked on the other hand the ruffian he is, with large, coarse head, pasty face, and thick lips.

Extracts from contemporary reports continue the story.

From *The News of the World*

George Oswald, an American, told of meeting Chicago May and Smith in the Provence Hotel on the night of the shooting. "'Guerin and Emily have been here,' I said. 'Lucky for you you didn't meet them.' 'He wants to throw acid on me,' said Chicago May. So Smith said, 'She's my friend and while she's with me he will not do anything to her. If he's going to be a bad man I'll be a bad man, too—I'll fix him,' and he tapped his breast pocket."

I take it that May and Charley heard that Eddie had been released, and that they were convinced that Eddie would come looking for May, either to disfigure her or to kill her, and that what Charley was tapping was the gun with which they hoped—panic-stricken, and not thinking beyond the short term—to attack Eddie before he attacked May.

From *The Times*

The first witness called was Emily Skinner. She said she resided in Coram Street and had known Guerin for seven or eight years. She had known the female prisoner for eight years. About six weeks before, she met Churchill in the street.

"She told me that she would like to prove to me that she had not put Guerin away. She gave me an explanation but I did not believe it."

"Do you know the male prisoner?"

"Yes, as Clarence Caldwell and as Cubine Jackson. He is an American."

"When did you first see him?"

"He called at my flat about four months ago and in the course of conversation he referred to Chicago May. Smith told me that he wanted to find Churchill in order to throw acid over her. I told him he was very silly. He said it was a shame Guerin was in custody but added, 'He is sure to get off.'"

"Did he see you again?"

"Yes. He came down on several occasions. I did not know he was living in the same rooms as Churchill."

The witness then went on to describe the movements of herself and Guerin on the night of the shooting. She saw the prisoner Smith alight, and saw a revolver in his hand.

"What was Guerin doing?"

"He was jumping about trying to avoid the shots. May Churchill ran across the road to a doorway and crouched down. I saw the prisoner stopped. Churchill was still in the doorway and Guerin had got hold of her arm. When I came up, Guerin exclaimed, 'I'm shot. I give this woman in charge.' Churchill retorted, 'I was with nobody, I was in the cab by myself.' She had a bag in her hand. I seized hold of her and then she exclaimed, 'Let me get my handkerchief' and tried to open her bag. 'You'll get no handkerchief here,' I said."

The witness identified the bag produced, in which an open knife was found.

Several witnesses to the fracas were called, and it was impossible to deny the facts of it. But when May's lawyer cross-examined Emily

Skinner, it became obvious that he was going to argue that May and Charley were engaged in a kind of anticipatory self-defense. They would establish that May had long been in terror of Eddie, to explain at least why Charley had been armed.

From *THE TIMES*

"In April last [Emily Skinner was asked] did you see Churchill near the Provence Hotel?"

"Yes."

"Did you say, 'I am no particular friend of yours but I don't want to see you blinded and that is what Guerin is going to do to you'?"

"No."

"Don't you know that in consequence of what you said, she went to Inspector Simmons, who set officers to watch you?"

"I did not know that."

May must have been very anxious to get this point into the record. It was very telling that months earlier, and even when he was confined to Brixton, she'd been in such fear of Eddie that she'd gone to her traditional enemy, the police, for help.

Then Eddie Guerin took the stand.

From *THE TIMES*

Guerin was asked, "You took the view, rightly or wrongly, that you were denounced to the police by Chicago May?"

"She told me so herself."

"And that in all probability you would be sent back again to Devil's Island?"

"She took that view."

"You have a very strong feeling against this woman?"

"Naturally I have."

"Did you tell Mrs. Skinner you would blind the woman with vitriol?"

"No."

"Or that you would cut her ear off?"

"No."

The case was then adjourned until this morning.

As Chicago May left the dock she nodded her head affably to the magistrate.

Under cross-examination, Eddie tells such blatant lies about the American Express job that he's almost being insolent. The following is what a reporter who was there in the courtroom wrote—in Eddie's own account, in his book, he's even more debonair.

From THE NEWS OF THE WORLD

Eddie Guerin, a slim, well-knit man, strode smartly to the witness box. Telling of the quarrel when he made up his mind to leave May, he said with a slight American accent,

"May threatened to send me back to Devil's Island to die like a dog."

Mr. Purcell (for Chicago May): "Wasn't it in Dublin you first met?"

"No."

"You know she is Irish?"

"Yes. I met her first in the Horseshoe in Tottenham Court Road. She told me she was married in America but separated from her husband because her husband's family would have nothing to do with her."

"Where were you yourself married?"

"In Leeds."

Guerin would not admit he knew May was fond of him.

"Is she not very strong in her likes and dislikes?"
  "More the latter!" (Laughter.)
  Counsel brought up the American Express job.
  "I had nothing to do with it."
  "Was the other man in the affair of great daring?"
  "I think Miss Churchill can tell you that. He was her lover."
  "Where is he now?"
  "He is in Devil's Isle. If he is still alive."

Eddie denied that May's return to Paris was to help him.

According to Guerin's statement, Guerin was desirous of break-ing off his relations with the female prisoner and she was, not unnaturally, very angry about it. She then said to him that if he did not continue to take charge of her and look after her, she would send him back to Devil's Island, or if she could not do that, she would do for him in some other way.

About the beginning of this year, the male prisoner appeared in London and not long afterward he was in Brixton Prison, where Guerin was awaiting the decision of the High Court. Smith shortly afterward left the prison and made the acquain-tance of a Mrs. Skinner, who knew Guerin and Chicago May. According to Mrs. Skinner, Smith appeared to be sympathizing with Guerin and made an observation to the effect that he (Smith) would like to throw acid over Chicago May for putting away a man like Guerin.

Shortly afterward, Smith made the acquaintance of Chicago May and became very friendly with her. His sympathy with Guerin seemed to have disappeared.

Police Constable Boulding, who was on duty, heard the noise of the shots and ran toward the spot whence the shots came. He arrived on the scene before the last shot was fired and saw the male prisoner pointing a revolver at Guerin, who was leaning on an umbrella. Smith ran away after the last shot was fired.

Guerin went up to the female prisoner and said, "When you could not succeed on sending me to Devil's Island you would stoop to murder?"

According to Guerin she replied, "Yes, and I am sorry that we did not succeed."

A crowd then assembled and the female prisoner said to them, "I know nothing about it. I was in the cab alone."

The prosecution contended that the defense that Guerin was the aggressor was wholly unfounded. Guerin had no revolver and no vitriol in his possession.

From *THE TIMES*

Mr. Gill, in summing up the case for the prosecution, said he did not dispute that the prisoner Churchill was in fear at the time. The suggestion on the part of the Crown was that she determined to be first in the field and employed Smith for that purpose. Although she might have been afraid, it did not follow that her fears were well founded.

Mr. Purcell, addressing the court for Churchill, said that from the life Guerin had lived in the past he was evidently a man who would stick at nothing to get his revenge. The woman had a reasonable belief that she was in deadly peril.

From the *DAILY EXPRESS*

Until the very last moment, May bore herself defiantly. She was the central figure around whom the whole drama of crime, love and hate revolved. She sat throughout, smiling and self-conscious, dressed to look as alluring and as fascinating as of old and apparently well pleased to have every eye in the court fixed on her. With her wealth of auburn hair piled high over her ears, her smiling, babyish face, and her frank and engaging appearance she seemed more like the accepted picture of innocence than the blackhearted adventuress and traitress witnesses alleged she was in reality. At every story to her discredit, she simply smiled or pouted, and when the evidence sounded overwhelming, she turned a fascinating glance on the jury as though to reassure them.

The members of the jury, at the end, indicated that they didn't need to leave the courtroom. They began to consult with each other in the box.

I SUPPOSE the court was cleared, and that the pavements outside were packed with a milling crowd of reporters and spectators. The newspapers had been running sensational background articles about the trial. One of these was in the newspaper *The People*. It printed the three letters that I quoted in the last chapter—the letters that express, to three different correspondents, May's fear of Eddie. I think she wrote them when she was in custody awaiting trial, in answer to letters from people she'd once known who'd contacted her when they saw in the papers that she'd been charged with Eddie's attempted murder.

I also think these letters of May's were stolen or copied by someone in her remand prison, and sold to *The People*. How else would it have acquired private letters to three separate people?

And we know that the police had been reading her letters. The prosecution read into the trial record a note that May had dashed off to Baby Thompson, and it, more than anything else, I'm sure, was the reason why the jury didn't even need to retire to discuss their verdict.

From *THE NEWS OF THE WORLD*

When the female prisoner was in the police station she wrote a letter to a Mr. Thompson. Perhaps she was not aware that letters were inspected before they were sent out. In the course of the letter, she said, "Goodbye. You may never see me again. This fellow Smith was the one Eddie got to throw vitriol so you see I lost no time in turning the tables."

I hope there's an element of tough-girl bravado in this. I hope she was showing off to Baby, and I think, on the basis of the dramatic opening sentence, that she was. And there was, after all, something to boast of in the way Charley had turned right around when he met her. The words *this fellow Smith*, I believe, are a way of conveying to Baby—a former or an occasional boyfriend—that Charley is not important to her. But he was important to her. She wouldn't have been secretly living with him if he was not.

The note, unfortunately, is a virtual confession. Again, as in the American Express affair, not even elementary attention has been paid by a crook to the saving of her own skin.

The verdict of the jury was announced after "a short consultation." It found both the prisoners guilty.

From the *DAILY EXPRESS*

Mr. Justice Darling in passing sentence said the jury had returned what to his mind was the only possible and logical verdict. Guerin was a bad man in many respects but he was entitled to the same protection in regard to his life as the best of them. It was not for the prisoners to judge him or to seek to take his life. He thought there was a difference between the case of Smith and that of the female prisoner although they were both undoubtedly guilty—the one of having shot at Guerin with intent to murder him, and the other of having counseled and procured the shooting with that intent; and therefore they were equally guilty of the criminal act charged. Smith had no excuse whatsoever; it was no quarrel of his, but he took it on his shoulders. Churchill had this—he could not call it an excuse, but this extenuating circumstance—that she was, he believed, although without reason, in dread of what Guerin might do to her, because she had done her best to send him back to Devil's Island. He should therefore make a distinction between the two prisoners.

He sentenced Charley Smith to penal servitude for life with a recommendation that at the end of his sentence, he be deported to America—in other words, at a certain point, maybe after twenty years, if Charley was of good behavior, he'd be returned to the States.

May was sentenced to fifteen years penal servitude. And the judge specifically made no recommendation of deportation in her case. Her address in America was still, I presume, c/o the Sharp household. "It is inexpedient," Mr. Justice Darling said, "that she should be sent back to give trouble at a home which is no doubt happier without her. She is better off in jail."

From *THE NEWS OF THE WORLD*

"May God's curse rest on you and your family for ever!"

Then followed a torrent of unprintable expletives. The speaker who was livid with rage as he clung to the ledge of the dock in front of him was Charles Smith who with Chicago May had been found guilty at the New Bailey of attempting to murder Edward Guerin, and his execrations were addressed to Mr. Justice Darling. Blank consternation seized everyone in court including the warders, who, taken aback by the suddenness of the extraordinary outburst, seemed for a time oblivious of their duty. Then as the infuriated man kept on piling anathemas on the judge's head they made a rush toward him and hustled him out of the dock amidst a scene of intense excitement.

In *Her Story,* May revised this scene. *I laughed and laughed,* she said about the moment when they heard their sentences, *so as to show the minions of the law that they hadn't broken my spirit, and to show my sympathy to Charley, to encourage him.*

That's how she wished to present herself to him—as proud and strong and insouciant. But the account in *The News of the World* is more convincing because it's more commonplace:

Smith continued his abuse as he was removed down the stairs leading to the cells, and his angry accents were distinctly caught by the persons outside the building.

Chicago May heard her fate without flinching and afterward quietly left the dock.

AN UNUSUAL FEATURE of the trial was that sitting as an observer with Mr. Justice Darling was a judge of the New York Supreme Court, who told *The New York Times* that evening that he had been "profoundly impressed." America, he said

"is the victim of her *causes célèbres.* Everyone in America reads the newspaper—not one, but many. . . . The result of this is that it is almost impossible to get twelve intelligent men who have not studied the case and reached a judgment unfitting them for service as jurors.

"How different here in England! Today's case had all the elements of sensation, yet the jury was selected in exactly two minutes. . . . As there is no Appellate Division here, there are practically no objections [from counsel] and the trial proceeds rapidly and smoothly."

"Do you believe that such speed is likely to result in the miscarriage of justice?" [the reporter] asked.

"Certainly there was no miscarriage of justice today," said Justice Davis.

There was, however, the influence of current prejudice. A book on female criminals by a London lawyer is typical of the time. "The woman Churchill," it said,

was a thorough-paced criminal of a very dangerous type. Again we find the female criminal with an attractive exterior and with considerable influence over men. She was born in Ireland— Ireland, by the way, has given us many notorious female criminals—but married an American and became an American subject. When you have a combination of Ireland and America in a female subject, you may be sure that you have something fiendish to deal with.

Mr. Justice Darling was presumably not immune to beliefs of this kind. Some years later, he dealt with the Irish patriot Sir Roger Casement's appeal against being hanged with ostentatious speed. After six and a half hours of legal argument from Casement's counsel, he dismissed the appeal in twenty minutes.

NOW MAY is led away.

She had been on the move ever since she slipped out the door of the house in Edenmore, seventeen years earlier. She had never stopped until she was forcibly stopped, by Montpellier jail. Now, after not even two years of liberty, she is stopped again. The momentum of her life, that picked her up and propelled her into the hasty assault on Eddie and through it and past it, has slammed her onto a barrier of punishment on which she must now hang for years and years. She has to come to terms, now, with whatever guilt she felt at what she had done to Charley. She has to forget whatever chance of love there was between them. She has to cope with the bitter chagrin of knowing that Eddie walks away, free. There is very little to comfort her in thoughts of the past. The future is too terrible to think about.

One newspaper commented with satisfaction that "the bronzed hair of Chicago May will be colorless and there will be no sweet roundness to her features when she comes out of prison." Eddie gleefully pointed out in his book that "imprisonment takes nasty slices out of the life of a woman whose principal assets are her charms."

She was taken off to serve her fifteen years of hard labor. And not a soul in the world, except perhaps poor Charley, pitied her.

PART FOUR

1907 to 1917

Eight

~~~~~~~~

Aylesbury

If May's jail had been an American one, the deprivation of liberty would have been the main thing she had to bear. But being imprisoned in England lent an extra dimension to her punishment. England conquered and occupied Ireland in the seventeenth century, planted its good land with the incomers who became the Anglo-Irish landlord class, and sustained the plantation by discrimination against the native Irish in every field—religious, educational, commercial, and political. The resentment the Irish feel toward England is therefore very deep, and the condescension of England toward the Irish is just as obdurate. It was irrelevant that May had committed a crime on English soil and was properly punished on English soil. At at that time, and even now that Ireland has long been independent, it galls an Irish person to concede authority to an English institution.

The female prison, Aylesbury

May was well aware of Irish history. A particularly tragic rebellion against English rule, in 1798, had ended a few miles from her home. The France of the newly accomplished French Revolution sent troops to Ireland to help the Irish challenge England, but the small rebel force was driven by a superior British one to a place called Ballinamuck, which even today seems to hold the memory of how its streams ran red with blood when the foreign soldiers were made prisoners of war but the Irish soldiers were slaughtered. The Duignan family went to Mass in Ballinamuck. Their horse and cart would have jogged every Sunday through the somber valley where "the year of the French" had ended.

There was some kind of rising against England in almost every generation, though not when May was a girl, when Ireland was almost broken by famine and emigration. *Crime never occurred to me as being a sin,* she remarked in her book, and part of the reason for that must have been that she grew up taking it for granted that the people who ruled her were unworthy of obedience. The assurance of injustice among the colonized is not just a mirror image of the assurance of the colonizer; in Ireland, at least, it was incomparably stronger. Every Irish person was a victim, in the perspective familiar to May, and victims are entitled to cheat.

May learned history at school, but her teachers had had to pass exams in topics that mattered in London, like "Write a brief sketch of the life of Warren Hastings up to the time of his *first* departure to India." In Edenmore, history was about the land. In May's own parish, in 1839, a contemporary account says, "117 souls were turned out in one day and Protestants were put in their place. Some died through want, some went to America, some are going backwards and forwards in the country." When May was ten years old, a minor famine reduced three hundred of the local people to eking out bare survival on food distributed by the priest. The landlord—who like many of the Anglo-Irish landlords was an absentee who lived in London—instructed his bailiffs to order the people to sell their new oats and potatoes to pay him rent. They armed themselves as best they could to resist. "We will die fighting like men," they cried, according to a local history, "sooner than allow any rack-renter rob us of the food necessary for ourselves and our families. It is better for us to die fighting like soldiers than die of starvation like slaves."

And she would have witnessed evictions. Eviction was a weapon very much used against her class.

If tension didn't amount to all-out conflict in Ireland, it was because of the safety valve provided by emigration. Verses written by an anonymous woman from May's homeplace, which are printed in the parish history of Edenmore, make the link explicit. The author curses the English—"the tyrants who oppress"—and goes on,

> *They wronged your fathers long ago,*
> *They wrong you now. Why wait?*
> *Your father's blood for rights did flow,*
> *In seventeen ninety-eight.*

An eviction in County Longford, 1876

But since there's no hope of defeating the tyrant, she says, there is nowhere to go to live in freedom, except America. She sees as if in a dream "the lovely Stars and Stripes, wave proudly overhead." So,

With that flag where freedom smiles
For fortune I will look,
I will say goodbye to Erin's Isle
And my friends round Ballinamuck.

May had done it, of course, in her day—she'd got herself to America. But in Aylesbury jail she found herself back in the power of the ancient oppressor.

It is beyond me to imagine the depth of her despair. I can only salute her experience and step back, when I think of the whole of her life being reduced to one small, stone cell, for every hour of the year and for year after year. A few years ago in Berlin I picked my way through the Jewish Museum designed by Daniel Libeskind, half built at the time, and there was an opening into a narrow, very high room in which there was light impossibly far above and where the smooth walls slanted inward, and for one second even a privileged person could feel the terror of the fragile self in incarceration. The poet Gerard Manley Hopkins said,

> *O the mind, mind has mountains; cliffs of fall*
> *Frightful, sheer, no-man-fathomed. Hold them cheap*
> *May who ne'er hung there.*

He was able to imagine it—the self on the verge of splitting apart, the mind cowering as it waited to go mad.

MAY'S VOICE is plain, but wholly eloquent.

I stretched out the examination of my cell, she wrote, *to an unimaginable length of time, noting each little detail as carefully as if I was going to buy it and did not want to be stuck with flaws in my bargain. Many and many a time in the long years thereafter, I used to go over that same cell, hoping to find something new to occupy my mind. I knew every square inch of my particular home, could tell wherein it differed from every other cell I was privileged to enter and noticed the slightest changes which occurred in it. An unusual mark, or a crack, or spot, on the surface of my domain, was an event of real importance.*

A woman who had always been at the center of a small storm of life—someone I imagine pulling up her skirt to unself-consciously scratch the white skin above the black stocking while she goes on with some story she's telling, her bright head thrown back in a peal of laughter, a woman who has never been slowed by doubt or self-consciousness or introspection—is left to her own resources. She shrivels. Time passes without bearing any fruit except its passing. She would have learned out in the world how to become a handsome older woman who knew to sit whenever she could because otherwise her ankles swelled up, to pull the brush through her hair and slide it back into her purse in one almost imperceptible movement, to button her blouse in such a way as to allow the cream of a rising breast to distract from the hatching of wrinkles on the skin above. Out there she could make other people forget, and therefore she could forget, that she was getting older each minute, each hour and day; but not in here where the prisoners, she said, *dreaded the monotony of absolute idleness, alone with their own thoughts.* Perhaps in Montpellier she'd learned some tricks of the mind to help her—a creature of cabs and carriages and the first-class lounges of railway stations and glittering restaurants where she called the waiters by their nicknames—to bear the condition of aloneness. But there's horror to having no company, for years and years on end, but your own body and your own arid mind.

There were few flies, she wrote later. *They are rare in England, but I even tried to make friends with a couple of these insects which ventured into my prison. If only I could have had some sort of an animal to care for and love, it would have been of the greatest help in keeping my mind occupied and giving me something to do.*

She recalled something her newspaperman boyfriend had said back in the high old days of the Tenderloin. One morning she came back to their apartment after some typically turbulent event involving men, robbery, a courthouse, bail, and the theft of the judge's diamond tie-pin when he was drunk in Hudnutt's drugstore on Park Row. She had somehow escaped going to jail, and the boyfriend commented affectionately, "Bars and bolts couldn't imprison my redhead."

I thought of that many times, she says.

But would her way out of imprisonment be insanity? *Many were the times when I thought of poor Smith when things were going bad with me, wondering how he was getting along. I rather flattered myself that the dear boy was thinking of me. I was quite sure he was, because he was always considerate for women, being born and bred that way, tough as he might be with men. But what was the use of thinking? Oh hell, was I growing crazy? Was Charley as crazy by now as I was?*

She even had the mad hope that she'd be rescued from Aylesbury. She had done everything she could, according to herself, to get Eddie out of Devil's Island and *Guerin ought to have reciprocated and tried to get me out. Instead of that, he threatened to shoot anybody who raised a finger to spring me.* By the time she was writing her book she could forgive him—*I think his sufferings and privations while he was escaping from Devil's Island made him batty.* But not back in Aylesbury, when fifteen awful years stretched ahead.

Yet now, in a much more formal and punitive prison than any she'd been in in France, May discovered self-control. I went on a day trip out from London to Aylesbury and in a library not far from the jail, I looked through what remains of the ledgers where, in May's time, an External Visitor was supposed to record the complaints of the women. There were about 135 women in the jail when May was there, so there must have been many complaints, but the rote comment "I found everything in excellent order" is repeated daily for years. Whoever scribbled it on the pages I was turning must have cared for nothing but order, though the real life of the place reveals itself very occasionally in brief notes: "M. Skelton granted a letter on the death of a child"; "Daisy Ball restrained in the straitjacket at 8:05 a.m. for attempted suicide"; "J. C. Roberts sentenced to 12 days close confinement, she has no marks to lose nor any gratuity to pay for damages."

But May's name never appears on the record. She who once provoked violence wherever she went caused no trouble in Aylesbury. She bore with standing all day while she worked at making string and with scrubbing dungeon floors and stoking the laundry fire, and with the gnawing hunger against which she soaked her bread in water and with waiting eight years before she tasted a green vegetable. She was afraid to be troublesome. Because she saw what happened to other women if they complained or answered back. She saw sane women being taken off to the asylum for the criminally insane at Broadmoor. And she was terrified of Broadmoor.

She had learned terror, in fact. Her imagination had woken up.

That's what made me walk up the hill from Aylesbury Station to the jail, slowed by the heat of summer as she must have been when she arrived there in late July. Across from the jail, which is monumental and glowering and a prison still, there stands, still, a little building that May could see from her cell. In her time, it was the gatehouse of the poorhouse. She used to watch in the evening homeless, indigent couples separate, the women to go to one side of the poorhouse and the men to the other. *Both were in need of lodging, with breakfast in the morning,* she wrote. *They must disown each other, for the time being. They were probably honest and had worked hard all their lives. What bright prospects they once had and hopes for the future! And it had come to this! Did they wish they had been crooks? Could the thief's fate be any worse than theirs? Is it any wonder crooks are crooks, under society as at present organized?*

She had never pondered the mystery of life's random injustice before. She had never cared before what dreams the old might once have had. She had never proposed a social origin for crime. I felt that I was somewhere important when I was on the site of that awakening in her.

As a blackmailer and thief she had moved too fast to feel the pity that came to life when she looked out from her cell. She could see the morgue, where, she said, *two big, ugly, black cats always kept vigil at the door. They always appeared on the scene in advance of the stiff,* and she speculates that the cats are there to keep rats off the corpse. *When the corpse actually arrived, an armed guard marched sentry, round and round the place, day and night. This also may have been to observe the proprieties and guard against body snatchers. In any event, the dead were still prisoners.*

When the time comes, two old workhouse-men appeared, dressed in dilapidated, high silk-hats and old, torn, black frock-coats. Invari-

ably they had some weeks' growth of beard. They drove an old nag, spavined and back-sunken, attached to an old wagon which had apparently been in the service of a greengrocer. . . . They carry a cheap pine box into the morgue and when they carry it out again they have to be helped by others because it is too heavy for the old paupers alone to handle. Accompanying the black-thing were two wardresses and a nurse, with a bunch of wild flowers, which was thrown on top of the men's burden. There must be some sentiment about the affair, you know! Up into the "hearse" hobbled the two poorhouse bums. Off they drove, like mad. Rattle her bones over the stones. They're only a convict's which nobody owns.

James Joyce would have appreciated the bitter rhyme.

The idea began to haunt May that if she was buried from prison she would be a prisoner for all eternity. But she turned her fear to good account. *That dead-house helped me to pull my time,* she wrote. *I wouldn't die, no matter what punishment I had to take.*

And one of the punishments was particularly lacerating.

She believed that letters came for her, but that the wardresses, out of dislike of her, didn't give them to her. Many of the wardresses in Aylesbury were Irish—*in France,* May remarks bitterly, *they get Corsicans for jailers. In England they find quite a number of tinker-Irish to do the dirty work.* In all her years in Aylesbury, she never got a letter, though she was told they had been sent. *They were kept from me,* she wrote.

But defiance of the English authorities and their Irish collaborators also kept her strong. *Though there were times when I nearly lost my reason I never let myself go,* May wrote. *The best way to describe me is that I was getting colder and colder, as the years rolled slowly by. I got just as cold and mean as the English themselves.*

JOLTS OF ANGER keep the spirit alive, but anger cannot make time move faster. It was time that was her enemy. The hours and hours of every day and week and month that she could not fill threatened her sanity. But when she was a little girl, she'd run every schoolday for six years across the yard at home and past the well in its surround of mossy flagstones and out into the big field that stretches halfway up Edenmore Hill. The lane at the top of the hill is sunk so deep between grassy banks that the wind up there hardly troubled the sturdy child, though what she was expected to learn in school probably did. The curriculum was laid down in Westminster in perfect indifference to the experience of children like the ones in Edenmore. I read the reports of inspections of Longford schools in the 1870s. The inspectors saw that the Irish children were often cold and tired. "I have to milk eight cows night and morning," one inspector records a little girl as saying, to excuse her inadequate comprehension. Yet the inspectors can't understand that though a map of England might be on the schoolroom wall for years, the children will still not know where London is. They can't understand why the children were baffled, in May's time, by a poem that contained the lines

I have no mother for she died,
When I was very young.
But still her memory round my heart,
Like morning mist has clung.

"I observed from the countenance of the children," one inspector wrote, "that the words of the last two lines conveyed no idea to their minds, and on questioning found none could tell the difference between 'morning mists' and 'memory round my heart.'" It never occurred to him that sentiments that seemed uplifting in London did not necessarily seem so in May's culture, or that words like "morning mist" and even "mother" might have nuances in the world of embattled small farmers that they did not have at the heart of the *imperium*. Or that the life of the children might be so bare that metaphors were a luxury not often in use.

Yet—and this is what mattered in Aylesbury—the system that did not educate the children did make them literate. And when May discovered books in jail, she discovered her salvation.

She came upon a compendium of *Harmsworth's Self-Educator; A Golden Key to Success in Life,* a weekly magazine "designed to be a working school of life" that guaranteed "education, success and fortune for a halfpenny a day" through engravings illustrating orangutans, geological maps, sections of the brain, how to pan for gold, kinds of birds' eggs, and much more, and hundreds of articles on topics such as the Chlorine Process, the Roman Tyrants, Beekeeping, Philosophy, Military Engineers, Prime Movers, How to Enter the Ministry, the Stability of Structures, and the Qualifications and Duties of Every Kind of Servant.

All the information was presented with tremendous anglocentric confidence. The entry on Ireland, for instance—to which May might well have turned, her homeland being a much more precious place in her present situation than it had ever been when she lived there—is openly disapproving.

A whole family with its few domestic animals is often crowded into a cottage of one room, standing in the midst of a neglected and barren moorland croft. From the congested western districts the more capable emigrate in large numbers across the Atlantic, which seems to open a natural highway to a land of greater plenty.

I imagine it struck May as accurate to see herself classed among the "more capable," present circumstances notwithstanding.

Next she began to read fiction. "What is a novel?" the article on fiction in the *Self-Educator* asks, and answers itself in the words of that "charming exponent," Jane Austen: a novel is a work "in which the most thorough knowledge of human nature and the liveliest variety of wit and humour are conveyed to the world in the best-chosen words." *All of the classical novelists were mine for the asking if I did not ask for more than my allotment of two a week,* May wrote. *Brontë, Eliot, Fielding, Thackeray, Scott, Dickens, Hawthorne, Emerson and dozens more.*

I read everything I could get my hands on, good, bad, and indifferent, from Gibbon's Decline and Fall of the Roman Empire *and d'Aubigné's* History of the Reformation *to* Alice in Wonderland *and Grimm's* Fairy Tales. *It is unbelievable that I waded through Mommsen's* Roman History *not because it was heavy going but because it was a comparatively recent book for the prison to have.*

I reveled in Dickens, especially Oliver Twist, *and the parts in other of his books about crooks and lawyers.* She would, wouldn't she?

Burns and Tom Moore were my favorite poets. Of course; a Scot and an Irishman.

And her experience of Shakespeare was unique. It is wonderful to add May's account to the many high-minded ones that have described the impact on respectable writers of discovering Shakespeare. Few can match May's span. *I read all of Shakespeare,* she says, *and got so that I would make believe I was acting the parts, in imitation of what I had seen on the stage when I used to go to the play, occasionally, to see a great actor and pick up a john.*

To go from using the theater as a place to pick up suckers to acting every part in all the plays—there's something of Shakespearean inclusiveness itself about that.

She read from four o'clock every day, when the women were locked into their cells, till ten o'clock. *I used to pull my cot under the hole that was my ventilator and window, and read until the light would fade away. In the summer time, the light would linger until bedtime. In the winter, we had gas burning outside of a glass window which looked into the corridor. I would pull my stool to the wooden table, fastened to the wall. With a book on the table, I would read until the lights went out.* She concealed her book of the moment in her clothes so she could read in chapel. I know exactly that hunch of the shoulders, that turning of the page—silently, without moving the arms—down around the knees. I went to boarding school in a granite convent on the edge of a small town in Ireland, and every so often we were marched down the main street to some lengthy service in the cathedral, and during whatever parts of the liturgy I could get away with it, I pulled my white veil around me where I knelt, and read. And I saw my mother using books to blot out her surroundings—she escaped thoughts that made her desperate by bringing to even the most shallow murder mystery a total concentration.

But if reading saved May's mind—and left, too, a visible mark on the vocabulary of *Her Story*—her body was in a very bad state by the time the First World War broke out in 1914, when she'd been in for seven years. And it got worse. The prisoners' meager food rations were cut until, by 1916, they were near starvation. They were also locked in a dark cellar during air raids. *It was pitiful to hear the poor old women crying with fear the night through, when they heard the buzzers in the little town,* May wrote. *Oftener than not it would turn out to be a false alarm. Imagine what it was like in that dark dismal hole, to wake up and know that you were like a rat in a trap, and they would not let you out even if you could have helped yourself.*

AN ALMOST EXACT contemporary of May's grew up in the same corner of Ireland, but at the top rather than the bottom of society. Constance Gore-Booth could see over in the southeast, from her family's large estate at Lissadell near Sligo, the range of beautiful hills called the Curlews. Little May Duignan could see them to the northwest. But while May had an austere childhood, Constance's was full of governesses and tutors and tennis and riding and picnics and practical jokes and secrets shared with her sister, Eva. Her people had a house in London, too, of course, and that was where the two of them were expected to find suitable husbands when they "came out" at the court of Queen Victoria.

The Gore-Booth sisters, Constance and Eva

The young W. B. Yeats knew the sisters. A poem of his about them begins

> *The light of evening, Lissadell,*
> *Great windows open to the south,*
> *Two girls in silk kimonos, both*
> *Beautiful, one a gazelle.*

But Yeats, whose own Sligo relatives were merchants, was not, in fact, on equal social terms with the Gore-Booths. The landed families looked down on the Protestant bourgeoisie. And as for Catholic peasants like May's family—laborers for and servants of the gentry and creators of their wealth—they were hardly even looked at. It was simply impossible for the landlord class to think of people like the Duignans as human beings comparable in interest or importance to themselves.

Yet the condition of the landlord class in Ireland, alienated as it was from the culture of the country as a whole, sometimes acted as a stimulus to originality. Constance did not follow the conventional route into marriage. She was more seriously interested in sketching and painting than most upper-class girls, and in 1900, she subverted the expectations of her community by going to Paris to study painting. What was more, she fell in love with a married Polish count, Count Markievicz, and when his wife died, she married him although he was Roman Catholic. The dates suggest that she was pregnant when she married him, so marriage would have been judged the lesser of two evils.

As it happens, Constance and her husband were living the lives of comfortably-off bohemians in Paris on the night May waited outside the American Express office while the Dutch Gus gang blew the safe.

THE MARKIEVICZES and their little daughter moved to Dublin in the early 1900s and became prominent members of the arts coterie there. All around them the energy was gathering for the rising against England that had been delayed for half a century by the trauma of the Famine. But although she found herself in a ferment of cultural nationalism, which coexisted with and influenced a variety of more or less secretive political and militaristic groups, Constance herself was purposeless. She said much later that the kind of thing she thought at the time was that "Nature should provide me with something to live for, something to die for"—like any wan *fin de siècle* lady.

But then in 1906, she rented a cottage in the hills above Dublin. The previous tenant had been a writer and folklorist called Padraic Colum—a friend of James Joyce's and a protégé of Yeats's and once known to every Irish child for his poem "An Old Woman of the Roads." Colum had left behind in the cottage some copies of revolutionary publications—*The Peasant* was the name of one of them, *Sinn Féin* ("Ourselves Alone" in the Irish language) the other. Constance wasn't entirely unready for the effect these had on her—she was to write later that her "first realization of tyranny came from some chance words spoken in favor of woman's suffrage." But as she read the magazines, she began to see women's freedom and all worthwhile freedoms as indivisible, in Ireland, from freedom from England. And soon the cause of national independence became her passion.

Her husband was also responsive to the appeal of national self-determination, but in his own part of the world, and the couple separated amicably for him to return to Poland and the Ukraine. Their daughter was taken to Lissadell to be raised by Constance's mother—who had no sympathy whatsoever for her daughter's newfound enthusiasms and who didn't, in fact, have a meeting with her for twenty years. Now Constance was free to throw herself into the preparations for an armed rising which, though intensely serious, no one believed would overthrow England's substantial garrison in Ireland.

Once when I was a young woman in Dublin, I attended the old-fashioned salon an elderly lady used to hold in a drawing room that looked down on a Georgian square. During the evening I found myself sitting deep in a sofa with the very old man, back home after fifty years in America, who was that evening's honored guest. It was the same Padraic Colum.

The nearest I ever came to Constance Markievicz was when I shuffled through the rooms of Lissadell as one of a group of tourists continually ordered by the guide to keep behind the ropes. But now, it gives me great satisfaction that Padraic Colum was from north Longford and was born a couple of miles from May's homeplace, and must have known the Duignan family. And that he and May and the countess are linked again in pages of mine.

. . .

CONSTANCE'S MAIN CONTRIBUTION to the coming insurrection was the creation of Na Fianna Éireann, a kind of revolutionary boy scout organization intended to train patriotic Irish boys in paramilitary skills. She arranged—and subsidized from her diminishing inheritance—camps where the boys learned drilling, signaling, and use of firearms. She attended to every detail, including the design of the Fianna uniform, for which her fellow patriot Sir Roger Casement— soon to be condemned to death by May's judge at the New Bailey, Mr. Justice Darling—sent money for "kilts for the boys." Like many of the other self-inventing cultural nationalists of that period, Constance was very interested in the symbolism of flags and headgear and uniforms— revolutionaries, by definition, have to oppose the oppressor's designs with their own designs. But though she was very capable of sounding like an arty dilettante, she was completely committed to her cause. And a great achievement won her the love of the working class of Dublin. She ran a food kitchen during an employers' lockout that left twenty thousand workers and their families facing starvation. With a handful of other women she bought, prepared, and served thousands of meals a day. Her military work was effective, too, for all that some of the male leaders sneered at her and excluded her from their conspiracies. When it came to the Easter Rising of 1916, there was indeed a cadre of ex-Fianna young men trained in some of the ways of soldiery.

The Rising was small and confused, and a split within the leadership meant it was countermanded outside Dublin. But it was an admirable exercise in collaboration by men who, though equally brave, had different visions of what a free Ireland might be. The Irish Citizen Army, for example, led by James Connolly, was more influenced by socialism than were the Volunteers led by Patrick Pearse. Connolly wanted to free Ireland from England because independence would be part of a process that would also transform the condition of workers, and of Irish women, whom he characterized as "the slaves of slaves." His people commandeered buildings in the south inner city, while Pearse had his headquarters in Dublin's main post office. The Rising lasted only six days, but during its course, an Irish Republic was proclaimed. Then, hopelessly outnumbered by the local garrison that was quickly supplemented by troops brought in from England—about forty-five hundred troops, it is estimated, and a thousand police, compared to about a thousand revolutionaries all told—and so as to prevent the death of civilians, Pearse and the men he was with decided to surrender. Connolly accepted the decision.

During those six days, one of the commanders under Connolly of the two hundred or so members of the Irish Citizen Army was a woman, a handsome woman in her forties wearing a green uniform with an immense Celtic brooch of beaten silver on her shoulder, and at her side a holster containing a Mauser automatic pistol with which—legend in any case has it—she shot a British soldier. And this was the Countess Constance Markievicz. She fought, and she was willing to die, in spite of which she has been denigrated by faint praise or omission in Irish historiography, as has Maud Gonne MacBride, the nationalist activist—and great beauty—who was loved by Yeats. Both subverted notions prevailing then and—in Ireland—since then, of how women should behave and how upper-class people should behave.

"A bitter, an abstract thing," Yeats came to call the countess. And Cecil Day-Lewis (father of the actor Daniel Day-Lewis), who though born in Ireland became Poet Laureate of England, wrote a poem about Madame Markievicz which began by acknowledging

Fanatic, bad actress, figure of fun,
She was called each.

The Easter Rising failed. After their surrender, sixteen of its leaders, including Constance, were held in jail in Dublin, and every morning for a week were taken to the yard, two at a time, to face the firing squad. She could hear the fusillades from her cell, but nobody told

Countess Markievicz in a studio portrait

her who had been executed until one morning there were no more shots: the men behind the proclamation of an Irish Republic were all dead. She, too, had been sentenced to death, but now her sentence was reduced to life imprisonment—"solely and only by reason of her gender," the commutation order said. She was marched to the ferry-boat through the streets of Dublin, jeered at by women whose men were in the English army and who were dependent on army pay.

And so she arrived at Aylesbury prison.

MAY DUIGNAN, even in her remote cell, had responded to the spirit of the age. She was now in open conflict with the jail authorities. She wanted the Germans to win the war, and she said so. This had nothing at all to do with endorsing Germany's war aims, if, indeed, she knew what they were. It was traditional. For hundreds of years, Ireland assumed that England's enemies were its friends.

Women prisoners, who were allowed to save a penny a week, were asked to give up their pennies to buy cigarettes for the troops. May wouldn't do it.

Let the rich English government look after its own soldiers, she said.

But, the matron said, "The soldiers might be your own cousins."

If any relative of mine, May said—risking whatever comforts might be available under the jail regime—*has fallen so low as to wear a red coat, he deserves to go without smokes, and I hope he suffers much worse than that.*

May claims in her book that when she heard in prison that British troops were being withdrawn from Ireland to fight in the trenches in France, she whispered to her friend Annie Gleason—serving five years for shoplifting a pair of silk stockings and a panama hat—*if they take the troops away, our people are going to make one more attempt to free themselves.*

In less than a month I proved myself a good prophet.

THEN THE RISING HAPPENED, and the Countess arrived. *She was the grandest woman,* according to May in her book, *I ever saw* (the Irish use "grand" to mean wonderful).

In the letters the Countess wrote from jail she doesn't mention May—or anybody else—by name. But I'm sure the two of them did know each other. They would have been bracketed by the prison authorities, in whose eyes they were both vile traitors to England in its hour of need. Constance was given the job of collecting and washing the tin cans used for eating. Tins marked "D" were supposed to be kept separate from the rest, but that was impossible, even though "D" probably meant "diseased," since many of the women were suffering from venereal disease. The tins were in a state of encrusted dirt and "I used to do 200 tins with another convict," Countess Markievicz wrote in an article years later, "and sometimes there was no soap or soda and many of the tins were red with rust inside." I feel certain that this other convict was May, who was also a "star" prisoner, that is, in the most serious category. The two Irish patriots would have been made outcasts together in the daily life of the jail.

The Countess had been in an Irish prison compared with which Aylesbury, in her opinion, was greatly inferior. "Extreme dirt," she wrote in a later newspaper article,

> was concealed under a parade of cleanliness. Every bit of brass was immaculate, the floors were scrubbed unceasingly, but the baths were so dirty that we refused to use them. Vermin was constantly crawling over one. The porridge ladle was left in a dirty pail with the lavatory brush.

She herself was a tireless worker for underprivileged people, but that doesn't mean that she liked their company, especially if they were English. "The women I am with," she wrote in one of the letters she managed to smuggle out of prison, "are the gutter rats of England, quite different from Dublin, prostitutes and widows for baby murder." Years later, however, she wrote about their desperation: "One girl tried to kill herself by cutting her throat, another set fire to her cell. Several tried to hang themselves with ropes used in the making of mailbags and more swallowed buttons and huge needles."

She gallantly tried to look on the bright side. "The one thing I am learning here is to watch everything closely, whether it is trees or black beetles, birds or women. The sparrows are delightful," she wrote to her sister, adding obscurely, "like men at their best."

But May says that the Countess told her—and I see no reason why May would have made this up—that she was tormented by the observation hole in the door of her cell, which was a carving of an eye painted like an eye, with a spyhole where the pupil of an eye would have been. *She said she had to walk the floor every night, trying to exorcise the devilish thing.* May felt the same about the spyhole. *You can get used to nearly anything, but you never quite got over the horror of being constantly watched and of having your privacy invaded.*

The jail grew more hellish as time went on. The suffragettes, arrested at demonstrations for women's right to vote, were on hunger strike, and they were subjected to forcible feeding. It's all there in House of Commons debates—how the old male nurses from the workhouse hospital were brought in to enter the suffragettes' cells and shove rubber hoses up their nostrils and back down their throats. The women cried terribly after food was forced into them this way. Most of them were of Constance's class, and I wonder whether May compared them with herself, now that reflection had been forced upon her. What did she think of their anguish after they had been forced to eat—she who had been hungry for years? What did she think of volunteering to suffer as they did—not for profit, not for survival, but for a cause? A women's cause?

But I don't know whom she could have talked to about things like that. Association was not allowed in the jail, and if she and the Countess whispered together, it was only because they worked together. There was the barrier of class, always. May says *we were great friends and I always took her part when the Englishers tried to ride her,* but the Countess, though she later wrote that she had "a certain community of hatred" with the criminal prisoners, says no such thing about May or anyone else. The Countess had resources, too, that distanced her from a street person like May. She spent a lot of time in her cell trying—and succeeding—to make psychic contact with her beloved sister, Eva. She embroidered, using her own hair for thread, until her needle and rags were confiscated. She had high culture to sustain her. Her dreams—though one was of playing billiards with the moon—were of such things as the view of Florence from Fiesole.

Whereas poor May dreamed of food, and of belonging.

In sleep, her family came back to her. She saw her parents and brothers and herself all gathered around the kitchen table.

With what pleasure, she wrote, *I ate the well-known meals! How we talked and joshed the table round!*

The two women were comrades on at least one occasion.

The Germans were making a successful push in the war and all the prisoners were ordered to go to the chapel and pray for British victory. The Countess and May and one other woman, jailed for spying for Germany, refused to go. So the wardresses made them deliver gruel to all the prisoners, which meant dragging hot, greasy vats up the stairs and along the corridors of the prison for many hours. The Countess, May says, got through the punishment by reciting Dante, aloud, in Italian. It is one of the most bizarre images from the long struggle for Irish freedom—the prostitute and the lady clattering along the stone passages of an English jail inefficiently ladling out gruel at each hatch, while Constance intoned lines from the *Inferno* in her Anglo-Irish accent.

I don't think that May could possibly have invented this anecdote, and I don't think she'd have known how to tell it if she hadn't been part of it. It was an unexpected kindness done to May by history that she was allowed make common cause with a woman like Constance. It returned May some reward for her personal bravery in standing with Ireland, powerless as she was. She had always thrilled to the upper classes. To have been associated with a titled lady who was also a heroine of the Rising—how the combination must have stirred May's bruised heart!

IN 1917, after a year in Aylesbury, the Countess—sixty pounds lighter than when she went in—was returned to Dublin under a general amnesty for republican prisoners. As the only survivor of the 1916 leaders—whose summary execution had won a sympathy for their cause they had never known in life—she got a welcome such as no Irish person, woman or man, had ever known before. The people of Dublin took to the streets and made Constance the focus of their growing pride in the Easter Rising.

In that same year, 1917, May, too, was released, after serving ten years.

America had come into the war and May claimed to be an American citizen by virtue of marriage to Jim Sharp—though the particulars on her marriage certificate, as I mentioned at the time, were completely invented. She was released on condition that she go back to the United States and never return to Great Britain—of which at that time, Ireland was still a part. She was lucky to be deported. She had no money at all. She could not have afforded the fare to America herself.

In *Belle of New York,* she'd been costumed as a Salvation Army girl. Now Salvation Army officers escorted her up to London on the train, seated between two wardresses and still wearing prison clothes. She couldn't stop laughing and crying. The other passengers, she said, thought she was a lunatic. That same scene—an Irish prisoner half-delirious with the joy of release—had been played out ten years before when Oscar Wilde was released from Reading Gaol. "Beautiful world! Beautiful world!" Oscar kept exclaiming when he was brought to the train, and his guard remarked that he was the only man in Britain who would say that to a railway station.

May herself had kept her verbal nimbleness. When the Salvation Army people gave her dowdy clothes, she hated them. Someone exhorted her to be good: *As if I could be anything else,* she snapped, *in the rig I have on.*

THE MEANING of Irishness was very different in the lives of Oscar Wilde, of the Countess—a friend of Oscar's wife, by the way, who had rejoiced with her when his apparent affair with Lillie Langtry ended and they believed that he would now be a faithful husband—

and of May. And in the life of Stephen Dedalus, speaking for James Joyce in *A Portrait of the Artist as a Young Man,* published two years earlier. Stephen arrives at the belief that to become an artist he must escape the nets Ireland has laid out to trap him. "You talk to me of nationality," he says, "language, religion. I shall try to fly by those nets."

May was compelled by the deportation order to be free of Ireland, but she was in any case strikingly indifferent to these nets. When her ship docked for a few days in Belfast Lough, she was looking out at the country where her parents and siblings and a whole community who knew her were a couple of hours away by the trains of the day. When the anchor was lifted and the ship steamed out toward the west, it would be the last she would ever see of her homeland. But May doesn't even mention Ireland. Her eye is always for the immediate, and what she wants to describe to the reader are the people with whom she sailed through the U-boats and mines of an appallingly dangerous wartime Atlantic. They included the drug addict wife of a Washington diplomat. *One day as we were passing her stateroom there she was on the floor, dead to the world, with her long beautiful hair all awry. I was told most of the men had been intimate with her. She was a lady, so nothing was said.*

"You talk to me of nationality," Dedalus said. May had never moved in educated circles where she might have had conversations about politics. *My friends and my family were fighting for our freedom at Easter week,* she announced to the warders in Aylesbury, but it wasn't true—there was no rising in Longford. She said it to provoke. And if her family were active in the subsequent guerrilla war of independence—and north Longford did contribute a famous "flying column" to it and did have the highest proportion of Sinn Féin voters in Ireland at that time—May would not have known it. She was heroic in her own way when she defied her jailers in an England at war. It never crossed her mind to go further. Penniless women of little education rarely do find a place in an independence struggle.

Stephen Dedalus wanted, of course, to express himself "in some

mode of life or art as freely as I can and as wholly as I can." When he
stated, "I will not serve that in which I no longer believe, whether it
call itself my home, my fatherland or my church," it was so as to
serve the higher calling of art. May's only claim to artistry is that she
had lived more like an artist than anything else—she had lived by im-
provisation, and perhaps that was what she had, however vaguely, in
mind when she gave her occupation, at her New Bailey trial, as
"Artist." But we can hardly feel today how original it must have been,
in the days when the territory of individualism had not been well
mapped, for Irish people in as humble a social position as May and
even Stephen Dedalus to reject the pieties of the tribe. She was au-
thentically naked of the clothing Stephen had to go to pains to shed.

She had no fatherland, no home. Soon after her ship arrived at
Ellis Island and she was held by Immigration, she had to fill in a form
that asked her to give the name and address of the nearest relative or
friend in the country from which she had come. Because the ship had
docked in Belfast, that country was Ireland.

What she wrote was, *None.*

What of church? She was an Irish Catholic by upbringing, and
other prisoners had given her holy medals when she was leaving
Aylesbury—I suppose they had little else to give, and were also su-
perstitious, and holy medals are thought to keep a person safe. On
board ship she got rid of them to Irish-American sailors on their way
back to join the U.S. Navy from working on oil rigs in China. The
men thought, she says—I take it that this is her joke—that she was
some kind of Catholic missionary. Stephen Dedalus gloried in the
language of the Church and identified with the priestly function and
was fascinated, intellectually, by Catholicism. But May disposed of
belief as briskly as she disposed of the holy medals. She might as well
never have been in a church for all the reference she makes to it,
though when she and Joyce were growing up, the liturgy was one of
the few symbolic and theatrical dimensions of a plain world. She
seems to have been entirely uninfluenced by the priests—as many

Irish Catholics are who let the whole thing fall away with the first sin, as if the authoritarianism of the Church was so absolute that no part of the person had been in any meaningful way engaged.

May didn't pray, even in emergencies. She doesn't believe there's a hell and she doesn't mention heaven. She's impervious to remorse and coolly astonished, the several times she mentions it, at the notion of turning to religion late in life. She really did fly by the net of religion.

The only aspect of the Irish Catholic tradition that survived in her was a robust anticlericalism. Her grandfather, she tells us, when instructed by the priest in the time after the potato famine not to plant seed potatoes sent by well-wishers in the States—presumably because the well-wishers were Protestant—planted them *and got a bigger and better yield than usual*. Her grandfather also admired the local Presbyterian pastor, though the latter preached that the Catholic Church was the Red Whore of Babylon. The same grandfather also said that *the priests sold Ireland to the English*. There could hardly be a worse charge.

When Countess Markievicz was in Aylesbury, she was receiving instruction in Catholicism and the local bishop came to see her and said a special Mass for her. May attended the Mass, too.

When the bishop met her, "Were you baptized a Catholic?" he asked.

Sure, May said, *but I'm not to blame for that*.

Her grandfather would have been proud of her.

Studies of Irish Catholic immigrant women in America show them remaining faithful in worship, but those were women with home-based jobs, either in domestic service or as wives and mothers, and they needed to go to church, if only to get out of the house. May had had her own community—her thieves, her blackmailers, her fellow-prostitutes. She was one of the few Irishwomen who really did emigrate from Ireland to America instead of to Irish-America. But now she needed the ethnic connection. This reentry to America is almost grotesquely different from the first. She's not young anymore and yet she has nothing at all to show for her years. And any friends who might have helped her in New York have long disappeared, along with the raunchy Tenderloin in which she and they had flourished. There is nowhere for her to turn except the ethnic network.

The cop who went out from Sandy Hook and boarded the ship to take her off to interrogation was one of the Irish ones she knew from way back. He was *so drunk he could hardly stand up. "Hello, May!" he said. And he kept impressing on me how good the boys were going to be to me.* He gave May *an image of Saint Anthony. I told him I did not like that saint because he was a woman-hater.* She might have meant this, though Saint Anthony of Padua was not a notable misogynist and he preached so beautifully, it was said, that even the fish gathered to hear him, but more probably this is an example of the kind of sassy repartee she used to exchange, when she was young and pretty, with policemen from home. Two more of them were there to greet her on Ellis Island—*Quinn and Marty Sheridan, who was the Irishman who threw the discus at Athens and beat the Greeks at their own game, a gentleman at all times.* But they couldn't protect her from suffering during her period of detention there. She hated being with foreigners *with great long beards, who ate with their hands.* She couldn't sleep where there was noise—after the solitude of Aylesbury, she must have experienced the crammed dormitory as torture. She got up *and sat on the cold stone floor by the door*—reaching back, though she may not have seen it, to her cell.

Eventually a matron put her in a room with some other women. *"I try to keep white people together,"* she said.

Another Irish person, a nurse called Miss Daly, took the clothes May had arrived in to keep as curios and, out of kindness, fitted her with underclothes and a hat and *a nice tailor-made gown.*

May was three weeks in hospital on Ellis Island. She wasn't ill. What they were doing with her was feeding her. She had been plain starved in Aylesbury. This time she had arrived in the New World with malnutrition.

. . .

A DETECTIVE known as Handsome Jimmy Dalton took her to the Catholic Aid Home, where she began her round of applications to the Catholic network, which meant sitting decorously and humbly in the waiting rooms of clerics and nuns. I can smell the chilly air, the furniture polish, the wax candles, the varnish on the pitch-pine wainscoting. I can hear the squeak of her boots on the shining linoleum floors that look as if they have been polished by maids—as they probably had been; nuns always had a supply of orphan girls and simple women to toil in their institutions.

Plaster statues looking impassively down at prie-dieux. Crucifixes with gouts of red blood falling from the nails in Christ's hands. Murmurs from behind high closed doors where fates are being decided. I know those hallways where supplicants like May waited to ask for work, lodging, alms, references, food, intercession with the authorities here on earth and with the Almighty above.

The nuns have the politic gift of making other women long for their approval. May herself, when she invented an idyllic childhood in the first—fantasy—chapter of her autobiography, sent herself to a convent boarding school where she was a rebel but a cherished one. I'm sure that in the presence of the sisters, May sincerely wanted to reform. But they knew better than she. They had the calm of observers rather than participants in the ruck of life; they knew which people would serve their interests and which would not. They knew, even as she twisted her handkerchief in front of them and turned out her empty pockets, that May was a woman on the most relaxed terms with her own flesh and all flesh. They knew that the attraction of discipline would soon wear off.

She went to a priest. *I told him I did not want money from him, just some kind of work, no matter how menial, just enough to let me live decently. He said he was sorry but that kind of help was out of his jurisdiction.* He asked her whether she needed a nickel for the ride home.

The probation service sent her to Saint Elizabeth's Hospital in New Jersey.

An old working-nun with a brogue as Irish as the pigs of Shute Hill took me downstairs to the refectory and I had a good meal of fresh fish, potatoes and good tea. After eating, I started to put on an old dress I had in my bag, to help the waitress.

They sent for me to go upstairs. There were two young, very snippy sisters, dressed in white in the office.

They asked me if I could cook for forty people. I told them that I did not know how to cook but that I would be willing to do any other kind of work. They then told me they had no other work for me to do and that I ought to go home before it got dark. I explained that I had no home and that if I was arrested, no one would believe I was innocent. I also told them no one would believe me if I said Catholic nuns had turned me out into the street, a poor woman with no money for lodging, just out of jail. But I couldn't move them, so I left.

She did not give up, though she gave up on Catholics.

Out from the Brooklyn shore in the lively waters of New York Harbor, where the East River mingles with the ocean in the Buttermilk Channel, there's a low island called Governors Island. One end, where the lawns are shaded by chestnut trees and surrounded by handsome historic houses, is like a fine college campus. The other end is workaday. An old prison converted from a fort, a horrible place of stone blocks and rusting iron doors, stands near a hospital which in 1917 was called the Soldiers and Airmen Hospital. May got herself a job there. It was an unpaid job, but it provided board and accommodation. She worked as a kind of nurse, which must have perfectly suited the aspects of her personality that were jovial and entirely unsqueamish.

Out in the clean breezes of the island, she had an excellent chance to recover herself. Her instinct had placed her exactly where she could best learn how to manage Manhattan—apart from it, and safe, but not five minutes by ferry from its teeming streets.

Because she needed to learn how to be in the world. What had been a dizzyingly irresponsible and chaotic metropolis when she left in 1900 was now the major city of a nation at war, and one that was about to attempt to reform itself through Prohibition. She needed to learn this mood. She needed to learn how to hurry, preoccupied, from one place to another, how to make a cup of coffee for herself, how to look at a man without catching his eye. Horses had almost disappeared: she needed to learn how to cross a street crowded with motor traffic. She had to come to terms with things—jars of mustard, paper towels, brassieres, the spacious interiors of cars. And connected with this, there were new manners to be learned. The Americans around May would have been sweeter than she. It would take a while for her to trust that she could eat slowly and leave some of her food, that there'd be no punishment for waste. Deprivation makes you wolfish; abundance helps you to be gentle.

The prisoners in Aylesbury used to peer from their cells at women visitors and tut-tut at the new fashions—shortened skirts, loose bodices, short hair. On Governors Island, May could have practiced dressing like that, stifling her giggles so that nobody would hear her. She could have begun to estimate, through listening to the people around and watching them, how not just women's clothes and bodies but women's whole presence in public life had changed. If she had been allowed to stay on the island, she might have turned in time into a decent, wide-hipped woman, competent, if slapdash, at her nursing chores—a woman who sometimes suddenly lost her temper or went off into a fugue of paranoia but otherwise never betrayed the extremes of experience that had left deep marks on her being.

But "Chicago May" caught up with May.

I went up on the roof with the nurses and volunteers and one of the doctors made a group photograph of us. In a couple of days they called me into the office, paid me the few dollars that were coming to me and told me I had a nerve to crash in there. Perhaps someone saw my rogues gallery picture and recognized me in the snapshot. I don't believe it was the police. It might have been a stool pigeon.

She cried in her room from despair. The woman next door heard her and sent her to an address on the Upper West Side where she could lodge temporarily with her daughter. So May left her healing island. She had fourteen dollars in the world. But on the way to her new place, a pickpocket on the bus lifted her ten-dollar bill. So when she began again, she had four dollars.

I couldn't help but laugh, she wrote, *to think of me being nicked.*

WAS THERE any other path she could have taken? Could she have gone home, for instance? A family will usually take in even its most deviant member if he or she is truly broken—if she can be shown to the community, as she wanders the lanes of her birthplace, to have been made so vacant by life as to be harmless. I heard it said in Edenmore that when May went back that one time after Montpellier, she arranged to have a room built onto her brother's house—as many emigrant women fearing a lonely old age in America did. I went to see the remains of what is said to be that house, which is used as a farm building now. Vistas of quiet fields open out on both sides, but the place itself is set back a distance from the road and it gives the impression of being half buried. All I could make out was a high stone wall, a rain barrel, something straggling—hydrangeas, maybe—in a strip of grass in front. I could not imagine her taking up hermitlike residence in that spot. Not only because ten years in an English jail for attempted murder was too great a disgrace to bring back to Edenmore, not only because there were practical impediments, such as not having the price of a ticket to Ireland and not legally being allowed to go there. But because dwarfing the low buildings was a huge gray sky, indescribably oppressive. May couldn't have lived under that dull sky.

She had no fixed address and—to put it mildly—she had no references. But though the Catholic convents in New York turned her away, perhaps some other institution would have given her refuge. She could have been the pale lady who sits in her cubicle beside her bed—neatly made by regulation before seven a.m.—a book open on her lap, who after some months is trusted with a key to the canteen kitchen so that she can slip down and make a cup of tea at a time of her own choosing—not that she had the money to buy even one cookie to dip into the tea. She could in time have been given a function—been appointed, for instance, to answer the bell of the heavy front door. But even if the management of the charitable institution paid her a few dollars a week, she would not have been free. Nobody in the institution would have wanted from her what she still had to give—the use of her body, and what was left of her spirit. She'd have had no leverage, no hope of exercising power. She'd have been broken, at last.

There was a young man living in the room next door to her lodging on the Upper West Side. *He took me out to supper one night and believe me I was glad to get a big square meal.*

Soon, she moved in with him. Of course she did. What could possibly have made her not choose whatever caresses she could get, whatever company, whatever protection after so many years of deprivation?

But now she has to keep herself in the style of a woman who has a man.

I became bad again.

IT WASN'T as easy as it used to be. The Manhattan streets in her heyday had been thronged with women offering themselves for sale to married men with pure wives. But I saw it estimated in a history of prostitution that between 1900 and 1909—in just that one decade—sex with prostitutes in New York decreased by 50 percent. Men had just as much sex, no doubt, but with girlfriends and fiancées. I presume that condoms were becoming widely available.

Streetwalkers like May were largely a thing of the past, if only because the telephone and the automobile had taken a lot of prostitution off the streets. Selling her own body was not now the venture of an individual woman; prostitution was becoming an industry, controlled by pimps and other criminals. And the locales of prostitution had changed since May was last at work. Timothy J. Gilfoyle in his book *City of Eros* shows that in Manhattan in the 1890s, there were twenty-four "panel houses"—houses where an accomplice stole a man's valuables by sliding back a panel and getting into the room where the man was having sex. After 1900, there were no panel houses. Old-fashioned brothels, too, had all but disappeared. When May went back on the game, there were only two brothels in Manhattan but there were seventy-seven "tenements," which I suppose are houses controlled at a remove by men, where prostitutes had rooms.

The police, too, in 1917, were nothing like as tolerant as they had been when they themselves half-belonged to the underworld.

But there is always demand, and May still had skills.

The first touch I made in New York after my ten-year bit in England was that of an old man in the park, near Madison Avenue.

She only got thirty dollars out of that.

But her second attempt was just like it used to be—raucous, half comic.

He was a hotel proprietor with a beautiful home in Harlem. He told me to say to his housekeeper that I was his niece. When we went into the house the worthy lady saluted him with a punch on the nose.

She said to me, "Madam, you look different from what he usually brings in. I know you are not to blame."

He hit her and I went to the poor woman's assistance. In pulling him away from her I yanked the pocketbook out of his back pocket. On my way out, I picked up two gold watches which were lying on a table. The lady told me to send in the police, which I did not. In the leather was one hundred and fifty dollars and one of the watches was no good. From then on, I worked at the old rackets and felt that my nerve was still good.

She got the bus out to Newark—to start again, perhaps, at a distance from the old Irish-American cops who had tried to help her. She rented a room there and *within an hour I dropped into the backroom of a saloon in Payne Street and relieved an old bozo of a hundred dollars. Then I beat it, and got a few drinks and a swell meal.*

"And so to bed," as Sam Pepys says, "and fair contentment with a day's work."

The quotation came, I suppose—the only good thing to come—from prison, from the reading she did there to save her sanity.

PART FIVE

1917 to 1929

Nine

Downward to Detroit

The man next door took her out for supper.

So began the relationship with Avery—sometimes known as Kelly—that was like a continuation of the sufferings of prison, but which May clung to as fiercely as an institutionalized inmate clings to prison.

She had lost her nerve. For example, in the move to the apartment the two of them were going to share, a twenty-dollar bill of Avery's went missing. *I was upset and nearly fainted. What would Avery think, knowing about my past? Would he think I had stolen the money and gypped him? Would I lose my protector? I went to the phone, crying, and told him all about it. He reassured me, said there must be some mistake and ultimately straightened out the whole affair, leaving me clear of all blame. I could have wept for joy.*

She had no money and no possessions. Out in the world, her legend lived on. The English poetaster and satanist Alastair Crowley wrote—and offered for sale on condition that it was kept under lock and key for fifty years—an immensely long poem which was an outpouring of fascinated disgust at a woman's body, and he called his monstrous seductress "Chicago May": "The great sow snores, / Blowing out spittle through her blubber lips, / Champagne and lust still oozing from the pores, / Of her fat flanks. . . ." Meanwhile, the real May was pathetic. She says that Avery *got me a winter coat and promised to take me downtown in a few weeks and get me a winter hat*. She could hardly have had lower expectations.

Her looks, of course, were not what they once were. Eddie Guerin says in *I Was a Bandit* that when Lord Rothschild, whose mansion was near Aylesbury, used to visit the jail, May would "tone down the somewhat muddy color of her skin by a judicious application of whitewash from the walls of her cell." He meant to sneer at her, but there was nothing indulgent about May's relationship with her looks. They had been her capital. They were her tutelary presences, giving her the confidence to run away from home and from then on allowing her such independence as came from being able to earn her living. They were her mint, coining money for her every time a man followed her to a room. They were her accomplices, every time they and she persuaded a man, scrutinizing her face, that she was telling the truth. And now they were deserting her. The statistics were recorded on Ellis Island. The color of her hair when she arrived there was gray. She weighed 160 pounds after they fed her for a few weeks—heavy for her height of five-foot-six. She gave her age as forty-one, but in 1917 she was really forty-six. The menopause must have been doing to her whatever it does to a woman whose reproductive organs are scarred and slack from years of inviting and then preventing conception.

She so badly needed someone to care for her that the newspaper cutting in the Pinkerton archive comes as a sad shock.

Chicago May, Notorious International Criminal,
Is Nabbed for Stealing a Dog

May Churchill is known to the police of two continents. She is a powerfully built woman of typical Irish type and speaks with a smooth dialect of Erin's Isle. When she faced the court she was neatly dressed and wore a broad grin.

Detective Fitzgerald, of the Fourth Branch Bureau, told the circumstances of her latest arrest. He said she broke into the apartment of Mrs. Lillian Avery at 1459 Amsterdam Ave. on Friday morning and departed with an English bull terrier, the property of Mrs. Avery's husband.

Mrs. Avery and her husband separated about three years ago and Avery, who had been living with "Diamond May" during that time recently returned to his own wife.

He owns the terrier and while living with May, the dog was sheltered in "Chicago May's" home at 105 W. 129th St. When Avery returned to his wife he took the pet with him, causing "Diamond May" much grief and disappointment.

When asked by the judge if she would return the canine, "Chicago May" said she would. The defendant was then released from custody.

The shock is that Avery had a wife, and went back to her very soon after he and May got together—the date on the newspaper story is April 16, 1918.

But this was only the first episode in a saga of jealousy. Stealing the dog was nothing compared with the next thing that got into a newspaper. On March 5, 1919, the *Daily Post* reported:

a woman calling herself Mrs. James Montague Sharp was charged with having fired a shot at William Avery and owning a deadly weapon without a permit. May took a wing shot at

William Avery, the shot being fired as a slight mark of protest because stories had reached her that Bill was lavishing attentions upon another lady. His feelings were so injured that he gave testimony against May, which was chiefly responsible for her not being discharged when she was held for violation of the Sullivan law.

She answered Guilty when arraigned in court and was patiently awaiting sentence as Mrs. Sharp yesterday when Denny Murtha brought to light the fact that Mrs. Sharp was a regular *Who's Who*. Mrs. Sharp having no place to go while awaiting sentence was sitting in her cell yesterday when Keeper Denny Murtha of the Tombs happened to wander by. Denny stopped short.

"Well, if it ain't Chicago May!" cried Denny.

And sure enough seated in the cell were May Churchill, May Wilson, Diamond May, May Avery, and Chicago May. The Tombs had thought it was merely housing an Upper West Side lady who recently had had an outbreak of temper, a running target and a gun.

I don't know which is the worse aspect of this—that May has had recourse to a gun again, or that Avery testified against her. Though there's a gleam of amusement at May's way with names; when did she confer that upper-class "Montague" on herself?

The fact that jealousy makes a person grotesque doesn't matter to the jealous person, who is in as much pain as if she were being burnt alive—who *is* being burnt alive on a pyre of insecurity and self-hatred. I remember—with awe—how a primeval fear of abandonment seems to take up residence and to be physically alive in the heart, gnawing on it like an animal. May never knew jealousy when she was a big, confident blonde with a fifty-dollar bill in her garter, but now she is an aging woman who for much of the last decade has barely staved off breakdown. She must have been painfully baffled by Avery's hold over her—Freud had been publishing since 1900, but his ideas had not yet filtered down into the kind of popular self-analysis that at least gave people words with which to describe themselves and their relationships. But she doesn't deceive herself. She never speaks of love. She doesn't say that Avery was handsome, like the bandit Dal Churchill, or a leader among his peers, as she thought Eddie Guerin was when she met him, still less instantly devoted like Charley Smith, in prison in England. She never uses Avery's first name.

Thoughts of the liaison with him, she wrote, *fill me with disgust for myself.* He's a thug. In James MacNerney's history of May's parish, it is suggested that the Molly Maguires—the secret society that tried to protect Irish miners in Pennsylvania—was started by men from Dromard, a village four or five miles from May's childhood home. Now she's clinging to a man who worked—one of the few times he did work—as a professional strikebreaker around those same anthracite mines. He was part, May writes, of *a wrecking-crew, armed to the teeth. If the poor miners opened their mouths, they were blackjacked. As a result of this rotten work, Avery got a scar on his nose and his cheek*—an Irishwoman, she says, threw a rock at him when he was evicting her family from a miner's shack in Pennsylvania.

May recognizes her own complicity. *He was a confirmed procurer and I was his willing slave, though I complained and got to have less and less respect for him as time went on. One of his women had an illegitimate child, a little girl, he boasted he was going to educate. The poor baby was born in a sporting-house in Albany, and no one knew who its father was.*

She is giving witness from the lower depths, not processing it through explanation or apology or repentance—a rare thing in autobiography, especially for the time. She draws no conclusions. Her staccato recitation of events is her only judgment on her years with Avery.

At this time I went out stealing and he was sharing the proceeds with me. [Her criminal record begins: New York City, May 24, 1918;

burglary, discharged.] . . . *I walked out; I got another apartment. It was not long before Avery phoned me at the new place. He told me to draw a hundred dollars from my account in the Post Office and to dress myself better. He used the money for his own purposes.* [New York City, August 1, 1918; vagrancy, sentenced to five days in work-house.] He beats her up with a blackjack and gets ninety days, and while he's in jail, he sends her word *to send him a little money so that he could buy smokes. Would you believe it, I did so! I knew what it was to suffer in prison, and I did not have the heart to refuse.* He lets her take the rap for something he's done, and she serves a sentence for him. [New York City; petit larceny, sentenced to Blackwell's Island Penitentiary, Court of Special Sessions.]

Around 1920, she's paroled on condition she leave the state of New York, so the record ends because in other states she used aliases now irrecoverable. Her wandering years begin in Weehawken, New Jersey, where she bought Avery a shebeen—an illegal drinking-den—at the jetty where the ferrymen drank, across from Manhattan. Think how hard she must have worked, how many men she must have had to handle, to earn enough money to buy a shebeen. But—and how many women have made this complaint?—he went out every morning after breakfast and she didn't know where he was all day. The simple words don't capture the hours, the days, of anguished suspicion.

Avery made money, then he lost money. He did this and that. Meanwhile, she traveled up and down the East Coast in search of suckers: Boston; Newark, New Jersey; Portland and Old Orchard, Maine; Cleveland; Erie, Pennsylvania. She's like any other jobbing laborer. It is now, it seems to me, that she really becomes an American—no longer a girl kept on the special reservation of a red-light district, but a worker, going about her business in streets and lobbies and furnished apartments she has reconnoitered for herself. She has put together her own professional whore's and thief's map and calendar. She knows the train timetables as well as any businessman and sits in compartments brooding about Avery as the dark fields and the lights of farmhouses pass by—so I imagine. And then she has to arrive in some town, pull herself together, lift her bag, and walk down the steps to begin her boring, alienating, uncomfortable, dirty, and dangerous work.

It was a gallant life in its way, and extremely lonely. But—*I stuck by Avery and worked for him,* she says, and any work is bearable if it's done to support the relationship that seems to make being alive worthwhile.

And it is worth asking—*was* the relationship with Avery nothing but destructive? Remember that back in Edenmore, May's brothers and her sister have children who are adults by now. Avery wasn't just "the man next door": the key word is that he was the "young" man next door. May is a childless woman. Avery may not have been merely the boyfriend over whom a middle-aged woman was frantically jealous, he may have been the nearest she ever had to a son, and she the kind of mother I've seen standing in the street calling after a sullen boy, oblivious to the display she is making of herself, the tears running down her cheeks. *If only,* May said about her Aylesbury cell, *I could have had some sort of an animal to care for and love.* She has had no experience of cherishing or being cherished, and she doesn't know how to attach Avery to herself except by throwing scenes and giving him things. But maybe what she most deeply wanted was to look after him. And maybe that was what kept him with her. After all, a typical anecdote of May's from that time ends, *I was told that he had gone east with a girl who was described to me. I checked into the Fort Pitt Hotel as soon as I landed in Pittsburgh and took a taxi and went out to the motor-terminal for western motors. He was alone, but I hit him in the eye just the same.* There must have been some reward for him, too, in a life with this demanding, aggressive woman, and it might not only have been that she was a meal ticket. He was in need, too, after all. He was imprisoned in the lower depths of society, too, blocked from fulfilling whatever his potential might be by being unskilled and uneducated.

He didn't mind writing to me and asking me for money, she wrote in one place, and *all the time I used to send him enough to live on,* in another. She mentions that he got a venereal disease and *after he left the hospital, he had the nerve to ask me if he could come to my apartment. As he was down-and-out sick and penniless, I told him to come on.* Another time, *when he was in jail once, I sent him a hundred and eighty dollars and put another hundred dollars in the Post Office in his name in case I got into trouble and could not help him when he got out.*

Is all that not maternal?

And maybe May's instincts were sound when she made Avery the center of her life. A bad relationship is dramatically full of immediate losses and gains, and May was always one for the short-term effect. And the only man who allows you to forgive him over and over like an errant child and whom you can consciously take back into your favor, as a mother does, is a bad man.

IN THE COURSE of her work, in 1922—that is, five years after she got out of Aylesbury—May happened to be in Philadelphia.

All I had was a tailored suit and some furs. I picked up a couple of men and robbed them the first night, so I had enough to rent a room and get something to eat. Then I started to work at my trade.

Imagine it! She lived so close to the edge that she couldn't even have food or shelter until she'd turned a few tricks. Perhaps she was trawling for custom—looking at, say, the jewelry in a display case at the entrance to a hotel, hoping to see in the glass a sucker approaching from behind—when she was distracted by the noise of a band and shouting and cheering. . . .

The immense popularity of the Countess Markievicz brought her to prominence in the first—largely aspirational—parliament of an Irish Republic, and she was made Minister for Labour. But Irish republicanism split on the issue of whether to accommodate with England or to continue the war of independence, and the split degenerated into civil war. Constance was an extremist, as converts are apt to be, and she allied herself with the more uncompromising faction—which was on the losing side in the 1920s, in Ireland itself. But it was the one that much of Irish-America, distant as it was from the immediate situation, supported. Constance's party sent her on a fund-raising trip to the States, and both as the only survivor of the Easter Rising executions and in her own right, she was welcomed like royalty everywhere she went.

Her path crossed May's in Philadelphia, in the Bellevue-Stratford hotel.

As soon as her eye lit on me, May said, *she left the people she was talking to and ran over to me and kissed me. We had quite a long chat, to the amazement of the swells, who did not know who I was.*

I've visited the site of this poignant reunion. The foyer of the Bellevue-Stratford had a vaulted ceiling lavishly decorated with gold leaf and that's still there, though the space below is a shopping arcade now. Back then, there were small tables and sofas and wing chairs in the lobby, and I wondered whether the hotel managers allowed May to sit there in the evenings—they must have had some policy about women whose work was picking up men. If they were Irish, they might have turned a blind eye as long as she was very discreet. But she was probably barred, and had to shout from the door to get the Countess to notice her.

May says that the Countess said that she was the same old May, only better, and why had she not come to Ireland to see her, which is exactly the kind of vague, gracious thing the Countess would have said. Then, they parted.

The Countess was to be escorted to church the following day in her green cloak by five hundred Irish Volunteers in full uniform. When she was, she "was greeted everywhere by enthusiastic crowds," one of the newspapers wrote. "Several pipe bands led her into Mass in the Cathedral but such was the crush of people thronging to see the famous Irish patriot that many were unable to gain entry to Saint Finian's."

The report also says that the evening before—the evening she must have met May—she was mobbed outside the banqueting hall where, at "a private dinner with the Ancient Order of Hibernians, attended by the Mayor and by Archbishop Moran, $50,000 dollars was pledged to the cause of a Republic for Ireland."

Fifty thousand dollars. I know that May hero-worshipped the Countess and would never have compared their fates. But I can do it for her. At that time, in downtown Philadelphia, the going rate for the use of a streetwalker's body, such as this patriotic Irishwoman's body, was four dollars.

THOUGHTS OF my brother Dermot often came into my mind as I followed May through her life. When she ran out of money as a new immigrant in America, I remembered his bewilderment and fear as a boy when he was packed off to England. I thought of him when May was in jail. He was arrested various times—for possession of marijuana, usually—and I have memories of his face with the paneling of various courtrooms behind it, and of him coming through a door into a remand center visiting room, unnaturally pale and tidy, his eyes somber, his mouth trembling. When he grew up, he did his best to overcome the lack of love in his childhood and the influence of his alcoholic mother, and he did hold down jobs for years. But addiction crept up on him, and his dealings with other people were dominated by it. He came to my mind again when I contemplated the length of time May and Avery were together—which was eight years, by far the longest relationship of May's life. Dermot was inseparable for much the same length of time from a woman who was also an addict. He was as angry with her as he should have been with his parents, and he assaulted her often and she retaliated in every way she could—not that either of them, usually, could remember the details of who had done what to whom. Yet they made attempts, over and over, to stop drinking. And they didn't want to leave each other. Who knows, ever, the secrets of a couple—the infantile language allowed in the night, the sympathy shown in illness, the shared love for a child or an animal?

But toward the end there was such aggression between Dermot and the woman that a court ordered him to stay away from her.

"He won't," someone who knew him well said to me on our way out of the courtroom. "He'll go on seeing her. He can't do without her. Who else *knows* him?"

And that must be true of many relationships that make no sense to the onlooker. There is an extraordinary intimacy between the couple in an abusive relationship precisely because the worst about themselves is known. They have abandoned themselves to vulnerability. May was *known* in this relationship of her decline as she had never been or wanted to be when she strode the red-light districts of the first world, the very picture of somebody who didn't need anybody.

AS PROHIBITION took hold, Detroit became the most rip-roaring city in America, and Avery and May were following the crowd when they moved there in 1924. *The New York Times* described the people of Detroit at that time as "the most prosperous slice of average humanity that now exists or has ever existed"—I came across the quotation in the library in downtown Detroit that I'd been warned not to walk to by myself. The splendid building was evidence, as were the stately museum across the way and the symphony hall, of the civic largesse of the city that got rich on cars. But I'd seen that a more tragic aspect of the Detroit of May's time had also persisted. I'd just been in a corner store where everyone in the shuffling line to pay the cashier, half hidden behind bulletproof glass, was swaying with drink or drugs. It was as if what flowed between the city Detroit once was and the city it is now was alcohol. The township in Canada that faces Detroit across the river used about nine gallons of liquor a year before Prohibition; it claimed it needed nine hundred thousand cases for "private consumption" one year later. Most of that, I read, joined the product of illicit stills in the thousands and thousands of speakeasies and shebeens that operated in cafés, the back rooms of hotels, upstairs in restaurants, in former bars that had never really closed, and in the basements of houses, in garages, in sheds and shacks up alleys, in the lofts of commercial buildings, and in the back rooms of ice-cream parlors. The lodgings of the men who came into the city to work in car factories were dirty, bare rooms, and in old photographs you see that they are dotted with empty bottles. The men lived in the drinking dens where they could get some kind of food, or a woman, or play a slot machine, or listen to entertainers. Liquor was sold from automobiles parked outside the gates of the factories, for the workers coming off shift. It was sold in shots in schoolyards. The whole population was addicted.

May set Avery up, again, in a shebeen—which she must have paid for with the use of her body pressed against the wall of a saloon or crushed in the backseat of a car or in the shadowy corner of the back porch of a dive. The police department of Detroit was famously corrupt, and Avery, according to May, *just coined money. It went to his head to really earn money of his own, without having a woman hand it to him. Then he started to stage parties where show girls and fairies of all sorts held forth. I told him it was all right to sell booze because everybody was doing it, but I drew the line at filth, vulgarity and degeneracy. He said I was a jealous crank. He would not let me come to the place, because he was afraid I would start something. One night I watched him. He went into a first-floor room. I knocked gently on the door and got into the place. Three girls, stark naked, were drinking and smoking, but I paid no attention to the little bums. They knew no better. I was sore on Avery and I hit him with the butt end of a gun, knocking out two of his teeth and I wish I'd knocked the lot out.*

Whisky pouring from a destroyed still, Detroit, 1929

Still, they stayed together, though they came and went from Detroit as she threw all her energy into trying to control him.

After one of those times away, they returned to the city—she by
train, he driving her car. I think I see her come through the station
that is now fourteen floors of monumental ruin, empty-windowed,
hollow and roofless above boarded-up pillared entrances that were
once as grand as temple gates. Her tawny hair, which had won such
praise for its abundance, is bobbed. The dropped waist, the sash
around the hips that suits the new ideal of a prepubescent girl, cuts
across her poor, tired belly. She looks her age; the boyish clothes of
the flapper era don't suit her generous body the way the high-necked
blouses and flowing skirts of the Golden Age had done.

Avery didn't turn up.

I waited three days, May says. *He had my car, money, jewelry and baggage. He had gained my confidence, because he had not touched a drop since the beginnning of our last stay away.*

As I had only fifty dollars I had to get out of the hotel and get cheap quarters. I thought the baby had been hijacked and thrown in the Detroit river, or maybe arrested, never dreaming that he might have beat it. Along comes a letter from him telling me he has been arrested in Toledo. It was a stall.

She went out and earned money.

As soon as I could manage to get a couple of hundred dollars together I started out to hunt for him. My investigator tracked him to Toledo. He was living in a sporting-house with a twenty-two-year-old girl. Then he married the girl, though he had a wife living in Sheepshead Bay.

I got a gun and started out for revenge.

She raved around the small towns on Lake Erie that the liquor mafia ran, searching for him, she and her gun, like Humbert Humbert going back with murderous intent over the trail of his lost Lolita. The nickname "Chicago May" makes May sound like a brassy, lip-sticked gangster's moll, but she was never that. She was a country woman—tough, but not sophisticated. She and her gun wouldn't have jumped in and out of low-slung automobiles with wire wheels—she'd have trudged on tired feet out of a local train station to make yet another frantic inquiry at the desk of a cheap hotel—not only a woman looking for her false lover but a mother bereaved. Her eyes would be red-rimmed and her hennaed hair gray at its roots. Her bag would have been a burden in the heat, because of the gun. At night she'd have had to keep it at her feet while she went out the back door of taverns with this man or that for a five-minute job. And the beds—I can only imagine her sleeplessness, as she stared up at the ceilings in those towns, in the heat, with the mosquitoes buzzing, and realized that this time Avery had planned it properly. This time he really was gone.

She never did find him.

MAY KNEW DETROIT when she was young, when *there was one gas machine in town and the citizens used to go to the curb to watch it when it ambled by*. But now—she reaches for a metaphor—*the field was ripe for the reaper, but my sun had begun to set.*

What I lacked in youth and energy, however, she adds in her book, *I more than made up in the cunning of experience.* But she wasn't cunning enough. She denies it, and in her autobiography she tries to cover up the next year or so of her life with some vague and evasive stories. But the truth is that after Avery left, she began to sink to the bottom.

She got together with another man for a while—*he was an Italian, this time.* But she doesn't care about anything anymore. *I earned money and I threw it away,* she wrote. *That's all I can say. I bought him a car and a radio set and I opened up a booze joint for him. He wasn't a crook or a brute, but he was stupid. Nothing came good. And I was sick. I was very sick. I was too sick to work.* She continually refers to the pain and weakness she had at this time, but she didn't fight even that. She went to Chicago to have surgery—I think on her kidneys—but whether from recklessness or despair, she didn't turn up for the operation. *I simply loafed around the Windy City and spent the money,* she wrote. *I checked into the Congress Hotel, bought some nice dresses, and bummed around the night clubs and resorts until the money was gone.* I sat in a corner near the reception desk in the Congress Hotel myself and watched women of today, in town to have a good time, as they came and went carrying parcels, bright-eyed and laughing. Maybe that was all she was doing—seizing the day, in the hope that tomorrow would take care of itself. But every so often, I'm sure, she had to slip away to the ladies' room to close her eyes and hold her stomach, and came out with fresh lipstick on but with beads of sweat still wetting her hairline.

When I came back he was sore because I had not done as promised. We had a fight so I took five hundred dollars and opened a nice apartment with another girl.

That's the end of the Italian.

I don't believe it about the nice apartment. Or the girl. May wasn't to know it, but her words now can be checked against her record.

One Sunday morning, she wrote, *I went to the drug store for medicine and for some reason a couple of cops pulled me in for soliciting which I was not doing.* But she was. She was a streetwalker now, because what else could she be? At her age, she had no chance of being employed by a "house." She's keeping going, like every stoic woman I've ever known—cleaning women, always borrowing on next week's wages; singers, with cracked voices and old faces under their makeup and thin hair under their wigs. Women who have no choice but to grimly pace the confines of their circumstances. May's work was hard and she was sick, and if there hadn't been a huge surplus of men in Detroit she couldn't have made a living. The working girls who today tout for custom on the sliproads of the expressway wear boots, but still, because they have to display themselves to the men driving by, their skin has a blue sheen from cold. They have their drugs to keep them going. But what did she have? She was out on the streets in her mid-fifties in all weathers. Avery took her furs. It rained on her, and she stood around in icy fogs, and she picked her way across hard snow, and hailstones sometimes pitted her cheeks. In summer, how did she— now permanently in some pain—endure the baking heat of the streets?

Her downward slide becomes a rout.

Aug. 25, 1925; Detroit, Michigan; accosting, discharged by
    Superintendent.
Sept. 7, 1925; Detroit, Michigan; common prostitute, fined $39
    or thirty days in jail.

Oct. 3, 1925; Detroit, Michigan; disorderly person, discharged by
Superintendent.

Oct. 30, 1925; Detroit, Michigan; disorderly person, discharged
by Superintendent.

Nov. 22, 1925; Detroit, Michigan; disorderly person, discharged
by Superintendent.

See how close together the dates of the arrests are. And think of
what each of the arrests must have involved. What does the word
"disorderly" mean? It means angry. Drunk. The old Irish woman
causing trouble again.

In the spring of 1926, she was picked up by *a young dick who
stopped me—I was talking when he walked past me and he heard my
accent and he came back. He accused me of being Irish, which I
promptly admitted and added that I was proud of it—*on suspicion
of an immigration offense. There was nothing to the charge, but the
publicity it attracted meant the Detroit authorities discovered her
identity. There was a warrant out for violation of probation, and the
next time she was picked up she was going to be in real trouble.

And she was soon picked up.

*I was too sick to work. One Sunday morning I went to the drug-
store in the 2nd Boulevard to get some medicine. A car drove up with
two rumrunners from New York. They knew me simply as a girl who
knocked about, not as Chicago May. They were driving my way and
gave me a friendly lift. The car was full of all kinds of booze.*

One Sunday morning, in other words, she was out on the street
hoping to pick up a man or a couple of men.

*Up came a law car, stopped us, and asked the boys if I had solicited
them. They had guilty consciences and became frightened. Seeing this,
I tried to make a getaway. The cops ran after me, and caught me.*

The final entry of the criminal record of May Duignan from
Edenmore, as furnished by the Department of Criminal Affairs,
Washington, D.C., is

Aug. 8, 1926; Detroit, Michigan; violation Act 231, Section 1, sentenced to sixty days in Detroit House of Correction.

May dreaded the House of Correction because, she says, *white and black lay down together* on the straw mattresses in the basement there. On the lowest rung of society, where she was clinging, color was the only advantage she had. She was afraid, too, of dying of exposure there—as, she said, the bandit Loretta Lee had done. In the dim microfilm annex of the Detroit Public Library, I found a trace of Loretta Lee. May was correct. She died at night in the House of Correction in that year, 1926.

May would not share with the black women, so it was *after a sleepless night that along came a matron and told me I was going to work in the laundry. I told her I was not going to work, but was going out as soon as my lawyer arrived. She told me I would have to do as I was told. I explained that I was sick and told her she could have me examined to prove whether or no I was telling the truth. She simply said, "Sick or not, you are going to work in the laundry or go to the dungeon!"*

The dungeon—a place of special punishment hollowed out beneath the basement in which the women prisoners slept—was literally as well as metaphorically as low as a prisoner could go. *Sure enough, they took me to the dungeon. I laid down on the flags and fell asleep from exhaustion.*

And there, on the stone floor, she reached the bottom. It is hard to imagine anyone with more of a past, and less of a future.

YET THERE WAS even a little further downward for her to go. There was rock bottom.

She must have hemorrhaged or shown some other alarming signs, because she was rushed from the House of Correction to the hospital in the county jail, where she had an emergency operation, though she was not expected to live. In fact, the *Detroit News* printed a kind of obituary that begins, "The old woman lying in the Detroit hospital, her face streaked with the toll of dissipation and prison walls, was born of a good family in Ireland."

My vitality was at a low ebb, she wrote herself. *I had little hope of pulling through but I still had the will to live. I saw neither priest nor parson for I feared a bad judge more than I did God. They strapped me on an operating table, gave me an anesthetic and I remembered no more for about ten hours. The coming back was worse than the going out. The first thing I remember was a nurse remonstrating with me for pulling off a towel and leggings, trying to toss them on the floor. My condition was good for a few days, and then I had a relapse. Then came the struggle with death. When I felt I was slipping I would tell them, and they and I fought off the enemy. The doctors and nurses were wonderful, particularly a good looking one.*

Near death though she was, she was chained to the hospital bed. She was, after all, a criminal.

In folktales, the lowest point is never the end of the story. Angels, when all is lost, hover near—for Jane Eyre collapsed in the heather of the desolate moor, and Hansel and Gretel asleep on the forest floor, and Fidelio abandoning hope in his prison cell.

Salvation approaches for May, too.

SHE DID COME BACK from the very edge of life. So it isn't fanciful to imagine her, even with her wrists bound, as very peaceful, her eyes resting on a languid fan that turns and stops and turns beneath the wooden ceiling, then closing of their own heaviness. The ward would have been quiet compared to the rest of the jail, and since it was late summer, perhaps in the afternoons the porter for the promise of a tip wheeled her bed out to a verandah and lined it up facing whatever bushes grew in the yard. I imagine the muted noises of the back streets coming over the wall, and in the evening, around seven or eight o'clock, dying away, and the night nurses when they came on duty leaving May alone for a while as dusk gathered.

UNTIL, ONE DAY—as if where she lay were a magic crossroads— narratives from three separate parts of the American experience intersected at May's bed.

These are the three.

The legend of the woman called Etta Place, who was the Sundance Kid's girlfriend and who was last seen in 1909, in Bolivia, at the ambush where the Kid and Butch Cassidy were killed.

The young film industry based in Hollywood, California.

The progressive police department of Berkeley, farther north in California, known worldwide at the time for what it had achieved under its innovative chief, August Vollmer.

The three combine to shape the fate of May Duignan from Edenmore.

When the outlaws Butch Cassidy and the Sundance Kid were finally killed in a shoot-out in Bolivia, they were with Etta Place, who was the Kid's girlfriend. She escaped, but no one knew to where.

In the 1920s, the early Hollywood movie industry was looking around for stories involving bandits and romance, such as Etta Place's. There was a playwright in Hollywood by the name of Elmer Harris who was an associate of Cecil B. DeMille's. Early in 1927, Elmer Harris heard that Etta Place had turned up in the hospital of Wayne County jail. That was where May was—Harris's informant must have confused the two once famous outlaw women.

Harris was friendly with August Vollmer, who had turned the police department of Berkeley into the most admired department, not only in the States but in the world. Vollmer was a maker of modern America, with his vision of police officers as professionals with an honorable place in the community. He paid his men well enough to be able to resist graft, he put them in uniform, he worked out a career

The Sundance Kid and his girlfriend, Etta Place, 1902

structure for them, he pioneered the use of a fleet of police vehicles and radios, and reformed the administration of police work. He was a pioneer forensic scientist, too, the inventor of the polygraph machine, an early expert on traffic control, a creator of systems, like the bureau of records that he was influential in setting up in Washington, and a gifted teacher—he set up the first ever criminology curriculum. But his real originality was to concern himself as much with the overall quality of civic life as with crime. He believed that policemen should be, in part, social workers. He promoted, for example, the view that the best way to handle professional criminals was not to continually incarcerate them but to "kill them with kindness"—to look at the conditions of their lives and try to change the conditions.

When Vollmer was coming to the end of his time in Berkeley, he was solicited as a consultant by cities all over the world. Cities with corrupt or chaotic police departments, especially, vied to have him address himself to their reform. Around the end of 1926, he finished a reorganization of the police department of Havana. And he moved on to Detroit, where the local chief, who had for many years been in the pocket of bootleggers and gangsters, had at last been instructed to take leave.

When Harris heard that Etta Place was in the jail hospital in Detroit, he contacted Vollmer. So Vollmer set up a visit to the hospital for Harris. And on the day, he went along with Harris.

The door at the far end of the ward must have opened, and loud voices startled the nurse-warders murmuring at a desk and the women half asleep in narrow iron beds under high windows that in those old-fashioned hospitals opened only inward and at the top. The doctor must have marched in as always, boots clicking on the tile of the floor, but this time there'd have been other footsteps, heavy but more tentative, behind his. Maybe May tried to turn her head on its hot pillow to see what was happening—cuffed as she was, she couldn't rise.

She'd have heard the men's voices coming near. Their faces would have come into view above her bed.

Elmer Harris gave her a quick scrutiny and turned away. This one wasn't Etta either.

The doctor would have said something like, I told you, this is the one who used to be Chicago May, and the bustle of the entourage would have retreated toward the door. But—I imagine it this way, and as I do, my lips involuntarily smile—when it seemed that the visitors were gone, a man's footsteps must have been heard again in the silence. They came back down the ward, slow and heavy, as if the person were thinking. They passed all the other beds.

August Vollmer

And then the bespectacled face of August Vollmer must have smiled down at May.

VOLLMER BOTHERED with May for the simple reason that he was a true idealist. Anyone else would have taken it for granted that after an outlaw career of nearly forty years—in which, in spite of spending more than half that time in jail, May always returned to criminality—there was no hope for her. It would have seemed ridiculous, even cruel, to talk about change to as hardened an old lag as she. But Vollmer wrote once, "You can never tell me what a man is able to do, but even though I recommend ten, and nine of them may disappoint me and fail, the tenth one may surprise me. That percentage is good enough for me, because it is in developing people that we make real progress in our own society."

Vollmer suggested to May that instead of going back on the hostile streets, she write her life story.

The wonder here is not only at him, but at May. How was it that she could listen to what Vollmer was saying? It's true that she must have known that she wouldn't last long at her old trade; the operation on her kidneys had not been a complete success and she was still in some pain. And it's true that when she got out of this hospital and then out of jail, she had no person to go to, and there was no money, no family, no friends—none of the normal supports of a life. But I'm sure social workers had already pointed all that out to her. Where fate was, for once, exceedingly kind to May was in sending a senior policeman to say it again. Because the police were not only her lifetime opponents—they were comrades of a kind, too, and in a way, peers. Policemen were just about the only people who impressed May.

Vollmer was *the good-hearted bull,* May wrote, *who showed me one way to make an honest living. He was practical enough to say something more than merely, "Go straight. It doesn't pay. You can't win," et cetera. Accompanying him was Elmer Harris, the moving picture director for Cecil de Mille. They came several times with beautiful flowers. It was the kindness and courtesy of these people, and others, which caused me to make another try to get on the band wagon with most of the people in society.*

Other people, perhaps set up by Vollmer, helped her get started. When she got out of prison, the prosecuting police officer and her social worker pleaded with the judge to give her a chance. A philanthropist undertook to pay for her board and lodging. And *the ladies of a Baptist Church were fighting on my side.* Up to now, she wrote in her book, *it had been the dames who, nine times out of ten, had treated me unfairly and tried to push my head under water*—in other words, respectable women had very understandably not wanted her around. But now *the question of creed, even, made no difference. It did not seem to matter to them when they came to see me every day and brought flowers that I had been a liar, a thief, a badger, a blackmailer and a conwoman. It likewise didn't seem to matter to them when I told them it was incomprehensible to me how criminals could get religion at the end of their careers.*

She set about trying to get a publication interested in her story, and soon moved back East—to Philadelphia—*this time to do a different kind of work than what I had been in the habit of doing.* And she succeeded in getting a journal called the *Weekly American* to take a series of articles about her life.

She paid a visit to New York.

The chief editor of the American *is a grand old man,* she wrote to Vollmer, *who treated me very kindly and sent me a ticket and twenty-five dollars for a pullman and looked after me and believe me I was pretty weak. It was the first time I rode on the elevated railroad. I made it all right. I still go to the hospital—my side is not healed yet. I told the boys they are going to mention you the great criminologist and how you showed me the way to be honest. I hope you will not mind as you sure did help me. I suppose you will say apple sauce.*

Vollmer didn't just encourage her with words. He used his influence to retrieve her criminal record from various jurisdictions, and then "the boys"—her editors at the *Weekly American*—were able to string her story around certain salient dates. That must have started a change in her—it does change a person when the chaos of memory is sorted into some kind of sequence. The journey through life may still not look purposeful, but it does at least resemble a path. Her experience would have seemed more valuable, newly coherent. In the backward perspective, too, fragments of the self begin to come together. Even as crude an author as May had to make herself, for the sake of the story, into a character. And intrinsic to that process is stepping—imperceptibly—away from what was there before.

Even more important, the *Weekly American* paid her very well for the articles—there were ten of them and she got $260 for each. So she had that money to live on while she turned the articles into *Her Story*.

THE AUGUST VOLLMER ARCHIVE is in the Bancroft Library at the University of California at Berkeley. The letters about May's book are scrupulously preserved there, beginning with a letter to Vollmer from Elmer Harris—Vollmer had evidently asked Harris to help May with her project.

"I tried you on the Eddyphone," Harris writes, and he says that he is too busy to help but that he's "of the opinion that if some competent author would interest himself in May's story and would handle it from the standpoint of sociology and psychoanalysis, something outstanding might be made of it." Luckily, this hoary old idea—that a man would do the writing for a woman, and that May would be an exhibit, not a person—was somehow bypassed. From Genoa Street, Detroit, in February 1927, in a lucid, flowing script that is a credit to her Edenmore teachers, May writes to Vollmer to say that she will try to write the book herself because

> I never want to go back to the old life if I can help it but I sure got to live and funds are pretty low.
> Excuse slang
> Yours truly
> May Sharp

This is confidence in herself returning in a massive way, given that it is about forty-five years since such schooling as she got, and that she never mentions reading again after she got out of Aylesbury and never mentions writing at all. Whatever made her think that writing a book was something she could do?

And where did she locate the "self" she might write about? I suppose she thought of her own story as the story of Chicago May, and she had a fair idea of what people expected from that. But even allowing for the fact that those were not introspective times, and that she wouldn't have sensed, except out on the edges of her consciousness, that she'd have to play complex games with self-knowledge, writing an autobiography was a huge task to take on. It is something possible for anyone to do, and something many people think they can do. But very, very few people do it. And why? Because it is truly laborious. Because it asks for a feat of memory retrieval, and the memories that return may still be full of unease and hurt, or simply resistant to words. Because not many people want to be, for the length of time it takes to write even a cursory account of a life, in the company of the simplified self the autobiographer leads through the narrative. "Myself" can easily become an unwanted fellow-traveler, in the way that slightly unreal, slightly insincere people are.

May wasn't completely unaware that she might fail. She said of Vollmer that he *put the bug into my head to at least try to write for a living.*

At least try, she says. In the context of who she is and where she is, those are heroic words.

It helped her to think that she was doing this purely for money—though from the beginning she had an exaggerated idea of how much money she might earn. But the real motives for writing an autobiography, it seems to me, are as deep and dark as an underground river fed by many streams. We can guess that memory was more vivid to May than to most people, because she had lived with nothing else in her years of solitary confinement. And—before Avery—she was proud of herself, and she asserts self-worth again by writing. I wrote my own memoir—though I didn't see this till afterward—in part because my pride was stung by knowing that in the eyes of the world I seemed to amount to nothing. I wanted to say that there was more to me than that. Perhaps May, too, wanted respect. Except that "respect" is not quite the right word for what an autobiographer is seeking: it is more that the forever vociferous ego seeks a listener.

If you have been compellingly attractive, as May had been, and if your name was once on everyone's lips, as hers was, and if you have within the limits of your time and place on the planet lived as willfully as a woman can well live, how can you slip into obscure old age without a protest? Vollmer and May thought they were talking about a practical, moneymaking venture. But the actions of her life said from the very beginning that she thought she was exceptional. Writing about herself gave her a chance to say that again, and get the crowd looking up at her again across the footlights.

I'm sure May meant at the beginning to cheat the task. But though she did have the help of the newspaper articles, the book is far more packed than they are with names and places and details of scams and jokes and opinions and anecdotes and reminiscences and digressions that are hers alone. It is amazing that this book came from where its author had been. What man, haggling a price with a prostitute on a Detroit street corner, would have guessed that in her head she had the hundred thousand words of *Chicago May, Her Story: A Human Document by "The Queen of Crooks"*?

IT WAS a great day for me when I went to read May's letters to Vollmer. It was like the brightness that opened in May's life to find myself on the Berkeley campus, where glossy birds skittered between luscious trees and the sky sang with blue. I'd come from the plainness of the west of Ireland, the stone walls, the biting wind, the marks of poverty. Maybe Vollmer's vision was so generous, I thought, because he lived in a climate as paradisal as this. In the library, May's letters waited in a box. I've seen wonderful things in libraries—a doodle Saint Robert Bellarmine made in a school text, for example, when he was a schoolboy, where the rude caricature of the teacher's face and bulbous nose is wearing a seventeenth-century hat. The manuscript of the Aeolus episode from Joyce's *Ulysses,* covered in the author's thrilling corrections and additions. But that May's letters survived is a most moving thing. She dashed them off—on blue paper with a deckle edge, on pink paper, on stationery engraved with the old-fashioned letterheads of the hotels and lodging houses she lived in as she moved around—and as she did, she brought herself back from the dead.

And brought herself forward, to my time and time to come.

BY JUNE 1927, she's writing to Vollmer, *I have been living in Ocean City for the last five weeks. I am trying hard to get well you really would not know me I have gained in weight 168 pounds I hope to be well in a few months more.*

She moved on to "Pinehurst, In the Poconos, Electric Lights, A Home-like House"—a Quaker lodging house, since converted to apartments. She must in that austere atmosphere have been working on the chapter about Eddie Guerin—*Guerin—of course you know that he was the cause of all my trouble?* a letter from there says. In July, from the Spruce Hotel in Philadelphia, she tells Vollmer that one of the matrons from the jail wants to come and stay with her—her old charm must have been blossoming again. The matron tries to shame May into sending her the fare by pointing out that May's medical care cost Detroit a lot of money, but May doesn't lose her good humor. *She is a very fine woman as a jail matron but no use to me,* she writes. *I do not need a chaperone.*

In the next letter, her joy at the direction that her life has taken bursts out.

I look wonderful, she writes. *I take the best care of myself.*

Copies of Vollmer's replies to May are also in the file, and they are continually encouraging.

"Your story is full of romance," he wrote, "and also has the additional attractiveness in that you are dealing with facts not fiction."

And when in January 1928, the Philadelphia police found out that May was in town and told her to get out, we hear his sensible voice again. "Dear friend," the great man writes to her,

> you will find the road that you are now traveling the hardest that you have ever traveled in all your existence. Nobody can beat it back or attempt to beat it back without finding all sorts of obstacles in the way; and as long as you live, you are going to be hurt from time to time. But if you let them whip you, you will have a yellow streak in you—and I don't think you have.

He writes again,

> Don't forget that old English coster song, "I Laugh When I Think How I Cried about You." There is a good deal of sound philosophy in that song and when one can get far enough away from his troubles they don't seem large at all.

May goes to the chief of police in Philadelphia and the chief calls the cops off. But all the same, May takes off across America as if she's on the run. And since she doesn't need to do that, I think that she was responding to a deep impulse to cover America, to equate her discovery of the shape and value in her own life with a discovery of the great continent. *Excuse writing, train going fast,* her next letter begins.

May forges ahead with her writing. *I am going to get Jack Black's book to see how he put it, I mean the style,* she writes to Vollmer— endearing herself to me by adding, *I really do not know how to express myself.*

But Vollmer reassures her again. The series of articles about her life has just appeared in the *Weekly American,* and Vollmer tells May, "You are a front-page author now, whether you are able to write or not, and all you need is some person who can take your stuff and put it into readable form and these people are generally found in every city."

For the next couple of months she keeps writing and keeps moving. She writes in Albuquerque, New Mexico, for example, where she arrived *after much hardship. The bus broke down and I walked eight miles down the raccoon pass.* Picture that—a woman who's nearer sixty than fifty, walking down a road between foothills of sage and cactus, pages covered in her big handwriting weighing down the bag whose contents, at this time, are her entire home.

She passes a milestone in the Hall Hotel, Denver—"Denver's Most Economical *Good* Hotel, A Pleasant Place to Make Your Home"—when she sends Vollmer a progress report. *I have six chapters of my book ready.*

Eventually, she wants to negotiate a contract for the book and finds a lawyer who'll do it for her—*Mr. Henry John Nelson is a Quaker so he will not lie,* she says when she asks Vollmer for a reference to give to him.

Vollmer's splendid reference is copied in the folder in the Bancroft Library.

Mrs. Sharp has asked me to express to you my opinion regarding her desire to go straight and her ability to do so. Let me say this: this woman has the fighting qualities that make her very dangerous or very good. If she desires to go straight there is nothing in the world will stop her from traveling that path. On the other hand, as you know from her history, when she decided to go wrong the hangman's noose and penitentiary and all the rest of the bugbears didn't deter her from going in that direction. There is nothing of the psychopathic nature in Mrs. Sharp's makeup; she is one of the truly professional class of criminals who entered the game knowing that in many instances they were able to outwit the officials and that it was a very easy life which paid well if they were not caught. She gambled with her liberty and lost it on many occasions. But I am convinced that this woman is now determined to go straight if the world will let her.

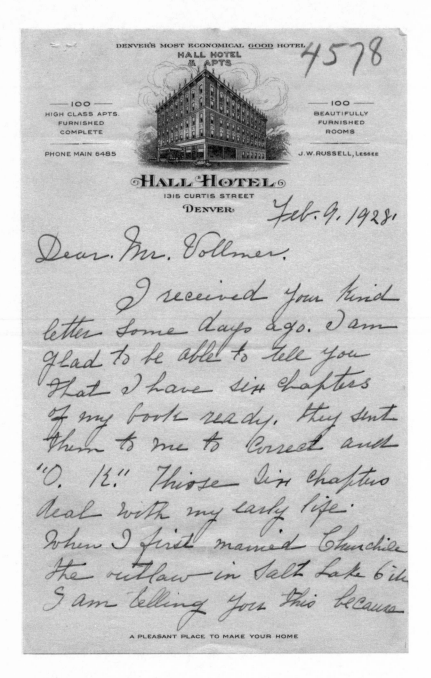

DENVER'S MOST ECONOMICAL GOOD HOTEL
HALL HOTEL
& APTS

— 100 —
HIGH CLASS APTS.
FURNISHED
COMPLETE

— 100 —
BEAUTIFULLY
FURNISHED
ROOMS

PHONE MAIN 6485

J. W. RUSSELL, Lessee

HALL HOTEL
1315 CURTIS STREET
DENVER

Feb. 9. 1928.

Dear. Mr. Vollmer,

I received your kind
letter some days ago. I am
glad to be able to tell you
that I have six chapters
of my book ready. they sent
them to me to correct and
"O. K." those six chapters
deal with my early life.
When I first married Churchill
the outlaw in Salt Lake City
I am telling you this because

A PLEASANT PLACE TO MAKE YOUR HOME

". . . I have six chapters of my book ready."

At times, now, May grumbles like a seasoned author. *I just received a letter from Boni & Liveright publisher asking for the manuscript. I also had a letter from Putnam's in NY asking for a manuscript. It is tough when the publishers want your stuff and one cannot prepare it. Though they will pull it to pieces themselves still they want it in proper form.*

Later she writes that any deal she's been offered *takes everything from me except the libel suits, if any. I really am very discusted after trying to do the right thing. Here I might as well be at the game.*

But on March 21, 1928, she sends Vollmer the great news that there is a contract. *I think I have scored. I am enclosing you the letter as you are the first I want to know. Also if you don't mind I am going to dedicate my book to you.*

The book was almost finished when she reached the Maryland Hotel, San Diego, where the chief of police was more than nervous at having Chicago May on his turf, and wrote to Vollmer about her. Vollmer was too honest to be completely reassuring. "It is reasonably certain that she will continue to live honestly," he replied, "despite the handicaps of her criminal past and the world's suspicion."

And her run across the whole continent ends when it must, when she reaches the ocean. From the Silver Spray Hotel, Ocean Beach, San Diego, she writes to Vollmer, who is going away on a trip. *I am not much on the prayer stuff but I asked God all the same to bring you back safe.*

I can stay out here by being very careful until Labor Day.

She's wondering what the cheapest route back East is *because now I look twice at a dollar before I spend it, not like when I could jump out and get it quick.*

Although I am not tempted one bit. Nothing can turn my path.

At one point in this odyssey, May was living in great simplicity on the grounds of a hotel in Flagstaff, Arizona, and she might have stayed there a long time had her cover not been blown. *I would not have left the desert so soon as I would not let a little hardship beat me,* she wrote to Vollmer. *Only the man who owned the camp and*

hotel, he says to me, do you know Chicago May. I nearly dropped.
He starts and tells me how smart she is etc. I said in a careless way
that I read something about her in the papers—that night I got sick
for an excuse and then it poured snow. I thought the best thing to do
was to leave.

She gets a characteristically sensible response from Vollmer. Why
not shout who she is from the housetops? What does it matter if anyone does know who she is?

But it does matter to her. She has abjured the persona of Chicago
May. She is a changed woman.

The May who toiled as a prostitute for Avery, who hit him and
threatened him and bribed him and was blackjacked to a mass of
purple bruises by him and still clung to him, the jealous woman who
went after him and his girl with a gun, the woman who was made ab-
ject by his leaving her and was arrested over and over on the streets of
Detroit—this May has fallen away. She has been replaced by the
woman who wrote from her cabin in Flagstaff: *The landlady has*
made me very comfortable, with regards to linen etc. I do my own
cooking—as I do not eat meat, so I can manage. . . . The air is just
wonderful. I sit on my cabin door and look out on the desert. My
friends the bulls—East cannot injure me here—they would not be-
lieve I would live the simple life.

This is the first time I saw a response to the natural environment
in May. And as for not eating meat—it's also the first time she took
any care of herself.

A biography lends a misleading solidity to personal destiny. A
process like healing, to take an example, is too subtle to be confidently described. We have only the most primitive and superficial understanding of the dynamics of the exchange when a personality
encounters an opportunity, but so much of the worst of May—the
violence, the restlessness, the callousness—was like an expression of
soreness, as if her being was always profoundly chafed by her life.

March 25. 1928.

Mrs Smith has made me very Comfortable, with regards to linen etc I do my own Cooking — as I do not eat meat. So I can manage. The Harvey House is very expensive food nothing etra, only the service. Every thing is very dear here — and one has to pay for the water. They haul it from Flagstaff.

The air is Just wonderful. I sit on my Cabin door and look out on the desert. my freinds the bulls. East Cannot injure me here — they would not beleive I would live the simple life. Forgive me for bothery you with all this Junk — as I know you are a busy man —

Yours resp —

May D Sharpe
Gen Del —
ask for long

Perhaps she's in the right place at last. Perhaps, even, she began to move toward it before Vollmer arrived, and that was why she could be receptive to his suggestions. Even the years with Avery—perhaps they were a cover for healing. I mean that she couldn't invest in Avery, to say the least, and so part of her core was left untouched, and during what seemed like time wasted with him, that part gathered strength.

She wrote a second letter from Flagstaff, just as pleased with herself. *People does not trust me,* she said, *but they should see me carrying wood and water into my little cabin. My health is fine and I think I will camp here for a time.*

But the admirable Vollmer wrote back gently, "Friends of mine tell me that the desert has charms that are not known to any other place. On the other hand, one can't live on cactus and fresh air so unless the desert offers you an opportunity to earn a living I presume it will be necessary for you one of these days to pull up your stakes and go elsewhere."

He was right to hint that there might be problems ahead.

TO ME, it was a bad omen that the place where she ended her on-the-road writing was Ocean Beach, California. It is not more than a co-incidence, I know, but once, when I was in my thirties and my life had lost all joy, I tried that very place—a nondescript, modest suburb on the Pacific, south of San Diego, with small, bright houses on dry grass and an occasional strip of stores, their concrete cracked and dusty in the white sun, and old people in shorts moving slowly toward their cars, and surfers padding down to the sea, rapt. I went there in the hope of never coming back. I'd already tried going back to Ireland from London, where I'd left behind Dermot, the nearest thing to a human responsibility I ever had. He didn't have a home—he'd lived with me for a while and then moved out into various nearby squats—and he had dropped out of school. It was the era of big rock concerts, and he already had a record for possession of dope. But I didn't give him or anyone besides myself a thought when I left for Ocean Beach.

What I learned there is that a fresh start is the hardest of all things to make.

The past rises in you.

May had traveled all the way across a continent, but she was still herself. She still didn't know how to manage the straight world. She still knew only one way to survive.

She was not one for smooth transitions, May. Neither is redemption smooth.

Ten

Moving Toward Love

In August 1928, May's book came out. It even got some publicity, although crook-authors were part of the entertainment industry and the real May, by this time, was altogether lacking in glamour. But whether some PR person thought it up or whether May—ever the con woman—did, the occasion was given quite a spin. It was pretended May wrote her book with the help of a charming young Englishman called Netley Lucas, himself the author of a memoir about his life as a con man. And it was pretended, furthermore, that in the course of working together they fell in love. And that furthermore, they were going to be married.

The New York Times greeted the news in sarcastic mode. "Lucas is only on the first few bookshelf feet of his confessions," its report ended.

At the Hotel Chelsea, where he lives, it was learned that he was engaged daily in the work of self-revelation. . . . Both of the betrothed have totally abandoned their old professions . . . and intend to devote the rest of their lives to making amends by explaining to the reading public in some detail their thrilling and gorgeous exploits and why it was wrong to commit them.

May and Netley Lucas

And Lucas's claim to a lurid past was soon discredited. "If he actually has a criminal record and it is brought to the attention of the immigration authorities," the Immigration Commissioner said, "he would be deported, but I understand that his confessions are fiction."

But the papers liked the story.

The *Chicago Tribune* even printed an "engagement" photo.

May's book seems to have had a modest success in the United States—there was a second printing three months after the first—and it came out in England, too. There was at least one review. *The New York Times* was perfunctory but it wasn't unkind. "*Chicago May* is interesting," the review begins.

It is pathetic. It gives one food for thought. It bears the hallmarks of honesty. And one cannot read even the first few pages without hoping that this woman who is now in her 50s may succeed in making an honest living and keeping straight, even though she was so matter-of-fact and unremorseful about her career of crime.

But one review doesn't begin to fill the need the autobiographer has for reassurance.

Something was wrong.

May's letters to Vollmer, on the best writing paper that she could lay her hands on, had been written in a big, open hand. Imagine the shock, then, of coming on the last of them. Its date is that very August of 1928, which should have been a triumphant month for her.

I hope Mr. Vollmer you will give me a hand down there as the success of this book means life to me. Otherwise God only knows what will become of me as my health is gone and I never would be capable of making a living crooked or straight.

She's writing from the Philadelphia General Hospital. *I hope to be out of here by next week—it is the liver, and the kidney is functioning OK, and no TB, so that is good news—spinal fluid negative, so I will crawl again.*

But something else is wrong besides the collapse of her health. She's disillusioned, it seems, and aggrieved. It's as if she's warning Vollmer, or even saying goodbye.

PS, she ends, *Believe me up to this time I have gone straight, So Help Me God. I promised you and I have kept my word, not only in the letter but in the spirit. I have just enough strenth left to help myself, and hope kept me up.*

With her book, she had harvested her own history, just as she had once harvested her good looks. She owns nothing more. Did that make her fear the future, now that she was sick again? Was the issue money? She seems to have expected to make more from the book than it was ever likely to make—she knew almost nothing, after all, about normal commerce. It may have been difficult for her to grasp that authors don't get any return for half a year or so, and then get only the surplus on whatever advance was paid. Money came and went from May all her life. She can't have known how to wait for it.

But maybe what's wrong, though she doesn't have words for it, is

PS

Beluve me up to this time &
I have gone straight, so
Help Me God. I promesied
you and I have kept my
word, not only in the letter
but in the Spirit, I have
just enough strenth left to
help myself, and hope
kept me up,

Lous McL—

". . . and hope kept me up."

disillusion with the act of autobiography itself—the speaking that is not completed until it is listened to. I didn't understand that I was expectant, when I began to write about myself for publication. But I look back now and my heartbeat quickens in fear at what would have become of me if I had recounted my life story—if I had taken that risk with self-importance—and no response had come back. You open yourself out, you tidy yourself and brush yourself, and you sit in the house of your autobiography, waiting for callers. And sales aren't enough—even good sales don't necessarily provide the writer with what, without knowing it, she is seeking.

The autobiographer presents herself to the world and, more specifically, re-presents herself to her own world. Can you write an autobiography and not wonder who in your family will read it?

Autobiographies are always, perhaps, addressed to the mother. May's mother died five years before *Her Story*, but May wouldn't have known that. There must have been some intimacy between the two of them, since they were the only two females in the household for nineteen years, until the night May's sister came along. They must have been, at the least, accomplices. But an American prostitute who was a contemporary of May's once said in a letter that the girls she worked with came from undemonstrative people, and that "it isn't for lack of love that the girls go astray, as much as for some evidence of it." I've often thought of that. I know how harsh family manners were in poor Irish households then, and even in my time.

What of all the others—the lovers and pals and accomplices and enemies? Now May has to register, consciously or unconsciously, that she has no world. Such worlds as she had are gone. Anybody who might have read her autobiography with knowledge and understanding and emotion of one kind or another is gone.

WHO CARED, for example, about what she and Eddie had done to each other?

May claimed to have forgiven Eddie for the violence toward her that drove her to get Charley to shoot at him. *He was never the same after Devil's Island,* she said. *He had the hallucinations is what I always thought. I have never blamed him.* Her book did him, at least, a favor; because of it, the kind of autobiography that *I Was a Bandit* is came out in London. Eddie would have got some money for his collaboration with the publisher, and he needed money. George Gissing chronicled the life of men in the seedy lower-

Eddie Guerin in old age

class half-world of London, and George Orwell said once that Gissing's work perfectly captured "the grime, the stupidity, the ugliness, the sex-starvation, the furtive debauchery, the vulgarity, the bad manners, the censoriousness" that was the flavor of that world. That was Eddie's world.

Soon after May and Charley were jailed, Eddie was charged with stealing, in the Metropole Hotel at Brighton, a dressing case and its contents. The newspaper report said, "He was discovered sitting in the lounge wearing a cap and glasses. He had taken off the hat he had been wearing and hidden it under a chair. When charged he said, 'I didn't steal it. I hadn't time.'" At the age of forty-seven he was arrested for hanging around a bank, and when searched, had only seven pence on him. At fifty-two he was in the dock after a fracas in Camberwell late at night. "The dispute was about money which the prisoner refused to give," a report said.

Guerin then struck the girl Cresswell in the eye causing her to fall down. Witness went to assist her, using a pair of tongs with which she struck the prisoner. Guerin thereupon hit her (the witness) with a vase taken from the mantelpiece. Prisoner threatened to throw both of them out the window.

The mean bedsitting room in South London—with no doubt a brown linoleum floor and a small cast-iron fireplace in which two or three carefully placed lumps of coal hardly warmed the cold air— could hardly be more like the milieu of Gissing's tales of hopeless male poverty.

In *I Was a Bandit,* Eddie was presented as a near-superman who fought hand-to-hand with sharks in his escape from Devil's Island. In real life, he's begging from "Dear Friend Billy"—who turns out to be Billy Pinkerton, apparently visiting London from his Chicago office. "I am writing over to George for a bit of stuff as I am broke," Eddie begins.

> I expect he will send it but it takes so long and if he should be away so I am asking you if you can oblige me even if it don't come before you go. . . . All from home would be delighted to see you for we all owe you a lot. I shall try to get away to a Hydro for a couple of weeks. I have been in a certain company where it is nothing but buze and it has near killed me so I am going to leave it even if I have to leave London.
>
> Yours Truly,
> Eddie

At least the Chicago connection still existed. But aged seventy-two, when he was caught stealing a purse, he had four pence on him. At seventy-three, he stole a checkbook and told the court with tears running down his cheeks that he had never had a chance. Aged seventy-four, he got three months for loitering. Aged seventy-seven, he was in court for frequenting Epsom Downs with intent to commit a felony. Aged seventy-eight, he was in court again for loitering with intent to steal from handbags. The next year he was sentenced for the theft of eight pairs of stockings. On his last court appearance—he had somehow wandered up to Liverpool—he pleaded for mercy on the grounds that he had had a hard life, and the magistrate must have warmed his heart when he said that he had indeed, that everyone knew who Eddie Guerin was, and that he was discharged now with a warning.

Soon after that, he was moved to the countryside as part of a plan to protect elderly people against the coming war. He died in 1940, in Suffolk. The *Manchester Guardian* reported the death, ending, "He will be buried tomorrow in a pauper's grave."

THAT SAME YEAR, a bit-part player in May's drama, the "ghost-writer/fiancé" Netley Lucas "died from asphyxiation in a smoke-filled room," according to the essay on May in a book called *The World's Worst Women*.

Dutch Gus, the instigator of the American Express job, probably died on Devil's Island. Today, the colony is a tourist attraction, and cruise ships send their passengers in launches to the offshore islet where Dreyfus was kept, for "a long lunch and a tour taking several hours. Lunch will be good: French cooking is the norm, and the mother country sends all the necessary ingredients for high quality dining." But thirty thousand of the eighty thousand prisoners who were consigned to Devil's Island before it was closed died there.

The one member of Dutch Gus's gang who got away from Paris, Kid McManus, May caught sight of sometime around 1920. *Outside 125th Street subway station I bought a bag of peanuts from a respectable-looking man in a black skull cap. It was Kid McManus. He took my money, returned my stare fearlessly, and did not know me. Roasting peanuts may not be the most profitable work in the world but it pays better than crime and he can sleep without dope.*

He was the only one of us who got away unpunished, she wrote.

AUGUST VOLLMER'S outstandingly useful career went on to include becoming professor of police administration at the University of Chicago, working for President Hoover's Crime Commission, and founding the Department of Criminology at the University of California at Berkeley. But in 1955, he took his own life. "He told his housekeeper," the *Berkeley Gazette* said,

> that he slept very little last night. This morning, hearing a shot from the yard, Mrs. Miller called police. Vollmer was pronounced dead on arrival at Herrick Hospital. "Although he has been in ill health for some time, all of us are shocked and saddened by his sudden passing," declared Police Chief Holstrom.

ONE OF the conventions of the crook's memoir is bitter repudiation of the crime that does not pay. But when May looks back at the friends she once had, she mourns them, but she never suggests that there was some other life they could or should have lived.

She's lost track of Annie Gleason, who was in Aylesbury with her. *My lovely Annie,* she calls her. *Margaret Reilly who got life in Michigan just had a baby in Detroit. I think it was a shame they sentenced her for such a long stretch. She had seven children.* Chrissie Carlile, who was in *Belle of New York,* was found dead with only a nickel in her pocketbook. May Bonner went to Auburn Prison for bigamy. Sweet-faced Anna Robinson—*I think her poor sister buried her. Poverty and disease had vanquished her whom the highest in society had worshipped.* Anna's pal Mrs. Wilson *lived in Chinatown. She sank lower and lower until she became a regular dope-fiend and bum, so poor she would sell herself to the devil to get a few dollars to satisfy her cravings.* Nell Weeks committed suicide at Dan the Dude's farm in New Jersey. Pretty Bessie *fell for a jockey, a colored man. Poor Bessie! She was so clever and so highly educated.*

May said earlier in her book that the *evil genius,* Emily Skinner—
a low-bred cockney from the purlieus of Whitechapel, she called
her—had thought that Eddie *would have her for his girl, out of gratitude. She was disappointed, because Eddie was still too conceited to
fall for Emily.* Emily's name comes up again at the end. *The last I
heard of my former maid Skinner, she and Blonde Alice who lived
with a Chink were palling it together, smoking opium and sinking fast.*

COUNTESS MARKIEVICZ probably never knew that the Irish-
American who doled out gruel alongside her had once been famous
as Chicago May. In any case, the Countess, too, was gone, and gone
defeated. Not because she died in a hospital for the Dublin poor—
she'd have wanted that—but because as the years passed she had become increasingly irrelevant to the political life of the new Ireland.
There's an account of her at an evening party in the mid-1920s by a
woman who knew her "in her vibrant maturity, at the height of her
youth and her courage. . . . It made me sad to see how little attention
was paid to her, sitting exhausted in the corner, the brown poodle at
her feet." The Countess was glad at the last to go to die among the
slum-dwellers on whom she had spent her inheritance and whose interests she had always tried to represent.

Her political opponents, who had concluded an independence
treaty with Britain, were in power, and they did what they could to
play down her death. As a combatant in the Easter Rising, she fully
merited being laid in state in a public building; instead, they dis-
played her body in the foyer of a cinema. But her death purged the
ambivalent feelings she had often aroused. The government could not
stop the crowds from coming out to honor her. Three hundred thousand mourners lined the route her coffin took, and the hearse was followed by truckloads of floral tributes. At the grave, the Last Post was
sounded by buglers of the youth movement she founded. A decade of
the Rosary was said in Irish—she'd taken instruction in Catholicism

when she was in Aylesbury. Her husband, her brother and sister, and her daughter were at the graveside to hear Eamon de Valera, eventually to be independent Ireland's most influential leader, speak of "the great woman's heart of her, the great Irish soul of her," and how "the loss of her is not to be repaired."

The poem by Cecil Day-Lewis, which began by acknowledging how she was caricatured by her enemies, ends with the triumph of her funeral:

When she died in a pauper bed, in love
All the poor of Dublin rose to lament her.
A nest is made, an eagle flown.

BELIEVE ME *up to this time I have gone straight, so help me God,* the postscript of May's last letter to Vollmer went. *I promised you and I have kept my word, not only in the letter but in the spirit. I have just enough strenth left to help myself, and hope kept me up.*

The confusion of tenses makes the meaning obscure, but there's no doubt that the tone is ominous. We don't know what May was doing for six months or so after the book came out, except that she was at Philadelphia General Hospital. But I think she must have gone back on the street. And if so, and if she allowed herself to remember it, the optimism of the character reference Vollmer wrote for her must have pained her very much.

Yet again she has to find a room where she can do business, and she has to put on makeup and suggestive clothes and wrest a patch of street from the pimps and her competitors. And it wasn't as easy to square a cop in Philadelphia as it had been. At the beginning of the '20s, thousands of people were arrested for running speakeasies there, but the numbers were for show—only four percent of those arrested were ever even charged—and the same went for prostitution; the madam of one brothel got two years probation every time she was raided, and at one point had stacked up eighty-four years. But as the decade went on, there was a push toward real reform. When May last worked in this city, she'd had to pretend to be a respectable housewife and send the man on ahead to her room and follow him with her arms laden with groceries; the irony of it—to sustain the way of life that preserved her from the Irishwoman's fate of domestic service, she had to imitate domestic service. By now, 1928 and 1929, reform was even more entrenched. She had an address in a building that was then an academy of music, and she must have had to take the men upstairs discreetly past the sounds of piano scales and scraped arpeggios on the violin. A room was better than the street. The big hotels in the city center would still have been opulent in those last months before the stock market crash, but the alleyways behind them, not their glittering interiors, must have been her workplaces now.

And yet—her story is like life. It stretches credulity.

The fact is that if there was ever a time in May's life when she was close to happiness, it was this time.

She was waiting for someone she loved.

MAYBE THE REAL FRUIT of May's autobiographical project was that it opened up emotional possibilities long closed off. Because when her book was coming out and she was pretending that she was involved with a much younger man, she was, as a matter of fact, harboring tender feelings toward a man much younger than herself. They peek out of her correspondence with Vollmer. She's afraid, for example, that when her young man hears about the mock-engagement to Lucas, he won't realize that it is a stunt and will take it seriously and be upset. *I got to be careful what I write to him,* she writes to Vollmer, *I shure hope you will talk to him and of course you can put him wise.*

Because her young man is Charley, Charley Smith—Charley who got twenty years hard labor for shooting at Eddie Guerin. He must have been telling the truth when he claimed to come from a good family in Virginia, because after he'd done fifteen years in jail in England, Lady Nancy Astor—who was an American herself, from a good family in Virginia, and was also the first woman ever to take a seat in the Westminster parliament—pulled strings to get him released and sent back to the U.S.A.

May and Charley hadn't met. *One of the disappointments of my life,* May wrote, *was when my lover, Charlie Smith, the man who shot Guerin, was watched so carefully by the dicks, when he came back to America that I could not meet him safely. . . . Since then, however, we have been in frequent correspondence.*

Now Charley is back in jail again, this time in Folsom, in California, not far from Vollmer in Berkeley, and May enrolls Vollmer in the project of reforming him.

I want to impress on my friend Charley Smith that Crime does not pay, she wrote to Vollmer. *When he served his years in lone Dartmoor it was not prison it was Hell.*

Vollmer was, as usual, helpful. "I promise you I will see Smith at the first opportunity," he replies soothingly, "and tell him what they are doing to you, how hard you are trying to travel the straight and narrow and what difficulties beset you in holding your own on this road."

All the same, May writes later, *I would like to know what he is in for now, if it is assault or killing as I do not like a killer.*

Vollmer, fortunately, was able to answer, "Smith was sent up from L.A. County for the crime of burglary. As soon as the deck is clear I will do what you ask me and let you know the result. There is a possibility I may be able to sow a few helpful seeds."

I am glad it was not for a stick-up, May remarks in her next letter. *Thank you for all your kindness. I know Smith looks forward to your visit. Poor chap. He did not get much out of life.*

Charley himself enters this dialogue with memorable hauteur for a man who has spent almost his entire adult life in jail.

"I received a letter from a very dear friend of mine in Philadelphia," he writes to Vollmer.

She informed me that you had befriended her when she was ill, and destitute.

You perhaps know that people of our stamp are sensible to kindness, when it is adminstered in the proper spirit. I can assure you that Mrs. Sharp is deserving of some human sympathy. Probably no other woman in the world today has been double-crossed to the extent she has, by friends in whom she placed implicit trust. That she was innocent of the crime which she was sent to an English prison for is the truth. I know, for I was sent to penal servitude for life in the same case. I was guilty.

I wholeheartedly appreciate what you did for her. At the same time, I want you to know that this appreciation is solely in her behalf. I need no help, by which I mean I am not "snooping" for sympathy myself. I feel no symptoms of reform myself, nevertheless, your kindness to my friend while she was in distress commands my admiration for your policy toward the fallen. Trusting that you will not consider my writing to you a liberty, I am,

Yours very truly,

Robert Considine

May tries to tell Vollmer why Charley matters to her. *You know he built a house in Los Anglos and had a girl—she stuck just three months and then wrote to him she had another Daddy. Smith was the kind to look after the woman not like the boys now who will take from the woman no matter even if they can get it themselves. If you should see him impress on him that what I tell him I mean about going straight. I would like to be able to pull this book through and I sure would help him.* Her dangerous ignorance of the business of getting paid for writing comes up again. She thinks that Charley can earn a living that way. He has *material enough to bring him in 100 dollars per month for ever so long. I will help him as I think I owe it to him.*

But the good Vollmer comes away from meeting Charley with a slightly more realistic plan.

Smith seems a very decent sort of a fellow and is looking forward with pleasure to the time when he will be out and with you again. He is a pretty good carpenter and believes he will be able to earn a living with his hands. He thinks that between the two of you, it will not be difficult to get along in this world without resorting to his old practices.

At this time, Vollmer was immensely busy and had momentous national and international work on his hands. It is a most impressive thing that he took such pains for these two obscure people.

May thinks they'll soon be together, but Charley fails to get parole. He has, apparently, a brother, but the brother won't fill in the parole form.

People in prison are like children, May writes, begging Vollmer not to lose touch. *When they receive a letter from a prominent person it tickles them to death. I hope and pray you can help Smith. I want to help him go straight. He learned I believe the carpenter trade in England so he can earn a living. Hoping and trusting you will try.*

I myself promise you you will never regret it.

I myself promise you . . . How grand her tone is when she is in earnest! But—why does she care so much?

She betrays her feelings, I think, when she sees a photo of Charley and makes the disappointed remark to Vollmer, *He is very homely, is he not, without his hair?* I think the memory of their living together in secret all those years ago in London was one of her good memories, and that she had remembered Charley as he looked then, when he was twenty-five.

I think she has romantic hopes of him. And soon, he can try for parole again.

She must have gone on working, trudging with the suckers past the shouted instructions of pianoforte teachers and the squeal of fiddles, panting on the stairs, grateful to peel the stockings down her veiny legs. But at some point around the beginning of 1929, her health broke down and she became an in-patient in the Philadelphia General Hospital. According to a self-congratulatory book of essays by medical men who worked there, this was a wonderful place, much loved by its kindly and brilliant staff, but an exposé in the *Philadelphia Record* of that same year accuses it of dirt, overcrowding, and sustained neglect.

My brother Dermot helps me to imagine May in hospital. When he came to the end of the road in England, forbidden to go near his girlfriend and owing money all around, he came back to Dublin, but soon he injured himself in a domestic accident. There was a chance he was going to die. I ran back to Dublin the way you run though you're in a plane, straining forward in the dark and the engine noise, and I went straight from the airport to the hospital and was there at dawn, slipping past the closed waiting rooms and clinics and offices until I found the right ward and tiptoed in. I saw my brother, propped up on a narrow bed beside a window. There were tubes coming out of his nose, and his hands were crossed on the counterpane, white on white, but his eyes were open in his thin face and he was looking away from me into the first gray light of the day. I invest my picture of May with the loneliness that stood all around him. And the patience.

No very sick person can do anything but wait. But people like Dermot and May, habitués of the streets, people known to the police, people expert in furtive encounters in the underworld of cities— when they are made scrubbed and neat under the watchful eye of vigorous nurses, they become pitifully passive. They become meek as refugees. My brother was eventually discharged, but he was never properly well again and he was in and out of hospital several times. May was in and out, too.

She's never explicit about what exactly was wrong, so I assume she had gynecological trouble. It is frightening to think of it, but when she was out of hospital she must have hauled her failing body onto the streets and sold it. She had no alternative.

I WENT to Philadelphia to follow May in the last part of her life—to look up at the windows of the former music academy and visit the site of the hospital and, when I was finished, to visit the site of her grave. My friend from Brooklyn was free to come with me because his little girl was with her mother. It was a day of iron cold and we were late getting away from the city. He's *always* late, I fumed to myself. If it was *his* work he'd make an effort, but because it's only mine he's taking his time. We carried our bags the five blocks to the snowy parking lot. He'd forgotten the car keys. Half an hour into the drive, he absentmindedly drove past the turn to the turnpike. The car was a pressure-cooker of my discontents.

Back at the beginning, when I used to go in on the F train to the New York Public Library at 42nd Street to read May's book, it had seemed to me I was starting on a venture that was work but that was also connected with my personal needs and hopes. I thought, for instance, that what I was going to learn about the social history of America would lend depth and eloquence to neighborhoods like the Brooklyn where my friend lived. Following May would cure me of being as Ireland-centered as I was, and that would make me more flexible in my relationship with him and the little girl. It had worked, on one level—there were five or six cities in the States now where the central library, at least, gave off a golden glow in my mind. I looked at everything American more closely—back streets, old theaters, the wooden booths in saloons. I was far more involved with American history—more appalled by what the country had been and impressed by what it had become—than I had ever dreamed I would be.

But this fractious expedition to Philadelphia might be an ending. I wasn't sure. I'd learned from my excursion into biography that beginnings and endings aren't half as evident when you're living them as they are on the page.

"What's the exit number?" he said.

"I don't know," I said. It makes me nervous, being asked that. I'm not used to American maps. "It doesn't seem to be marked—"

"Of course it's marked—here, I'll pull over—"

"Do not! We'll be killed if you stop here!"

And all weekend, though we did rewarding things, in my heart I stood further and further back from him. I could feel ending everywhere—maybe because my research was ending and I'd be going home to Ireland to write. Maybe because I could feel May becoming more and more ill, and I knew how little time she had left.

But when he went back to Brooklyn and I moved to a hotel—of May's time, and a block away from one of her addresses—the bleak side of independence wasn't long in presenting itself. I was free to work, but somehow I was too languid to work. I read all the advertising magazines in the room. I tried to imagine my own future. I ate downstairs in the hotel café—too early; I'd forgotten that detail, that when you travel on your own, the evenings are long, and you're inclined to eat too early. The man at the next table started talking to me—a pleasant man, and of no greater importance to me than I was to him. But that detachment wouldn't last if I was living on my own. I was not needy now, but if my friend and I parted, I'd be only a hair's-breadth from the usual humiliations. On the other hand, I was glad to be going to read in the Free Library in the morning by myself. I wanted to concentrate on May now without any distractions, because there was so little time left.

This kind of to-and-fro went on all the time at the back of my head.

I could feel—near—the loneliness that might have been May's fate.

But she sprang away from it.

May committed herself.

THE *PHILADELPHIA RECORD* reported that "after May entered the hospital, one of her first visitors was her old flame, Smith, who had taken up quarters—after roaming half the globe—on Spring Garden Street near Broad."

Her hospital room must have become their home when Charley got out of Folsom and came to Philadelphia to be with her. She didn't have to pretend with him. She didn't have to dress herself again in the costumes of seduction or contrition or false respectability. He was branded as she was by years of jail cells, stone corridors, tins of ugly food, the derision of warders. And as well as that, she owed him. And he needed her.

She surely cherished the man, even though he was bald and a head shorter than she, and his clothes must either have been years old or come from some prison aftercare supply. Anyone glancing at him in the street would have seen nothing but a nondescript little chap hurrying to a bus stop, his raincoat over his arm in case of a shower—perhaps counting out the coins to buy flowers at the hospital gate, because Charley would always have been one for a gentlemanly gesture. Anyone passing May's room would have thought nothing of the glimpse of her white face watching the door. Middle-aged people who love each other often refrain from any kind of demonstrativeness in public, not realizing that the way they meet each other's glance with unguarded openness gives them away.

Their manner to each other must have been as tentative as if they were young again. Charley had been in jail almost continuously since before he was twenty. May had, perhaps, known romance, but this would be the first emotional relationship free of the ambiguous element of sex. Sex would have been at the very center of the Nebraska fling, and it would have been what Eddie Guerin expected of her, and it was bound to be one of the ways she tried to bind Avery to her. But even if she had managed to preserve some sexual integrity for herself in spite of her occupation, intercourse would always have carried the danger of conception, and even when she got too old for that, the continuing threat of disease. It must have been quite new to lie in a clean, white bed and have her hand held by her improbable gallant knight.

Her life had been exceptionally solitary. She had never had a home of her own, unless you count the four or five furtive months with Charley himself, back in London. She'd spent most of her time alone—even during the years with Avery she'd earned the money that would attach him to her by going off alone, up and down the eastern States. So simply having someone to talk to was new to her. Yet I don't imagine that either she or Charley was chatty. I imagine him sitting quietly for hours in the little room that grew more and more stifling as the summer approached. Her hands would have taken on the pale hue of the sickroom. The fingers must have been thin by then, the flesh a little loose, the nails uneven and pallid—a sick woman's nails. I imagine him laying his cheek against those fingers. I imagine him wringing out a cloth in a tin basin of water and touching it to her forehead. I imagine them both looking up like startled children when a nurse came bustling into the room. Four wary eyes. They could show each other without shame that in places like this, where they were in the power of authorities, they became both alienated and dependent. I'm sure they lied in front of each other to everyone else, but they didn't lie to each other.

They were graduates of institutions. They both knew how to make a temporary civilization out of gossip about the staff and jokes about the food that was doled into May's bowl. Any topic—even sparrows, if sparrows came to the windowsill and Charley fed them May's crumbs—would have been inducted into their miniature world. And, of course, every day they had to continue the story of the life Charley lived after the porter clanged his bell and shouted "All out!" Where had he eaten? That dump! They charged him *what* for a hamburger? Why didn't he buy bread and cheese and bring it back to the room with a few bottles of beer? Had he written to Vollmer to give him their news? What did the weather forecast on the wireless say? Could he find some ice?

I suppose that her voice became more frail as time went by, and that it took more of an effort to turn her head to watch the door for him, but that she smiled at him from the pillow with ever more sweetness. Far back in her story, I wondered what she'd brought with her from Ireland as the meaning of love. Maybe this—this simple, tested thing was her best experience of love. Maybe for the first time in all her life, her eyes were loving.

Because—it may seem a small thing—but her hair, that in the bad time in Detroit was gray, is now auburn.

The nurses must have helped her to dye it for her big day.

She and Charley are getting married.

From the *CHICAGO TRIBUNE*

May Vivienne Churchill, known to the police of three continents as "Chicago May," blackmailer and underworld queen of a generation ago, is to be married here next Monday to Charles Smith, who served time with her for the attempted assassination of Eddie Guerin, according to Henry J. Nelson, lawyer, who said he is counsel to the couple.

She is reported to be a patient in a Philadelphia hospital, where she will probably undergo a serious operation. . . .

A common-law contract was agreed between herself and Charley, and because of her condition, the hospital authorities gave permission for the civil ceremony to be conducted in the hospital. It was intimated that the marriage ceremony will be performed in a hospital room.

The Philadelphia Inquirer took up the story:

Plans were made for a wedding in the hospital but when May took a turn for the worse the nuptials were postponed. Several days ago, when her condition became increasingly dangerous, Chicago May summoned her attorney Henry John Nelson and instructed him to make out a will whereby she left all her worldly possessions to her intended husband. On Monday, before an operation, she scrawled a note leaving everything she possessed to him in case she died.

May in middle age, in a Detroit police mugshot

She rallied. In the Vollmer archive in Berkeley there is a telegram:

1929 May 30.
CHICAGO MAYS OPERATION COMPLETE SUCCESS
LETTER FOLLOWS
ROBERT CONSIDINE

May did not, however, recover. There was some kind of hemorrhage, and they rushed her back to the operating table. I hope they pumped her full of friendly dope there and that, as oblivion stole upon her, the finger that would have worn a wedding band went slack. Perhaps her hand made a frail movement to clutch at the hospital gown, as if it were searching for the edge of the shawl that covered her bright head when she was a girl. It was an unseasonably hot day—85 degrees, and humid. A record number of motorcars, a local newspaper says, drove out of Philadelphia to the beaches that day. In

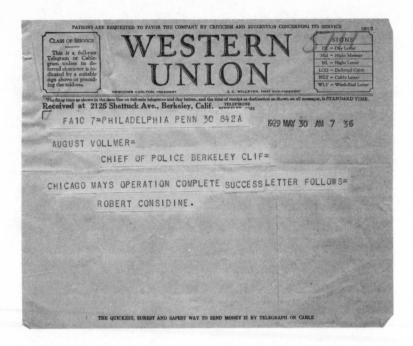

PATRONS ARE REQUESTED TO FAVOR THE COMPANY BY CRITICISM AND SUGGESTION CONCERNING ITS SERVICE

WESTERN UNION

CLASS OF SERVICE

This is a full-rate Telegram or Cablegram unless its deferred character is indicated by a suitable sign above or preceding the address.

SIGNS

DL = Day Letter
NM = Night Message
NL = Night Letter
LCO = Deferred Cable
NLT = Cable Letter
WLT = Week-End Letter

NEWCOMB CARLTON, PRESIDENT   J. C. WILLEVER, FIRST VICE-PRESIDENT

The filing time as shown in the date line on full-rate telegrams and day letters, and the time of receipt at destination as shown on all messages, is STANDARD TIME.

Received at 2125 Shattuck Ave., Berkeley, Calif.

FA10 7=PHILADELPHIA PENN 30 842A   1929 MAY 30 AM 7 36

AUGUST VOLLMER=

CHIEF OF POLICE BERKELEY CLIF=

CHICAGO MAYS OPERATION COMPLETE SUCCESS LETTER FOLLOWS=

ROBERT CONSIDINE.

THE QUICKEST, SUREST AND SAFEST WAY TO SEND MONEY IS BY TELEGRAPH OR CABLE

the white room, her confused head would have been made restless by the bullfrog hooters of those early cars—the last noises she was to hear on earth. They were heralds of the kind of innocent freedom her life had never allowed her. I don't think she ever swam in the sea.

Then death rose in her and brimmed like water over the bowl of a fountain. The wedding party of Charley Smith and the lawyer Henry John Nelson came to the hospital as arranged, but then went away. May had been having an operation on her fallopian tubes. The womanliness she had earned her living by killed her. She died on the day she was supposed to marry.

FORMER NOTORIOUS CRIMINAL'S HOPE SHE MIGHT WED FAITHFUL "PAL" UNFULFILLED was the headline in one of the Philadelphia papers, and CHICAGO MAY'S WEDDING BELLS TOLL REQUIEM AS DEATH HALTS OLD ROMANCE BEYOND THE LAW the headline in another.

The *Chicago Tribune* talked to Charley. "Smith learnt of her death when he called at Attorney Nelson's office. 'I'm sorry,' he said simply. 'I have loved her for more than 20 years.'"

Epilogue

Just being here is glorious. Even you knew that,
you girls who seemingly missed out on life and sank down
into the vilest streets of the city, that fester
like open sewers. For each of you had an hour—
maybe not quite an hour—some immeasurable span of time,
a distance between two whiles—in which you really existed.
Totally. Veins glutted with existence.

RAINER MARIA RILKE, seventh *Duino Elegy*
(translated by Gary Miranda)

Nobody owns their own story. Another person may come along and take it over, as a cuckoo takes over a nest. And stories have afterlifes, too. I see this one having one ending in America, and then, long after, a different one, in Ireland. And then there is its life within me.

America was where May was buried, after as perfunctory a funeral as there could be. In the pale, discreet archives of the Historical Society of Pennsylvania, among the records of the undertaking firm that buried her, there's a brittle envelope marked *Sharp, May C.* From it I know that she had a coffin, and was not shrouded and tipped into a pauper's pit as she used to fear in Aylesbury when she'd look out from her cell at the morgue cats, imagining they were keeping rats away from the corpses of the unrespected. But apart from the coffin, Charley ordered an extremely sparse interment. Headstone? Not ordered. Care of the grave? Not ordered.

He was characteristically grandiose in the letter he wrote to Vollmer. "The 'Great Spirit' of my darling has 'passed on,'" he wrote, and he says that he accompanied May "to the burying ground, as I didn't want my sweetheart to be buryed like a common Chicago gangster." But according to the undertaker's report, neither Charley nor anyone else she knew accompanied May. She went down into the earth by herself, just as she had run away from home by herself. She returned to the solitary confinement she knew so well. The undertakers do note that Charley was represented by a nun, a local Sister of Charity—some convents supply mourners in memory of Mary, who received her Son from the cross. But May wouldn't have liked having a nun there; not at all.

The belongings she left behind are itemized in the envelope:

eye glasses
tooth brush
1 pr. stockings
1 undershirt
1 drawers

Presumably she'd been brought into hospital by ambulance and this was all she'd had. Still—no slippers or robe? No rings? No purse? Did Charley take them? Of course he did—May would have understood that. And if he took them not only from her room but from her body, she'd have understood that, too.

And she'd have understood that he never paid the undertaker's bill—though, like a true con man, he went to great trouble to pretend he was going to. Three weeks after the burial, writing or purporting to write from Emmett, Tennessee, in a confident, educated hand in black ink on linen paper, Charley is "in receipt of your statement concerning the interment of Mrs. Sharp, and I assure you that the matter will be taken care of within the next thirty days or so. Taking the opportunity

5111

Philadelphia, Pa.
June 2nd 1929

Mr. August Vollmer
Chief of Police
Berkley Calif.

Dear friend:
      I suppose you know by now that the "Great Spirit".
of my darling has "passed on"

      I had visited her the evening before, and she seemed
to be recovering, so I wired you at her request, and as I learned
later she was dead when I sent you the wire.

      I had gotten up earley to go to the depot to meet
Mr. John Shuttleworth, editor of True Detective Mysteries, who
came over from New York to spend the week end with me, and the
hospital couldn't get me on the phone. When my editor friend
arrived we went to lawyer Nelson's office and was informed of
the sad news.

      I should have wired you, but I was in an awful
temper owing to the attitude of the hovnourable lawyer~~s attitude~~.
He refused to make any arrangement for the buryal. I curssed
him and left.

      Now the Catholic sisters and priests had been hov-
ering around May's bedside latly like a lot of vultures, and I
went to them. They were very sorry etc, but she had died out of
the church and theycouldnt do anything for a herdtic of course.
Very Christ like, wasn't it?

      I had a hundred and eighty dollars, so I then went
to Oliver Baur the largest undertakers in the city and explained
the situation to them. Gee what a good woyrld this is. They immediately claimed the body and told me to keep the money, and
pay them when things straighten out a bit. If I had been a mil-
lionair they couldn't have treated me better. I refused to allow
even the Lawyer to see her,. Only Mr. Shuttleworth and myself
went to the burying ground, as I didn't want my sweetheart to
be buryed like a common Chicago gangster.

      Considine isn't my right name, so please write to me
sometimes at the following address, as your letters give me confidence. Best regards

Robert Eutine   Emmett Tenn.

Charley's letter to Vollmer describing May's funeral

to thank you for your consideration and courtesy in one of the dark-est hours of my life."

The firm tried again in June: "Dear Sir, we have been hoping to hear from you before this regarding payment of our bill. . . ."

In July: "We would appreciate a line from you as to just when you think it possible to make a payment on account of our bill. . . ."

In October, they wrote to Mr. Charles Smith—this time, for some reason, in Des Moines, Iowa. The letter came back stamped with a red hand with a pointing finger—RETURN TO WRITER. UNCLAIMED.

They gave up.

But we know where he was, because the last two letters in the Vollmer "Chicago May" archive are from Charley to Vollmer.

The first is again from Emmett, Tennessee, but in the month or so since May's death, Charley has acquired a new alias. He says that he is with his people, and that they are

very religious, and have several boys and girls going to college at Arlington, Va. I didn't want the authorities to make any connection with the name Cubine—my right name. Only my sister here knows that I have ever been in trouble and consequently my life here is a lie and it hurts me to be forced to lie to children.

The pious remark seems to me to be very like Charley. But even more like him is the very last item in the file. It is a note scrawled in pencil on paper from a paper bag, and it was somehow smuggled out of a penitentiary in Missouri. His flowery phrases have all disappeared. He has been picked up for vagrancy, and he begs Vollmer to send him half the fare to Detroit. There's no date and there's no sign that Vollmer replied, and I know nothing more about Charley after this.

The note is stained and crumpled. That it ever got to Vollmer and that it still exists in this world amazes me.

But I'm not sure that Charley would have liked it that though in

Dear Mr Vollmer:

You have perhaps heard of my getting 30 days for vag, but I can assure you that I have committed no crime. I hope I am not taking a liberty when I ask you for some assistance— half of my fare to Detroit, where I have a very good friend. I wrote to Mr. Shuttleworth for the other half. Will explain everything to you when I complete

Charley's plea from the penitentiary

This few days. Excuse writing as I am very nervous.

Sincerely

Robert Guthrie

Municipal Farm

Leeds MO.

life he moved along the very seabed of society, today the traces he left are preserved in a fine library. "Mr. Nobody from Nowhere" is what he called himself.

He didn't want to be known.

THE STOCK MARKET CRASH came later in the year that May died; the world changed, and old-style crooks like her were completely forgotten. There was no one to visit her. There's nowhere, really, to visit.

The world was motionless with cold the day I went to where the cemetery map indicates she was buried. Her grave is somewhere in the bare grass between other people's headstones. There was a drift of snow where her face might have been. A cold wind humming in the wire fence. Back at the beginning, on the warm summer's evening I drove away from Edenmore, I'd been beckoned by the posters for a circus, but this was as far from lights and music and spangles as you could get. Away on the horizon the skyscrapers of Philadelphia were a glacial frieze in steel and glass. She belonged to the era of building high, I thought—over her lifetime the teeming life of cities was lifted off streets and ordered into apartments and offices. And she, chaotic as she was, was part of the push toward order. They were wild, the first city dwellers of America, and not just the crooks but the Pinkertons and the cops and the politicians, too—as late as 1897, Tammany ran an election in New York on the slogan "To Hell with Reform!" and the boys got back in. But the lawless, such as May, played their part in the defeat of anarchy, though they never meant to. It was they, raucous though they were, an underclass herded into and out of courts and jails, who pressed against the boundaries of law and order and compelled the invention of civic structures—

But no. No fine words could cover up the bleakness of this lonely place and the harsh, effortful life that led to it.

I had already seen the right memorial for such a life as hers. When

I was in Detroit I'd felt her presence everywhere in that city that lives within the ruins of itself—that keeps going only because it knows how to keep going. I'd taken a cab out through a district of trashed and burned houses to find a house that may have been the one where she wrote her first letter to Vollmer, when she was gathering herself to change her life after she came out of the jail hospital.

The cab passed an abandoned high school as big as a government headquarters. A conservation district of fine Arts and Crafts houses, and just beyond it block after block of derelict or burned frame houses, malls with every store boarded up, signs for small businesses abandoned behind rolled aluminum doors covered with graffiti. Then Economy Grocery, Money Orders Cashed, Cooley's Lounge, Blues Dancing. The B'nai David Memorial Park, glittering with smashed glass.

There was a handsome corner building that might once have been a bank where we swung off onto a rutted side road. So many houses ahead of us were missing, with whatever was left of them lying under the snow, that this could have been the outskirts of early Detroit, undergrowth still black on the horizon. Only one house was left on the block—a house so sad that it would be too melodramatic to use in a movie. The cabdriver climbed out slowly and stood in the snow, looking at this house—blackened evergreens growing through its porch, its walls bent out, its windows half rotted off, its basement gaping open to blackness. It had been both burned and trashed, and then time came for it anyway. There was nothing beside it or behind it. It seemed to stand in its white field as a terrible specter of destruction and decay come for the obscure. I knew that there was no proof that May had lived here, though the old cabdriver nodded solemnly, as if to himself. But wherever she did live was as indifferent as this to all that she had been.

I walked away from the cemetery in Philadelphia.

Adventuresses should prepare for this, I thought. No marker with your name.

Nothing.

HER FATE in Ireland was very different.

The Edenmore community was never more beautiful than at the death of someone it counted as one of its own. Her father died soon after May, and he'd have been helped by his neighbors to the end so that he could pass away in his own home. "The funeral of Mr. Francis Duignan to the family burial ground," the local newspaper reported, "was one of the largest seen in the vicinity for a number of years. Rev. F. Lennon C.C. officiated at the graveside. RIP." The motor hearse and the horse-and-carts and the bicycles and the men, women, and children on foot would have gathered at the tolling of the church bell to attend the liturgy in whose words, over and over again, is repeated God's promise of eternal life. "May perpetual light shine upon him. May he be one with all the angels and saints and all our brothers and sisters who have gone before us. . . ." The congregation would have risen, sat to listen, knelt during the sacred passages in a rhythm of language and movement so familiar to Catholics that they are unconscious of its power and their own grace. The crowd would have assembled around the grave—dug by local men—to see the holy water sprinkled and the coffin censed by the priest with his smoking tureen of incense. The dead were as familiar as the living—when Mr. Duignan was laid to rest beside his wife, he was joining people he knew. Birdsong would have started up again, leisurely and sweet, when the people dispersed. Otherwise there was quiet in that landscape of grass and lake water.

But the community was savagely punitive, too.

At the time May died, and for at least another half-century, Ireland was fully in the grip of an institutionalized fear of women; that is, of sexuality. One Irish male in fifty, then, was a Catholic priest; three-quarters of all men between twenty-five and thirty-four were single; there had been a fourfold increase in a decade in admissions of men to mental hospitals, and Ireland had the lowest birth rate in Europe. The clergy worked obsessively at controlling sexuality by diktat and by propagating disgust. In my lifetime, little girls were not allowed to participate in athletics because they would have had to change their clothes near boys. The Archbishop of Dublin forbade the use of tampons because it would familiarize girls with their own bodies. Pregnancy outside marriage entailed lifetime disgrace for the girl and her family. Contraception was forbidden, and so was knowledge of it. Women had to go to church to be cleansed after giving birth. And much, much more.

It was in this society that May had a posthumous existence. She lived on, tragically, in one imagination—not as the woman she was, but as the loathsome seductress of the priests' taboos.

I was told the following story by people in Edenmore.

AFTER MR. DUIGNAN DIED, May's close relations left the locality, all but one man who was her nephew—the son of the girl who was born the night she ran away from home. He was very intelligent, and for a time he was the most progressive farmer in the district. But he was never a robust personality. He was always a loner, and exceptionally sensitive. No one outside a small, in-turned agricultural community can appreciate how important it is for a man not ever to lose face there—never to give the others a way of getting at him. This man had no idea that he had a scandalous aunt. But sometime in the 1960s, in the course of an argument, his antagonist threw her existence up at him. He realized that his neighbors had always known about this terrible shame in the family, and that all his life it had been talked about behind his back.

No one can be sure what happened inside his head, but the people who told me this believe that his discovery of May accelerated a process of withdrawal in him. He stopped going to the fair, and therefore he didn't get rid of his cattle. They were bullocks, meant to be sold when they were young, but he kept them for ten years and more, and their hooves and horns grew thick and deformed. Sometimes on a Sunday,

I was told, his neighbors would stroll down to the little river that was the boundary of his farm to look across at the weird, neglected beasts.

Modern people may not understand that it would fester in your head, the knowledge that your aunt sold her body. But they never knew this man's Ireland. When he was young there was a fire in a convent orphanage in the town nearest to his home. Thirty-five infants—not orphans at all, necessarily, but abandoned babies—were burned to death, and one reason they died was that the nuns didn't want the firemen to see themselves or the girl children in their night attire. When he was older, the ruling ideology exacted another sacrifice, this time even closer to his home. He could see the spire of the church where it happened from his farm. In 1984, a teenage girl died one night in the grotto beside that church, in front of the statue of the Blessed Virgin that stands there. She was trying to deliver, alone, with a nail scissors, the full-term baby she'd been hiding under her school uniform. She died, and the baby died, too. These examples of the deformed attitude to the female body that was the result of poverty, ignorance, and the influence of a celibate clergy could be multiplied by hundreds and even thousands of examples, great and small. May must have been a scarlet blur in her nephew's consciousness, a lurid presence in his farmhouse during the years he sheltered there from his neighbors' jeers.

Eventually, he was taken into the mental hospital in Longford town and he lived there for many decades, often walking out to do his little errands—where he was greeted pleasantly by one and all, the same community that had damaged him with its malice, turning its kindness on him now.

He was a victim of the quarrel between that community and May. But he was May's last victim, too. The one proud thing he retained when his mind was mostly gone—and it made me shiver when this was said to me by people who had no idea that it was always said of her—was his upright walk. He was tall, like his aunt, and noted for the straightness of his back.

He died in 2004, and was buried not at the hospital but back in his homeplace, his neighbors, of course, attending.

THE STONE of the room May got built onto her brother's house, that time she visited home, is the only physical mark she left on Ireland. She was demonstrating, when she got that done, that she had money, but she was also claiming her place as one of the Duignans. And she still does belong to the Duignans, little as that tribe may like it. I don't think she is forgotten by her relations, and I fear that they may not like the attention I have given her. It seems to me perfectly natural that May should bring out such defensiveness—she was a dangerous woman and harmful and a transgressor on many, many fronts. But she was other than that and more than that. Should shame be her only legacy?

She lives within me, though our relationship is full of uncertainties. The one thing I know for certain—and this is surely the fundamental usefulness of biography—is that one word doesn't begin to sum her up. Bad, a sinner, evil, fallen—none of the words will do. They're used to demonize and dismiss, but even baldly told, May's story shows that her self and how she expressed it was a much more complicated matter than a single word can suggest. And the story of a life is nothing compared to a life.

Are life stories even tellable? I wrote my own—in fact, I've made two attempts at it, because I wrote two memoirs—but I can feel the unsaid and the unsayable pressing from behind all I said, though I never consciously kept anything back. Any single moment of a life is so magnificently various, so rich in material and at the same time so multiply and delicately insubstantial that it is hardly served by being placed in a simple, chronological narrative. The thinness continues into character. You read your own words and they seem displaced from yourself; a lighter, smarter, more shallow person than you seems to have written them. And how must other people feel, as you speed past them in the story of your life? How meager, the words seem to say, was your experience of them, compared to their experience of you.

I tried to escape my own perspective by imagining May's response to what I've said about her. But that brought up one of my most bitter memories.

In my first memoir, *Are You Somebody?*, I wrote about my brother Dermot and how he was neglected when he was a child by a mother who was drunk every day and a father who didn't sustain any effort to help him. And I sketched his difficulties later, in adolescence and young manhood—in part to reproach myself because I failed him, too, when our parents sent him to live with me in London. For one thing, I wanted him to know how sorry I was.

But when Dermot read the bits about himself, he said to me, with a shrewd, complicit leer, "You made all that up, didn't you?" He more or less winked at me.

I was stunned. First, I was stunned at his denying the suffering that I myself had witnessed. But above all I was stunned at his supposing that I'd been deliberately dishonest—that I'd dramatized his life for effect. He'd been for a long time a bit of a hustler, a borrower who didn't pay back, a liar to authority, perhaps a petty thief—a person who managed an addict's life on few resources by presenting himself this way or that, depending on the audience. He had literally forgotten the world in which people feel themselves ordinarily contracted to tell the truth.

And of course, May's world was much more like his than mine. She was blithely candid, but she had no particular regard for the truth. Would she have given me a friendly wink, too? Would this account of her seem so far from what she felt herself to be that she, too, would presume it was a scam?

I didn't know it, but Dermot was dying when I was coming to the end of my time with May. The doctors in Dublin had offered him a liver transplant if he could stop drinking, and he made a great effort.

On the day I visited May's grave in Philadelphia—I checked the dates afterward—he went into a rehab community. But it was too late. He asked for his clothes as soon as clothes were allowed, after one week. He made his way back to where he lived and sat on the old couch and drank. He couldn't resist anymore. And he did die, two weeks later. I got back to Ireland too late to say goodbye. All I saw was a glimpse of his face, grotesque with yellow makeup, against a satin lining, while the undertaker's men waited impatiently to close the coffin.

At that time I was beginning to ask myself whether I had ever understood May. And that got mixed up with the effort—which I suppose will always continue—to make some sense of Dermot's life and death. There was nothing forced about the two of them being in my head at the same time. I heard Ezra Pound quoted when I was a young student—the passage that begins "When, when and whenever / Death closes our eyelids"—and it has always consoled me to think that we cross the river to the afterworld on the one raft—victor and vanquished together, "one tangle of shadows."

Being dead is exactly the same for everyone. But—being alive? Orthodox biographers have an easy task because their subjects' lives connect outward into the wide world in which we all have a part. What we know about ourselves and what we can know of them is of the same order, even though they are extraordinary. But Dermot and May had in common with each other, and with billions of people, that they lived harsh lives full of punishment and they died bare deaths. What meaning can we take from that? May wasn't Everywoman—her path was too individual for that. There are lessons to be drawn from any unprivileged life about the nurture a child needs, and the absence of opportunity for young people with no money and little education, and the chasms that lie in wait for women on either side of a narrow ridge, and the inadequacy of the ways we define crime and punish people for crime, but May's life didn't mesh in any particularly illuminating way with these circumstances. Neither she nor my brother is a useful example.

May was fifty-eight when she died. Dermot was ten years younger. He left behind: a television set that leaped and gestured mutely in the corner when I used to visit him—reminding me, as if I needed reminding, that my visits and all the visits he got hardly interrupted his solitude; some clothes that had been secondhand to begin with; a pair of sneakers; and a few paperbacks he had not read. Worst of all, in all the poverty and neglect of his room was a small vacuum cleaner that he had bought with his own money about a year earlier, when he must have believed that there was a life for him somewhere ahead. May left behind her book, which disappointed her. Apart from that, her underwear and a pair of spectacles. I couldn't help but cry out— if a person accomplishes nothing in their life and then leaves nothing behind, why did they live? What was their life *for*?

IT WAS MAY HERSELF—it was thinking about her—that helped me to move away from that unanswerable question.

I still mourn all that Dermot never enjoyed—the support of a partner, status, the pleasure of education, leisure, joy in accomplishment, a home. But May didn't have any of those things either, and not for a minute did she think that her life had not been worth living. At the end of her book she says, *I never wanted to die, even in prison. Not that I was afraid to die, but because I enjoyed living.*

I accepted that; but first I had to wrestle with the word "enjoyed."

Any information Eddie Guerin gives about her in *I Was a Bandit* is not reliable, but when he says she sometimes had ten men a night, something like that might have been occasionally true. What could possibly make a life, based on such brutish, debilitating work, in the usual sense "enjoyable"?

She wasn't interested in money—she made no attempt to amass it for security or to take pleasure in its contemplation. She didn't hold on to it any more than she held on to her furs or the diamonds "big as hickory nuts" a newspaper of the time had said she wore when she was a figure in the Stephen Crane affair. Fame? I think she liked being a celebrity in her own world, but her legend was quite clearly a burden to her.

Her nationality? Did she enjoy that? Her Irishness was very important when she was in an English jail and she could express her hatred of the regime by flaunting it, but she was the very last person to live for a cause. The great anarchist Emma Goldman, when she was a neighbor of May's in the 1890s, once went out onto 14th Street to earn money with her body, but the first man she accosted gave her a few dollars and told her to go home. That would never have happened to May—she was as expert on the streets as Emma was on the hustings. But she could never have shared a revolutionary vision. She was a woman for what she could touch in the here and now. She had no use for what she might someday touch.

All the possible beginnings—the stage career, the marriage in New Jersey, the *succès de scandale* in South America after she queened it at the ball in Rio—she stayed with none of them. And as for pleasure, there's no sign that she valued the everyday, sensory pleasures that are what most people mean by enjoyment. Drink is usually associated with a hangover, and except for the time when, back from the dead after her Detroit operation and full of hope about her book, she savored everything about her shack in the desert, she never praised food. That was the only time, too, that the natural world delighted her. And as for sex—she made her living from the promise of pleasure. But can a person for whom sex is a commodity, like liquor is to a barman or cash to a bank teller, preserve a live sexuality? I think she and the women she worked with must have been perfectly matter-of-fact about lust in all its manifestations. Can appetite survive, of all things, matter-of-factness?

And the arts were meaningless to her, all but literature, and she forgot about that in the helter-skelter downhill of the years with Avery—years that may have been compensation for the living death of jail, but that nobody could call enjoyable.

I think that when May said, *I enjoyed living,* she was talking about something more elemental than pleasure. She had lived as indifferent to safety and security as anyone well can, and that must have meant that she relied on the present moment—that she leaned in against its grain—in a way the rest of us do not know. Maybe there's an identification with the flow of things that is more free than freedom. Freedom is a state that demands consciousness of itself, and maybe she rejected even that much definition. If she had been pursuing the goal of freedom, she would have had to mourn the failure of her project—when she went, for instance, to jail, or was imprisoned, psychologically, by Avery. But she doesn't mourn the failure of her project, because she never had any project. She embraced the random, the contingent, the chaotic. She carried economic survival with her in the form of her body—a snail complete in its shell—and that brought her into degraded and violent milieus, but she never stood in judgment on where she happened to find herself. Where and how she finds herself is where all of her is. Maybe as truly as any Buddhist, she was wholly unattached.

That could be what she meant by *I enjoyed living*—that she had no quarrel with consciousness, that she fitted the world. That her zest for life didn't demand the reward of pleasure—it was aboriginal. *Hope kept me up,* she wrote in her last, frantic note to Vollmer, and maybe hope is the one virtue she certainly had.

Saint Paul said the three great virtues are faith, hope, and love; and May's dash, her speed, her appetite for the future are surely a secular version of spiritual hope. And hope is life. Hope opposes itself to despair.

WHEN I LOOK BACK at what I thought I was doing when I began her story, I almost smile at my crassness. I patronizingly thought it would be a "moral challenge" to write about someone who wasn't exceptional, did I? Well, the moral challenge had reversed itself. Have I been as true to myself in my life as she was? Could I have endured what she endured—the nights on the streets, the furious men, the years and years alone in stone jail cells? Have I known what it is to live always on the edge?

I see now, too, that my journey toward her had no way of reaching her. For one thing, she was so exceptional that she's cut off from me—she's cut off from most people. And there's another thing, which I felt as a great mystery at the time when she and Dermot were jostling in my mind. I didn't understand my brother, and I know much less about him than I know about her, but I loved him. And I don't love her.

I could have loved her. The basis for it was there—she was a woman of great fortitude, much amused by the world, and though she had no pity, she was kind. But to love her I would either have needed to know her in the flesh, as I knew Dermot from when he was a baby. Or I needed to write a novel, not a biography. Love is a project of the imagination. You can manipulate a character in a novel so as to make her lovable—you can place her in situations where she is moving or enchanting or alluring. I did imagine small scenes in May's life, but only within the framework of available facts. When they strained to be enlarged into a fiction, I pulled them back. In a fiction I could have conferred consistency on her, and I could have arranged to have insight into her, and I could have swathed her in charm. But I stayed tethered. As well as I could, I wrote a factual biography.

Biography, however, is not just a leap in the dark. The dark is not the same, at the end of the biographical effort.

I believe that it was more respectful to bow before the facts of her life than to use them as a point of departure. And it is respect that matters. How much warmth I feel toward her doesn't matter to anyone but me, but whether I approach her with respect does matter. That's what I meant back at the beginning when I said that writing about her might be like a political act. This or that ideologue goes to great pains to deny women like May a common humanity with the rest of us. She was excluded from every community. She was thrown out of memory. Well, I want her back in, and I want her such as she was. And that's why I have followed her around, watching the clues she drops, patiently considering her meaning, caring for her history far more scrupulously than she ever did herself. I ran after her even though I knew I could never catch up with her—that the girl would stay effortlessly ahead of me on the pale causeway, though rain was darkening her red-gold mane of silky hair.

Whatever she did I paid attention to, and watching a person attentively is the beginning of love. It is practice for love.

A tired old prostitute is dust in an unmarked grave. But, see—you have been led to her. We know already how to have fellow-feeling with people we like and understand, but there is a territory beyond what we already know, and pioneer journeys to be made to it. Out there, people are waiting in the dark.

Shine the beam of attention out there. The dark recoils.

The site of May's grave, Fernwood Cemetery, Philadelphia

Acknowledgments

The photographs reproduced on pages 14 and 207 come from the National Library of Ireland; on page 33 from the Nebraska State Historical Society Photograph Collections. The image on page 36 is reproduced from a website called "The Wild Wild West" (www .gunslinger.com/west.html), for which I could not locate an owner. The photographs on pages 51, top and bottom, and 44—from *The Great War on White Slavery* by Clifford G. Roe, *War on the White Slave Trade* by Ernest A. Bell, and *Shepp's World's Fair Photographed* by James W. Shepp, respectively—were provided by the Chicago Public Library, Special Collections and Preservation Division, where I thank Glenn Humphreys. The images on pages 66, 83, 247, and 249 are from the Prints and Photographs Division of the Library of Congress; on page 69 from the New York Public Library, Astor, Lenox and Tilden Foundations; and on page 73 from the Museum of the

City of New York. The photograph on page 113 comes from the American Express Corporate Archive; on page 143, the image *A Farmhouse Near Bantry, County Cork* is copyright Fáilte Ireland. The photograph on page 190 is from the Buckinghamshire County Museum; on page 202 from the Sligo County Library; and on page 239 from the Reuther Library of Wayne State University—I thank Anna Savvides of the Burton Collection in the Detroit Public Library for help in finding it and for much more.

The images of May on page 98 are courtesy of the *Chicago Tribune*; the photographs on pages 100, 107, 269, and 285, and the press cuttings on which the endpaper design is based, are from the Pinkerton archive in the Manuscript Division of the Library of Congress, for help with which I thank Jeffrey M. Flannery.

The photograph of the site of May's grave on page 304 was taken by Edwin Robertson of Philadelphia, whom I specially thank, as I do Peter Farrell of Moydow, County Longford, for his loan of the rare early photograph of an eviction on page 192.

The documents on pages 258, 261, 267, 286, 289, and 291 are reproduced courtesy of the Bancroft Library, the University of California at Berkeley, where my very particular thanks are due to David Kessler.

I would also like to thank Deirdre MacNabola of the Longford County Library, Wayne Furman of the New York Public Library, and Tania Vladova in Paris.

The lines from the Seventh Elegy of Rainer Maria Rilke's *Duino Elegies* on page 287 are translated by Gary Miranda. My thanks to my friend John Mood for showing me that translation, and to Azul Editions for permission to quote from it.

SEAN MACCONNELL, with his gift for making connections, pointed me in the direction of Frank Columb's *Chicago May: Queen of the Blackmailers* (Evod Academic Publishing Company, 1999), the remarkable feat of research which started me on this project. James MacNerney and Tom Murtagh were the best of guides to Edenmore. Alex Poliakoff, in Washington, and Tony Laryea, in England, went to great trouble for me. I've had the pleasure of beginning to know Anne Tierney, Martha Cooley, and Carolyn Anderson through the writing of this book, and of drawing again on the generosity of old friends— Luke Dodd in London, Sheridan Hay in New York, and Helen and John Browne in County Clare. I think about each of these people differently, but about all of them with gratitude.

I have a very happy memory of my brother Dermot and my sisters Deirdre and Grainne cheering on this work at an early stage, when I told them about May over a picnic in Grainne's garden. Dermot is intertwined with the book. But the present claims a story like May's, not the past, and I offer it to John and Anna Low-Beer, who shared a home with me and with May, with heartfelt thanks.